THE DELINQUENTS

JAMES ASMUS | FRED VAN LENTE | KANO

CONTENTS

Collection Cover Art: Paolo Rivera

Editor: Josh Johns
Editorial Consulting: Alejandro Arbona
Editor-in-Chief: Warren Simons

The Delinquents™. Published by Valiant Entertainment LLC.
Office of Publication: 424 West 33rd Street, New York, NY
10001. Compilation copyright ©2014 Valiant Entertainment LLC.
All rights reserved. Contains materials originally published in
single magazine form as The Delinquents #1-4. Copyright ©2014
Valiant Entertainment LLC. All rights reserved. All characters,
their distinctive likeness and related indicia featured in this
publication are trademarks of Valiant Entertainment LLC. The
stories, characters, and incidents featured in this publication are
entirely fictional. Valiant Entertainment does not read or accept
unsolicited submissions of ideas, stories, or artwork. Printed in the
U.S.A. First Printing.
ISBN: 9781939346513.

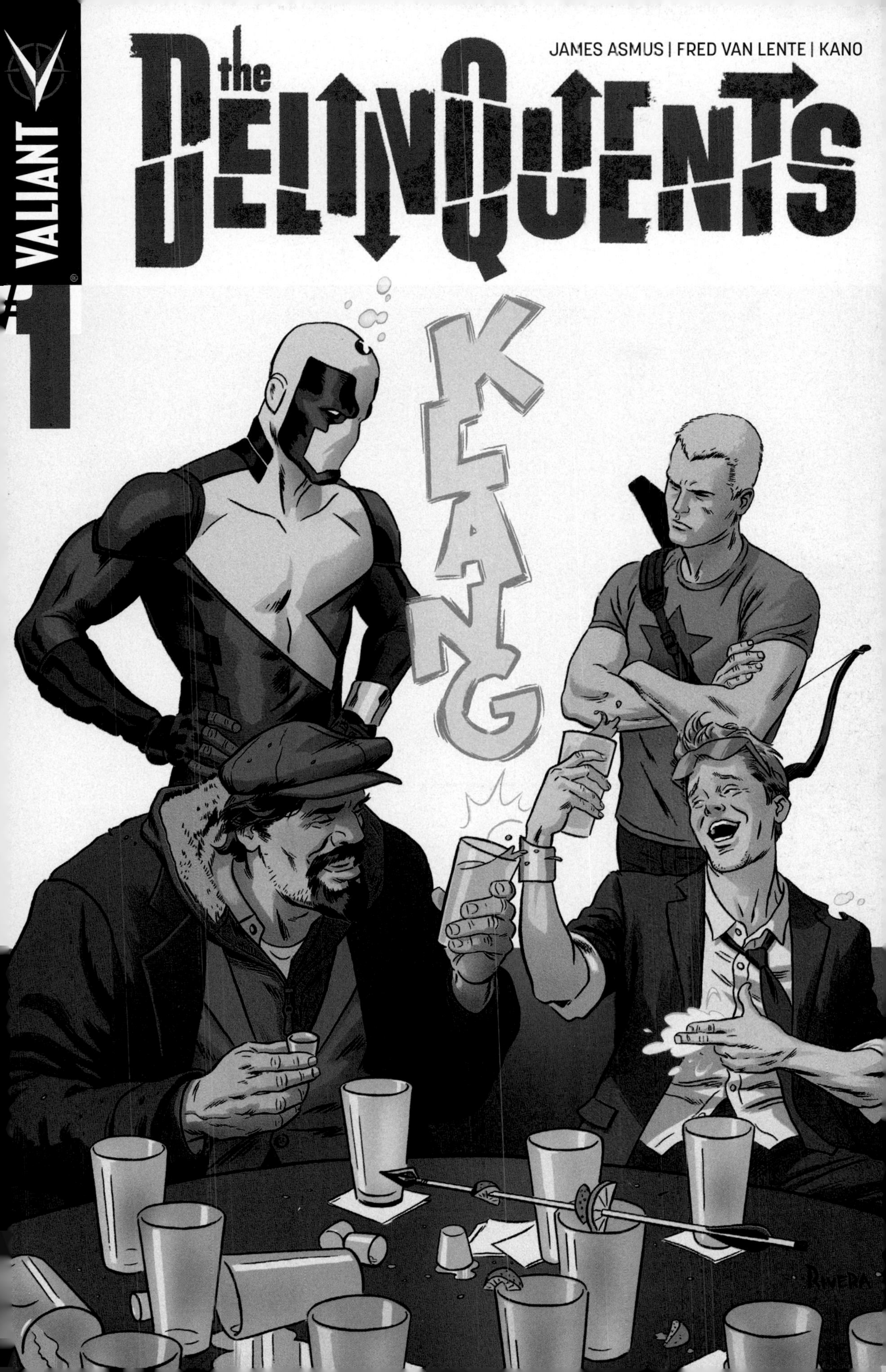
VALIANT
#1
the DELINQUENTS
JAMES ASMUS | FRED VAN LENTE | KANO
KLANG
RIVERA

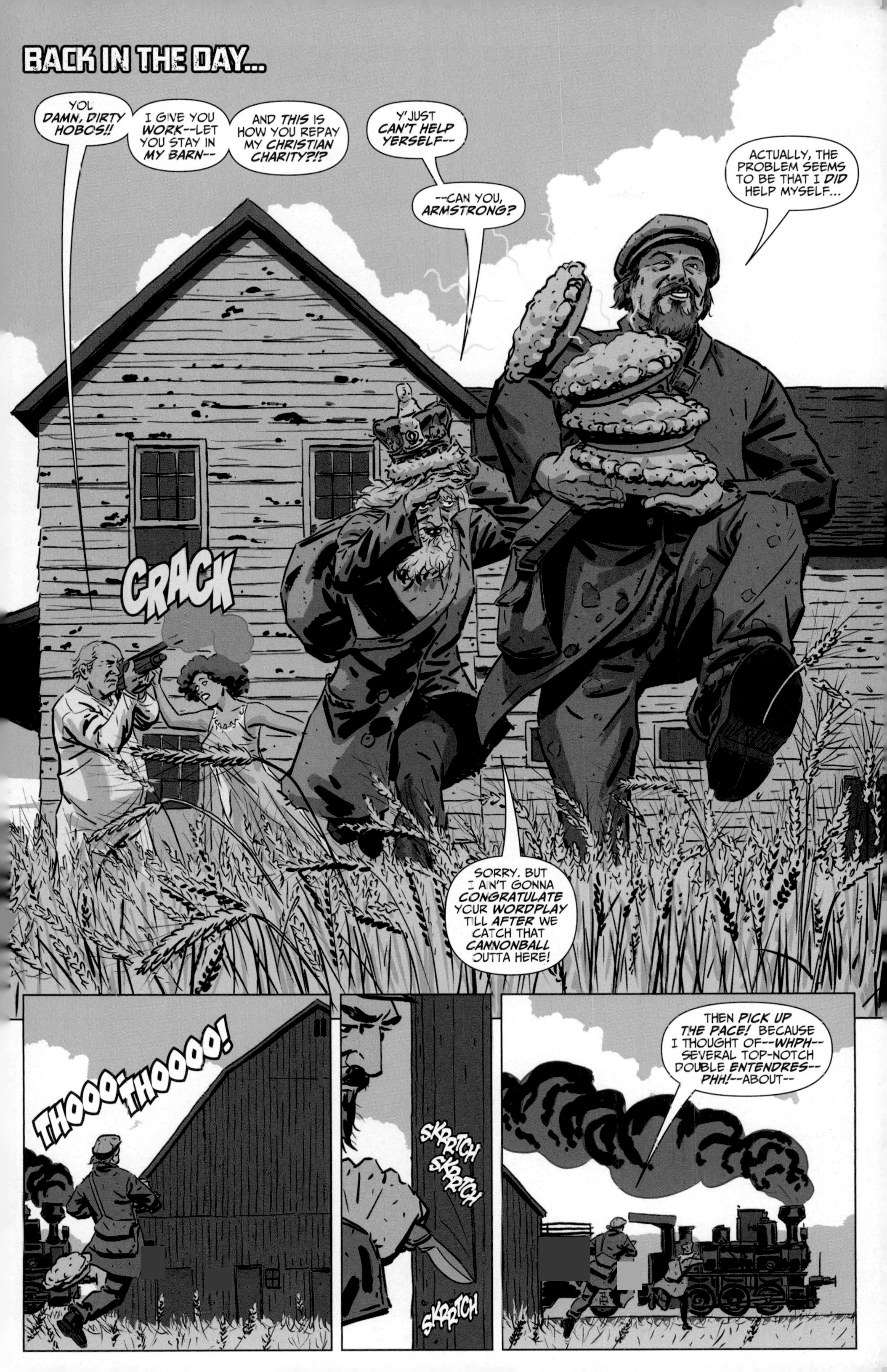
BACK IN THE DAY...
YOU DAMN, DIRTY HOBOS!!
I GIVE YOU WORK--LET YOU STAY IN MY BARN--
AND THIS IS HOW YOU REPAY MY CHRISTIAN CHARITY?!?
Y'JUST CAN'T HELP YERSELF--
--CAN YOU, ARMSTRONG?
ACTUALLY, THE PROBLEM SEEMS TO BE THAT I DID HELP MYSELF...
CRACK
SORRY. BUT I AIN'T GONNA CONGRATULATE YOUR WORDPLAY TILL AFTER WE CATCH THAT CANNONBALL OUTTA HERE!
THOOO-THOOOO!
SKRITCH SKRITCH SKRITCH
SKRITCH
THEN PICK UP THE PACE! BECAUSE I THOUGHT OF--WHPH--SEVERAL TOP-NOTCH DOUBLE ENTENDRES--PHH!--ABOUT--

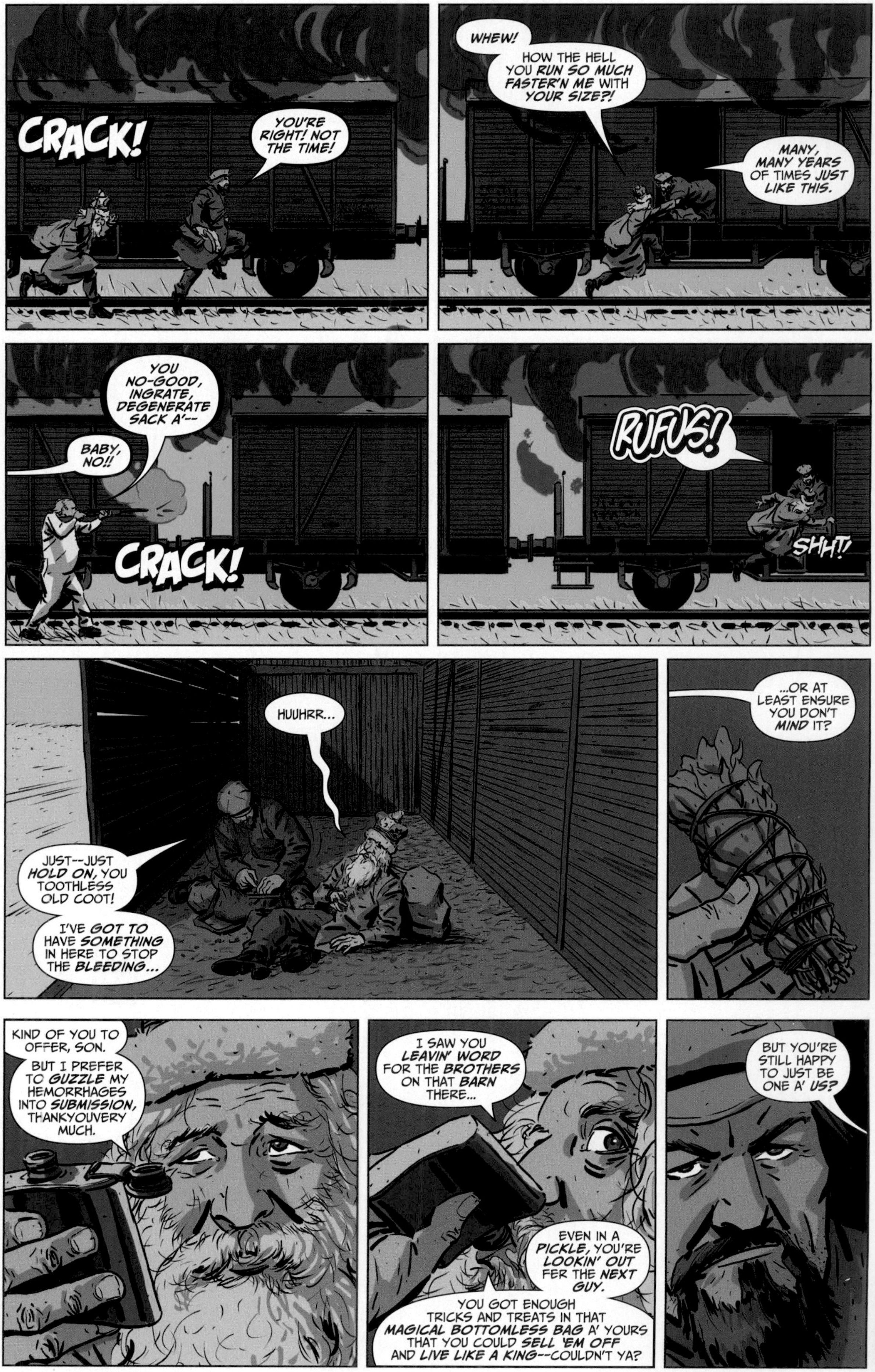
CRACK!
YOU'RE RIGHT! NOT THE TIME!
WHEW!
HOW THE HELL YOU RUN SO MUCH FASTER'N ME WITH YOUR SIZE?!
MANY, MANY YEARS OF TIMES JUST LIKE THIS.
YOU NO-GOOD, INGRATE, DEGENERATE SACK A'--
BABY, NO!!
CRACK!
RUFUS!
SHHT!
HUUHRR...
JUST--JUST HOLD ON, YOU TOOTHLESS OLD COOT!
I'VE GOT TO HAVE SOMETHING IN HERE TO STOP THE BLEEDING...
...OR AT LEAST ENSURE YOU DON'T MIND IT?
KIND OF YOU TO OFFER, SON.
BUT I PREFER TO GUZZLE MY HEMORRHAGES INTO SUBMISSION, THANKYOUVERY MUCH.
I SAW YOU LEAVIN' WORD FOR THE BROTHERS ON THAT BARN THERE...
EVEN IN A PICKLE, YOU'RE LOOKIN' OUT FER THE NEXT GUY.
YOU GOT ENOUGH TRICKS AND TREATS IN THAT MAGICAL BOTTOMLESS BAG A' YOURS THAT YOU COULD SELL 'EM OFF AND LIVE LIKE A KING--COULDN'T YA?
BUT YOU'RE STILL HAPPY TO JUST BE ONE A' US?

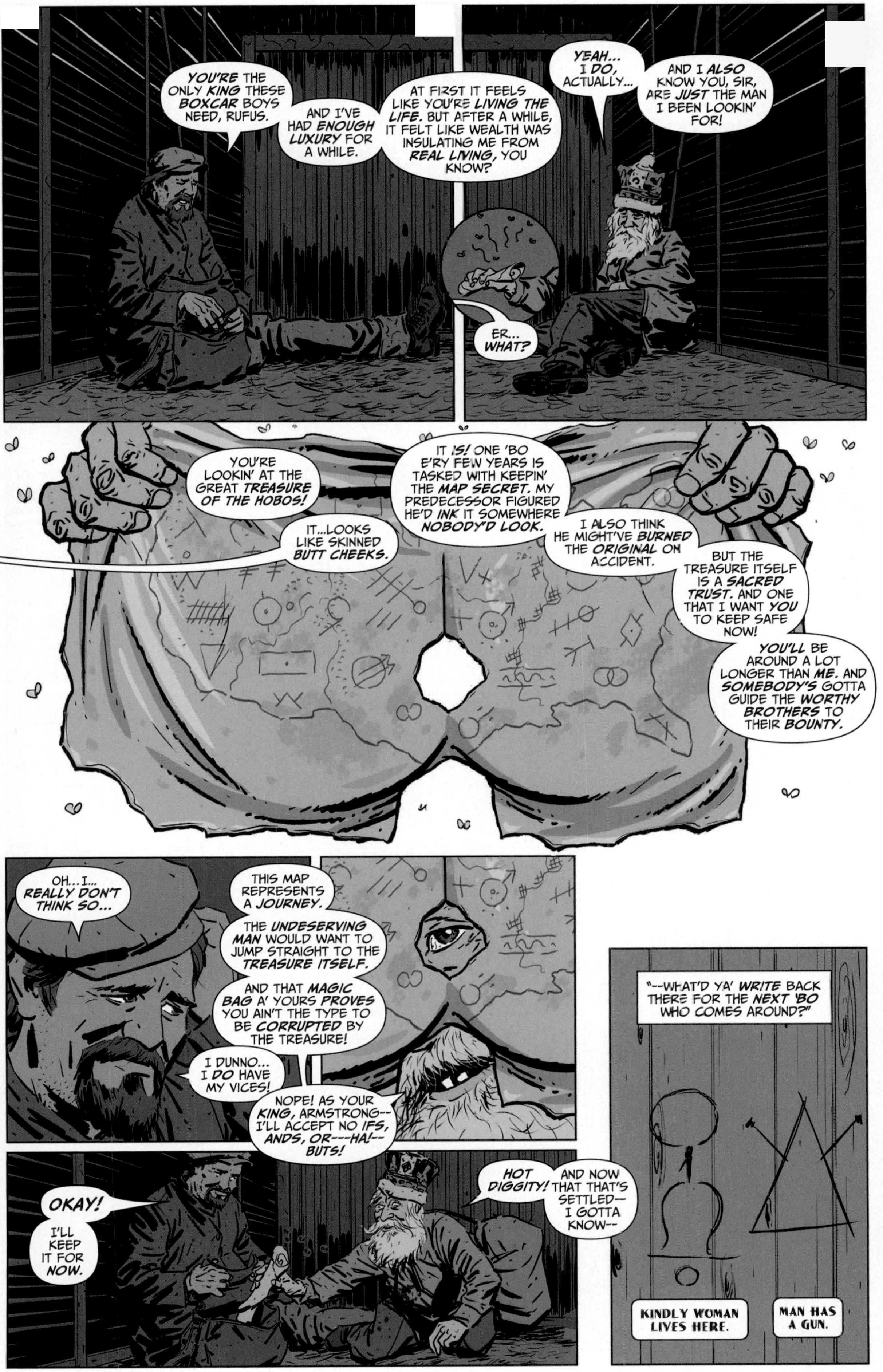
YOU'RE THE ONLY KING THESE BOXCAR BOYS NEED, RUFUS.
AND I'VE HAD ENOUGH LUXURY FOR A WHILE.
AT FIRST IT FEELS LIKE YOU'RE LIVING THE LIFE. BUT AFTER A WHILE, IT FELT LIKE WEALTH WAS INSULATING ME FROM REAL LIVING, YOU KNOW?
YEAH... I DO, ACTUALLY...
AND I ALSO KNOW YOU, SIR, ARE JUST THE MAN I BEEN LOOKIN' FOR!
ER... WHAT?
YOU'RE LOOKIN' AT THE GREAT TREASURE OF THE HOBOS!
IT...LOOKS LIKE SKINNED BUTT CHEEKS.
IT IS! ONE 'BO E'RY FEW YEARS IS TASKED WITH KEEPIN' THE MAP SECRET. MY PREDECESSOR FIGURED HE'D INK IT SOMEWHERE NOBODY'D LOOK.
I ALSO THINK HE MIGHT'VE BURNED THE ORIGINAL ON ACCIDENT.
BUT THE TREASURE ITSELF IS A SACRED TRUST. AND ONE THAT I WANT YOU TO KEEP SAFE NOW!
YOU'LL BE AROUND A LOT LONGER THAN ME. AND SOMEBODY'S GOTTA GUIDE THE WORTHY BROTHERS TO THEIR BOUNTY.
OH... I... REALLY DON'T THINK SO...
THIS MAP REPRESENTS A JOURNEY.
THE UNDESERVING MAN WOULD WANT TO JUMP STRAIGHT TO THE TREASURE ITSELF.
AND THAT MAGIC BAG A' YOURS PROVES YOU AIN'T THE TYPE TO BE CORRUPTED BY THE TREASURE!
I DUNNO... I DO HAVE MY VICES!
NOPE! AS YOUR KING, ARMSTRONG-- I'LL ACCEPT NO IFS, ANDS, OR---HA!-- BUTS!
OKAY!
I'LL KEEP IT FOR NOW.
HOT DIGGITY!
AND NOW THAT THAT'S SETTLED-- I GOTTA KNOW--
"--WHAT'D YA' WRITE BACK THERE FOR THE NEXT 'BO WHO COMES AROUND?"
KINDLY WOMAN LIVES HERE.
MAN HAS A GUN.

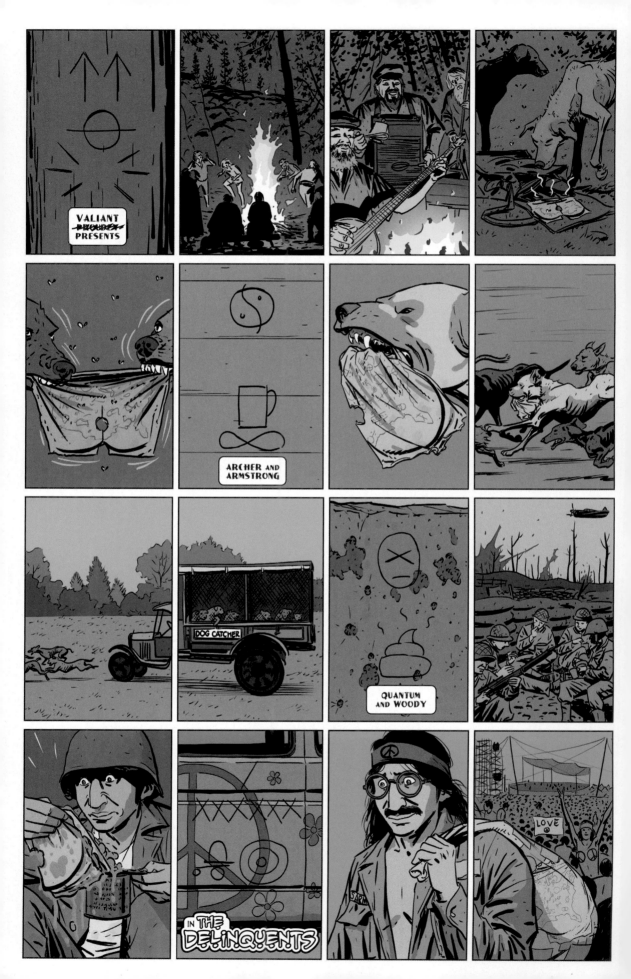

VALIANT ~~PRESENTS~~ PRESENTS

ARCHER AND ARMSTRONG

DOG CATCHER

QUANTUM AND WOODY

IN THE DELINQUENTS

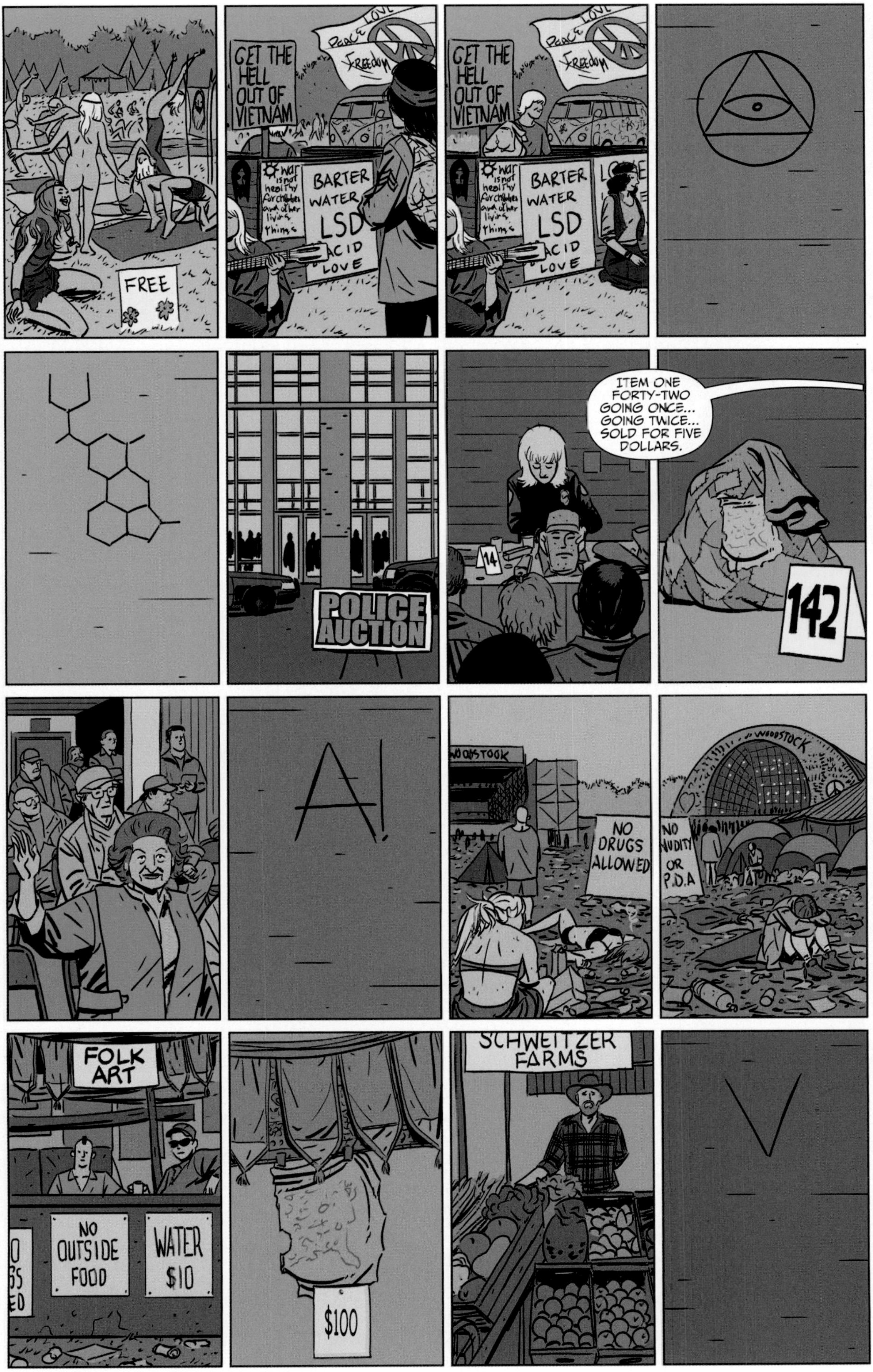
FREE
GET THE HELL OUT OF VIETNAM
PEACE LOVE Freedom
war is not healthy for children and other living things
BARTER WATER LSD ACID LOVE
GET THE HELL OUT OF VIETNAM
PEACE LOVE Freedom
war is not healthy for children and other living things
BARTER WATER LSD ACID LOVE
POLICE AUCTION
14
ITEM ONE FORTY-TWO GOING ONCE... GOING TWICE... SOLD FOR FIVE DOLLARS.
142
A!
WOODSTOCK
NO DRUGS ALLOWED
WOODSTOCK
NO NUDITY OR P.D.A
FOLK ART
NO OUTSIDE FOOD
WATER $10
$100
SCHWEITZER FARMS
V

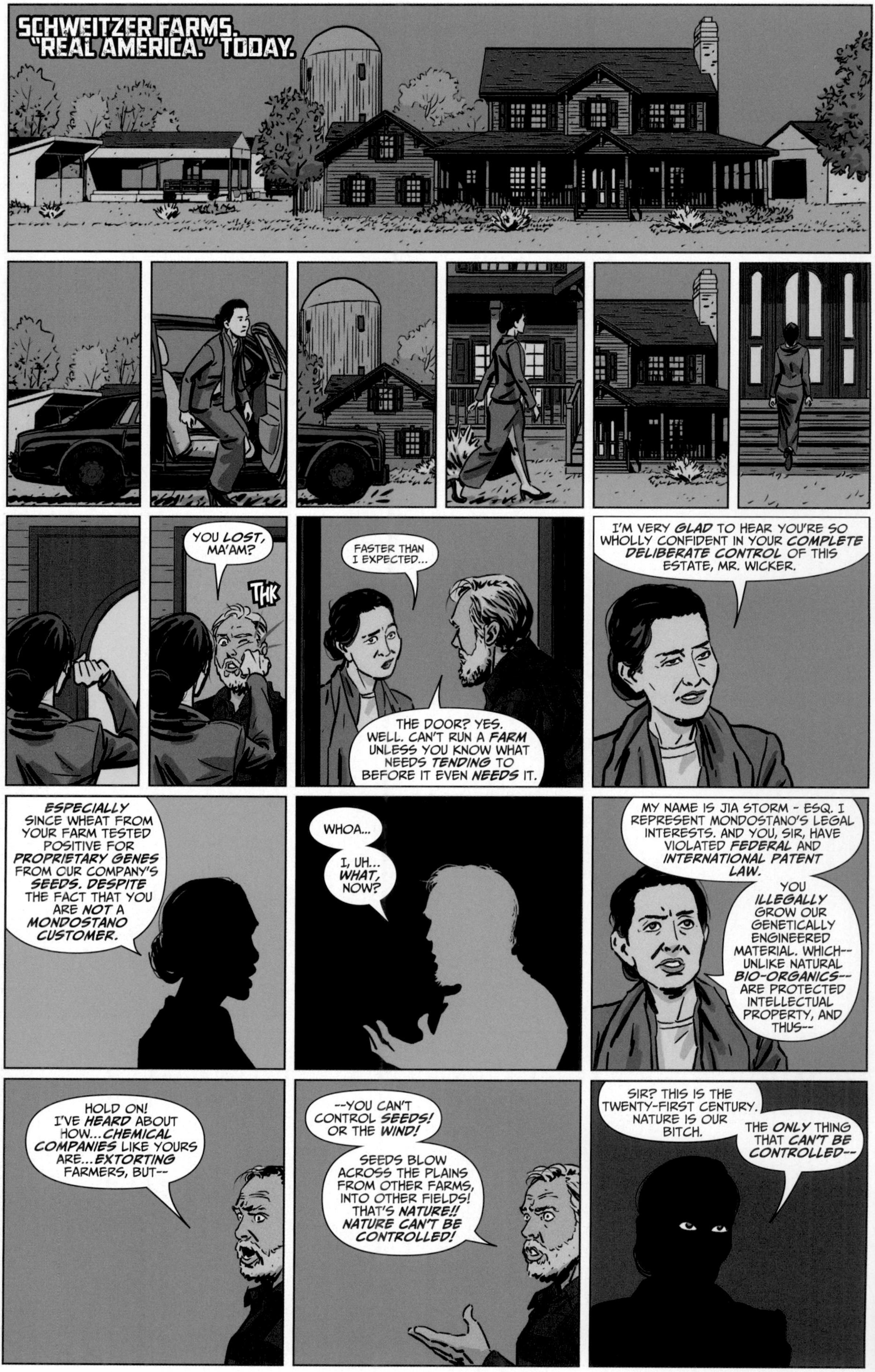
SCHWEITZER FARMS.
"REAL AMERICA." TODAY.
YOU LOST, MA'AM?
THK
FASTER THAN I EXPECTED...
THE DOOR? YES. WELL. CAN'T RUN A FARM UNLESS YOU KNOW WHAT NEEDS TENDING TO BEFORE IT EVEN NEEDS IT.
I'M VERY GLAD TO HEAR YOU'RE SO WHOLLY CONFIDENT IN YOUR COMPLETE DELIBERATE CONTROL OF THIS ESTATE, MR. WICKER.
ESPECIALLY SINCE WHEAT FROM YOUR FARM TESTED POSITIVE FOR PROPRIETARY GENES FROM OUR COMPANY'S SEEDS. DESPITE THE FACT THAT YOU ARE NOT A MONDOSTANO CUSTOMER.
WHOA...
I, UH... WHAT, NOW?
MY NAME IS JIA STORM - ESQ. I REPRESENT MONDOSTANO'S LEGAL INTERESTS. AND YOU, SIR, HAVE VIOLATED FEDERAL AND INTERNATIONAL PATENT LAW.
YOU ILLEGALLY GROW OUR GENETICALLY ENGINEERED MATERIAL. WHICH-- UNLIKE NATURAL BIO-ORGANICS-- ARE PROTECTED INTELLECTUAL PROPERTY, AND THUS--
HOLD ON! I'VE HEARD ABOUT HOW...CHEMICAL COMPANIES LIKE YOURS ARE...EXTORTING FARMERS, BUT--
--YOU CAN'T CONTROL SEEDS! OR THE WIND!
SEEDS BLOW ACROSS THE PLAINS FROM OTHER FARMS, INTO OTHER FIELDS! THAT'S NATURE!! NATURE CAN'T BE CONTROLLED!
SIR? THIS IS THE TWENTY-FIRST CENTURY. NATURE IS OUR BITCH.
THE ONLY THING THAT CAN'T BE CONTROLLED--

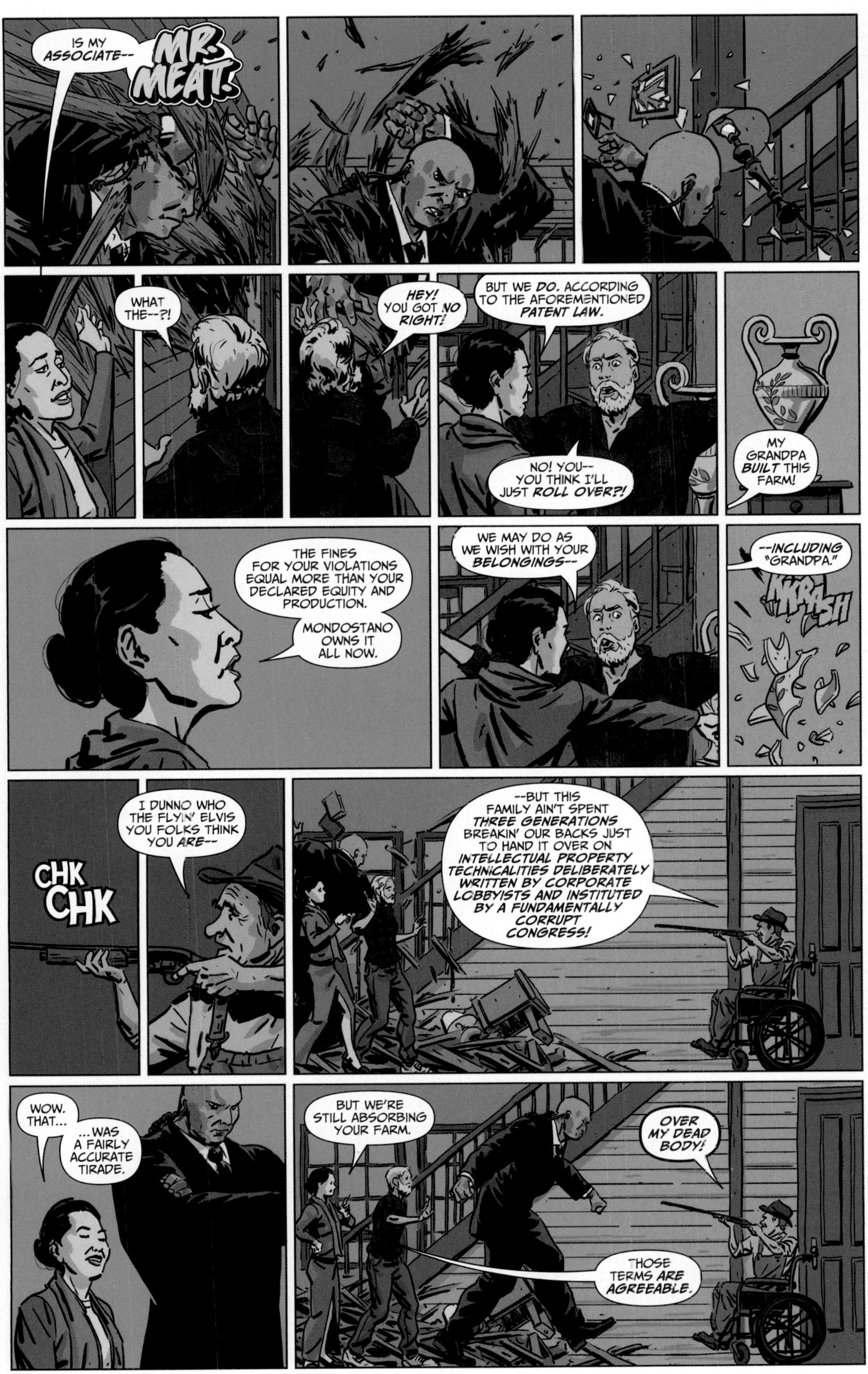
IS MY ASSOCIATE--
MR. MEAT!
WHAT THE--?!
HEY! YOU GOT NO RIGHT!
BUT WE DO. ACCORDING TO THE AFOREMENTIONED PATENT LAW.
NO! YOU-- YOU THINK I'LL JUST ROLL OVER?!
MY GRANDPA BUILT THIS FARM!
THE FINES FOR YOUR VIOLATIONS EQUAL MORE THAN YOUR DECLARED EQUITY AND PRODUCTION.
MONDOSTANO OWNS IT ALL NOW.
WE MAY DO AS WE WISH WITH YOUR BELONGINGS--
--INCLUDING "GRANDPA."
KKRASH
CHK CHK
I DUNNO WHO THE FLYIN' ELVIS YOU FOLKS THINK YOU ARE--
--BUT THIS FAMILY AIN'T SPENT THREE GENERATIONS BREAKIN' OUR BACKS JUST TO HAND IT OVER ON INTELLECTUAL PROPERTY TECHNICALITIES DELIBERATELY WRITTEN BY CORPORATE LOBBYISTS AND INSTITUTED BY A FUNDAMENTALLY CORRUPT CONGRESS!
WOW. THAT...
...WAS A FAIRLY ACCURATE TIRADE.
BUT WE'RE STILL ABSORBING YOUR FARM.
OVER MY DEAD BODY!
THOSE TERMS ARE AGREEABLE.

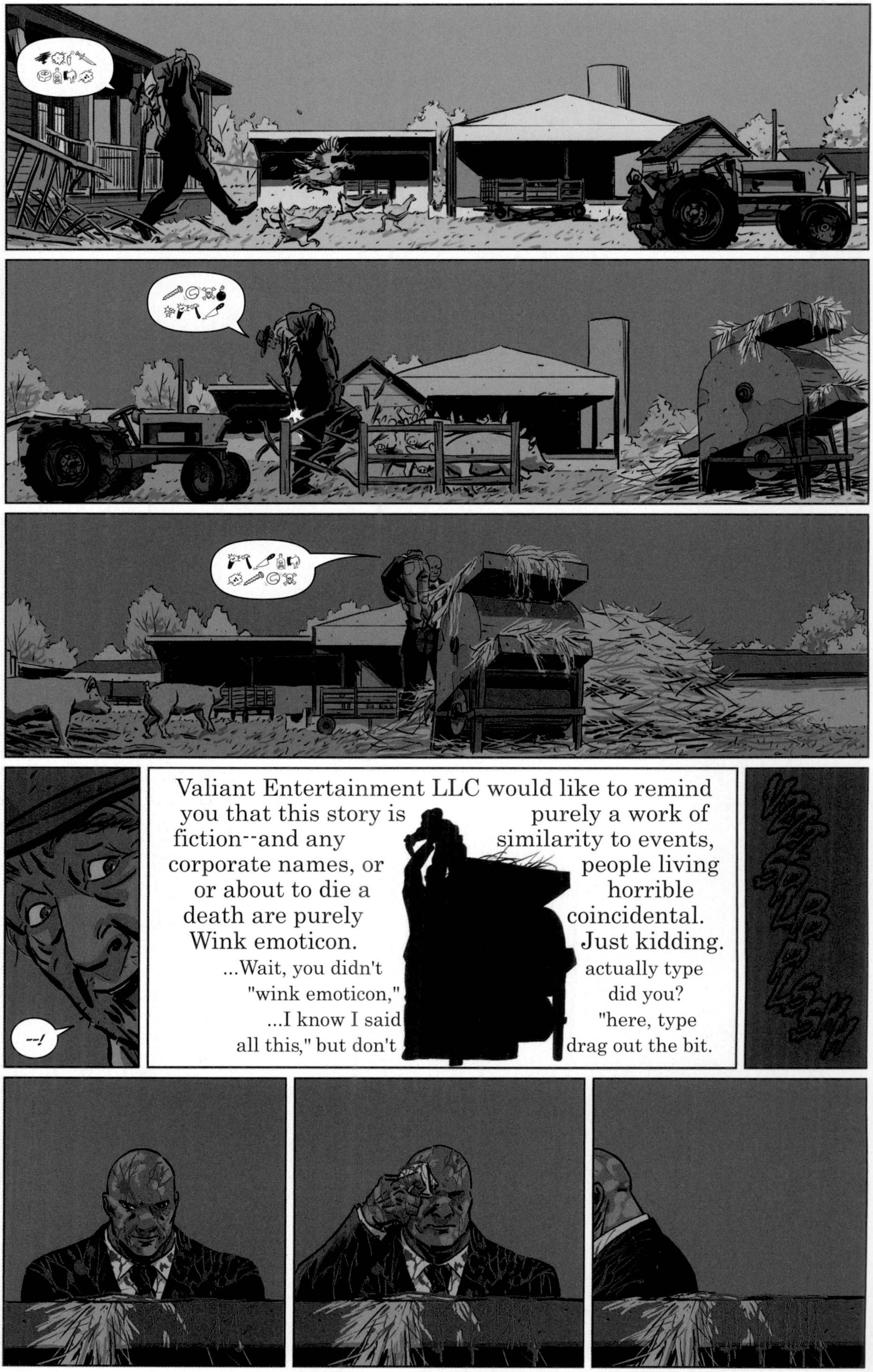
--!
Valiant Entertainment LLC would like to remind you that this story is purely a work of fiction--and any similarity to events, corporate names, or people living or about to die a horrible death are purely coincidental. Wink emoticon. Just kidding.
...Wait, you didn't actually type "wink emoticon," did you? ...I know I said "here, type all this," but don't drag out the bit.

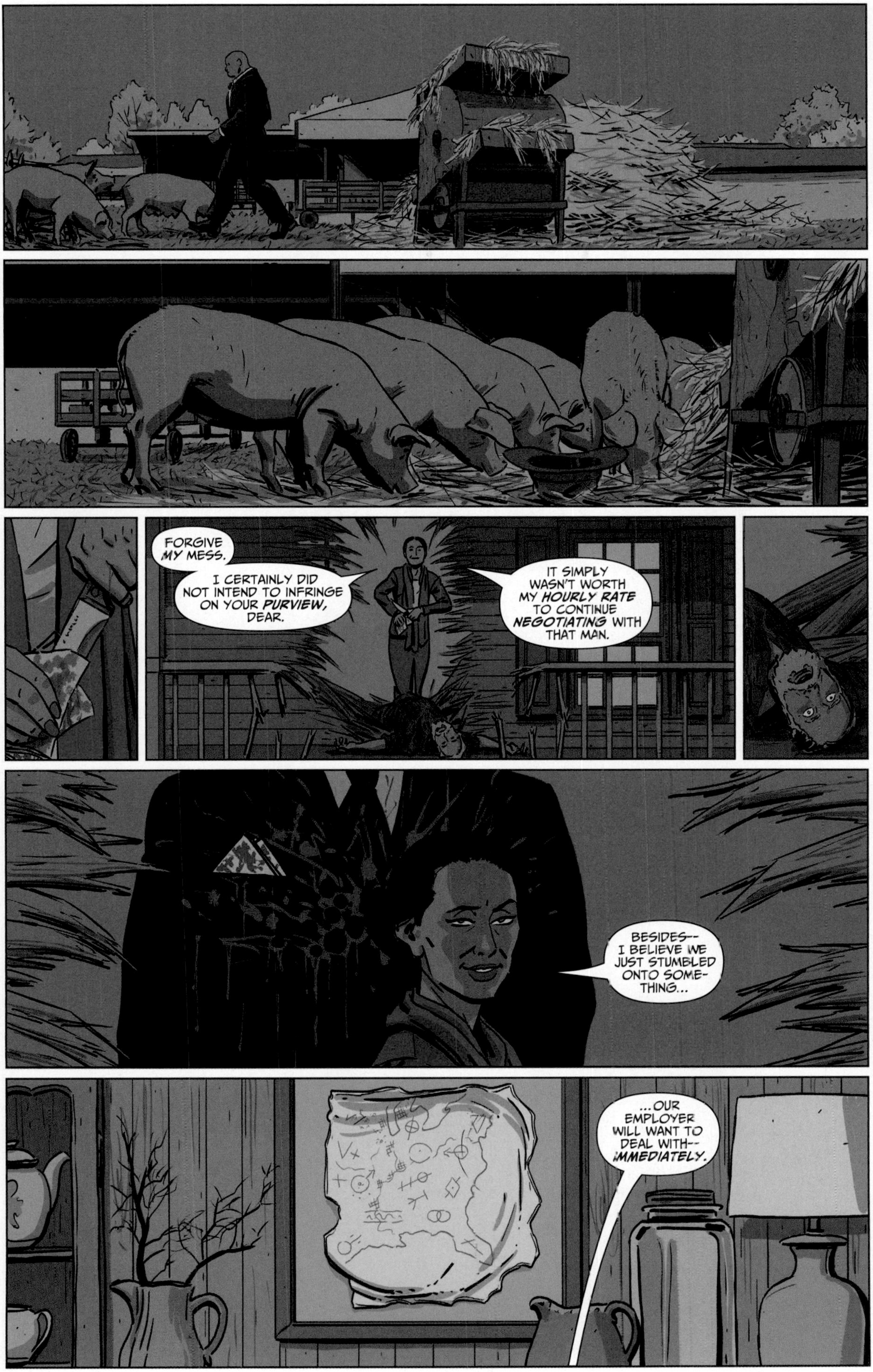
FORGIVE MY MESS.
I CERTAINLY DID NOT INTEND TO INFRINGE ON YOUR PURVIEW, DEAR.
IT SIMPLY WASN'T WORTH MY HOURLY RATE TO CONTINUE NEGOTIATING WITH THAT MAN.
BESIDES-- I BELIEVE WE JUST STUMBLED ONTO SOME-THING...
...OUR EMPLOYER WILL WANT TO DEAL WITH-- IMMEDIATELY.

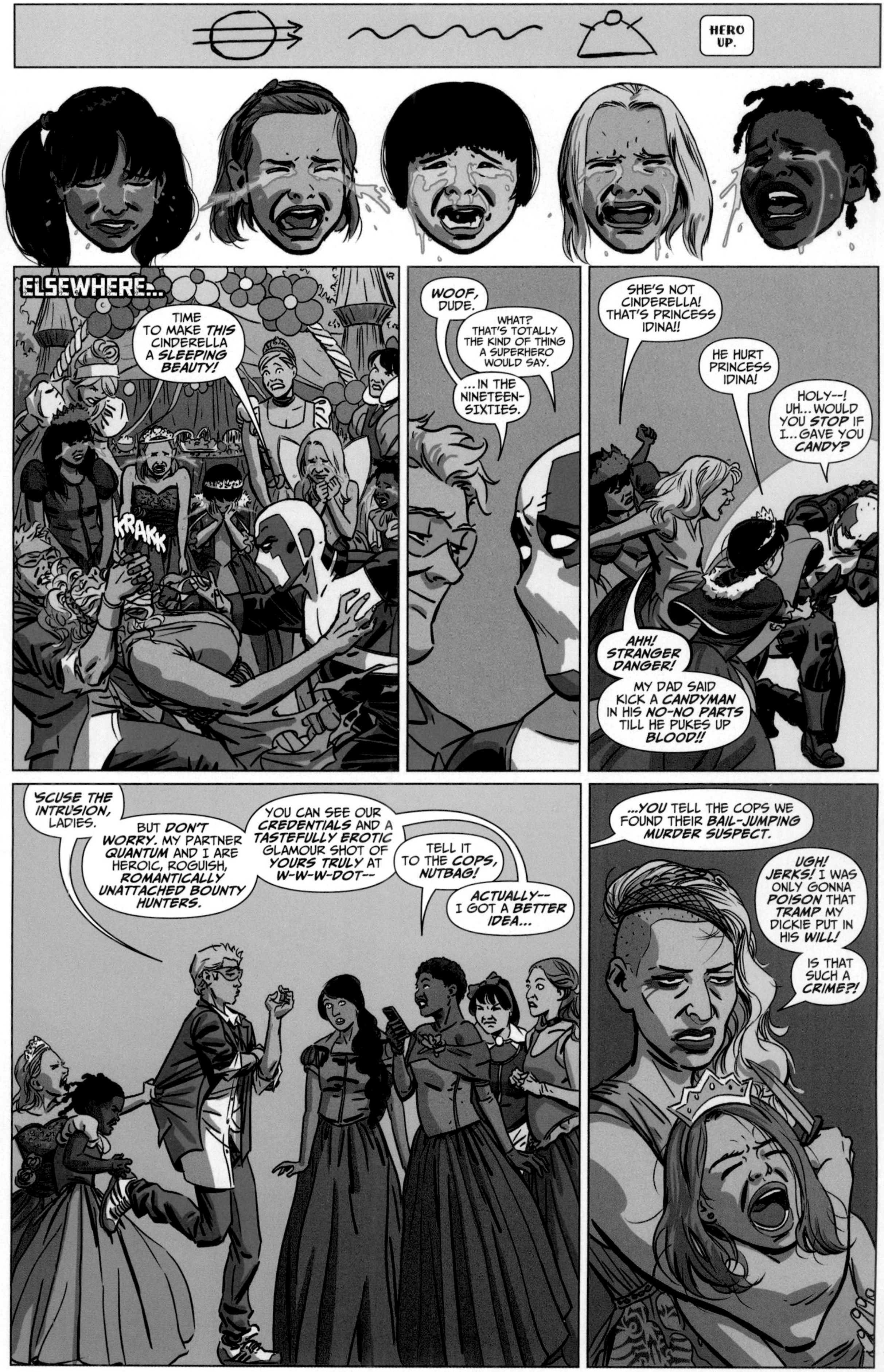
HERO UP.
ELSEWHERE...
TIME TO MAKE THIS CINDERELLA A SLEEPING BEAUTY!
KRAKK
WOOF, DUDE.
WHAT? THAT'S TOTALLY THE KIND OF THING A SUPERHERO WOULD SAY.
...IN THE NINETEEN-SIXTIES.
SHE'S NOT CINDERELLA! THAT'S PRINCESS IDINA!!
HE HURT PRINCESS IDINA!
HOLY--! UH...WOULD YOU STOP IF I...GAVE YOU CANDY?
AHH! STRANGER DANGER!
MY DAD SAID KICK A CANDYMAN IN HIS NO-NO PARTS TILL HE PUKES UP BLOOD!!
'SCUSE THE INTRUSION, LADIES.
BUT DON'T WORRY. MY PARTNER QUANTUM AND I ARE HEROIC, ROGUISH, ROMANTICALLY UNATTACHED BOUNTY HUNTERS.
YOU CAN SEE OUR CREDENTIALS AND A TASTEFULLY EROTIC GLAMOUR SHOT OF YOURS TRULY AT W-W-W-DOT--
TELL IT TO THE COPS, NUTBAG!
ACTUALLY-- I GOT A BETTER IDEA...
...YOU TELL THE COPS WE FOUND THEIR BAIL-JUMPING MURDER SUSPECT.
UGH! JERKS! I WAS ONLY GONNA POISON THAT TRAMP MY DICKIE PUT IN HIS WILL!
IS THAT SUCH A CRIME?!

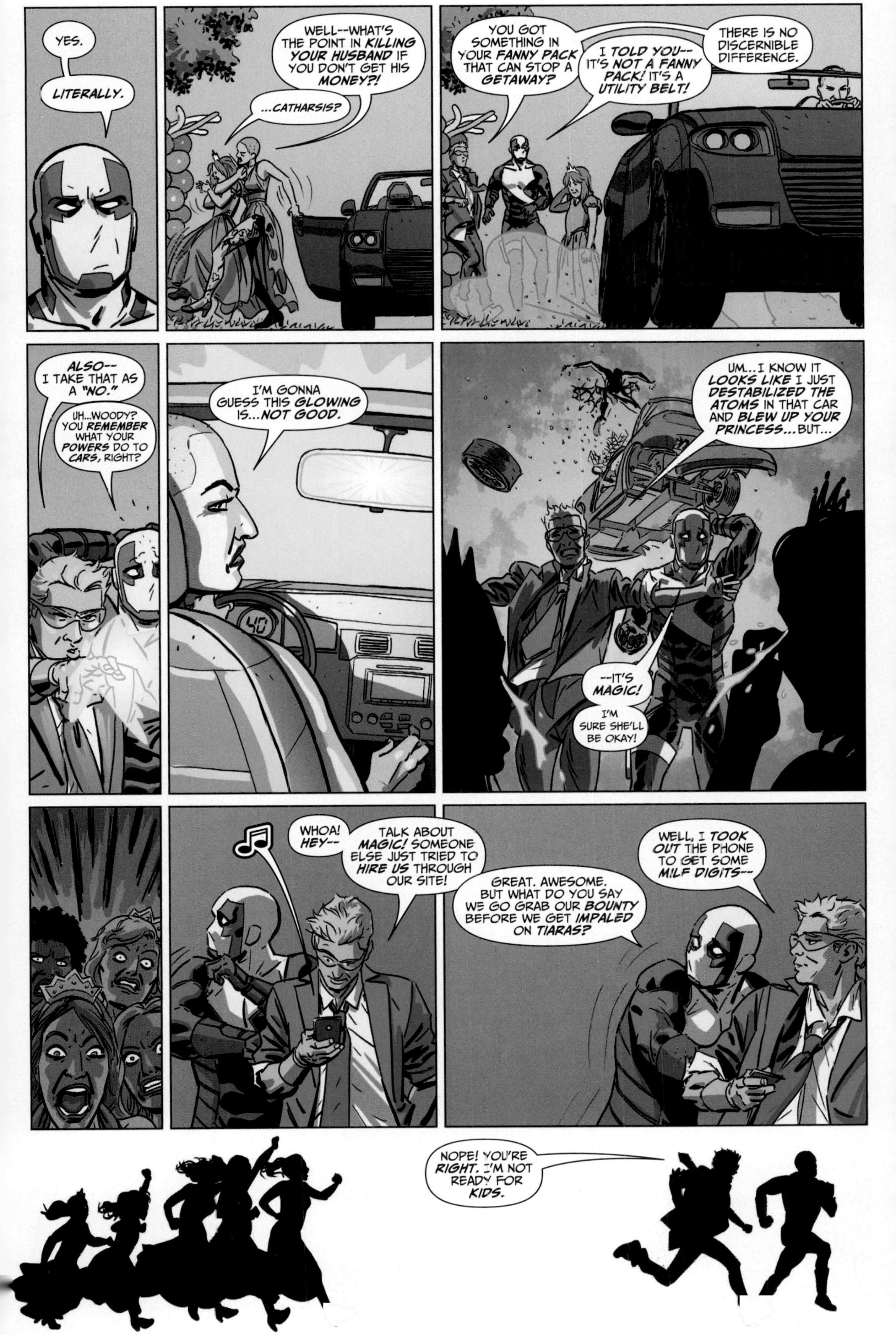
YES.
LITERALLY.
WELL--WHAT'S THE POINT IN KILLING YOUR HUSBAND IF YOU DON'T GET HIS MONEY?!
...CATHARSIS?
YOU GOT SOMETHING IN YOUR FANNY PACK THAT CAN STOP A GETAWAY?
I TOLD YOU-- IT'S NOT A FANNY PACK! IT'S A UTILITY BELT!
THERE IS NO DISCERNIBLE DIFFERENCE.
ALSO-- I TAKE THAT AS A "NO."
UH...WOODY? YOU REMEMBER WHAT YOUR POWERS DO TO CARS, RIGHT?
I'M GONNA GUESS THIS GLOWING IS...NOT GOOD.
UM...I KNOW IT LOOKS LIKE I JUST DESTABILIZED THE ATOMS IN THAT CAR AND BLEW UP YOUR PRINCESS...BUT...
--IT'S MAGIC!
I'M SURE SHE'LL BE OKAY!
WHOA! HEY--
TALK ABOUT MAGIC! SOMEONE ELSE JUST TRIED TO HIRE US THROUGH OUR SITE!
GREAT. AWESOME. BUT WHAT DO YOU SAY WE GO GRAB OUR BOUNTY BEFORE WE GET IMPALED ON TIARAS?
WELL, I TOOK OUT THE PHONE TO GET SOME MILF DIGITS--
NOPE! YOU'RE RIGHT. I'M NOT READY FOR KIDS.

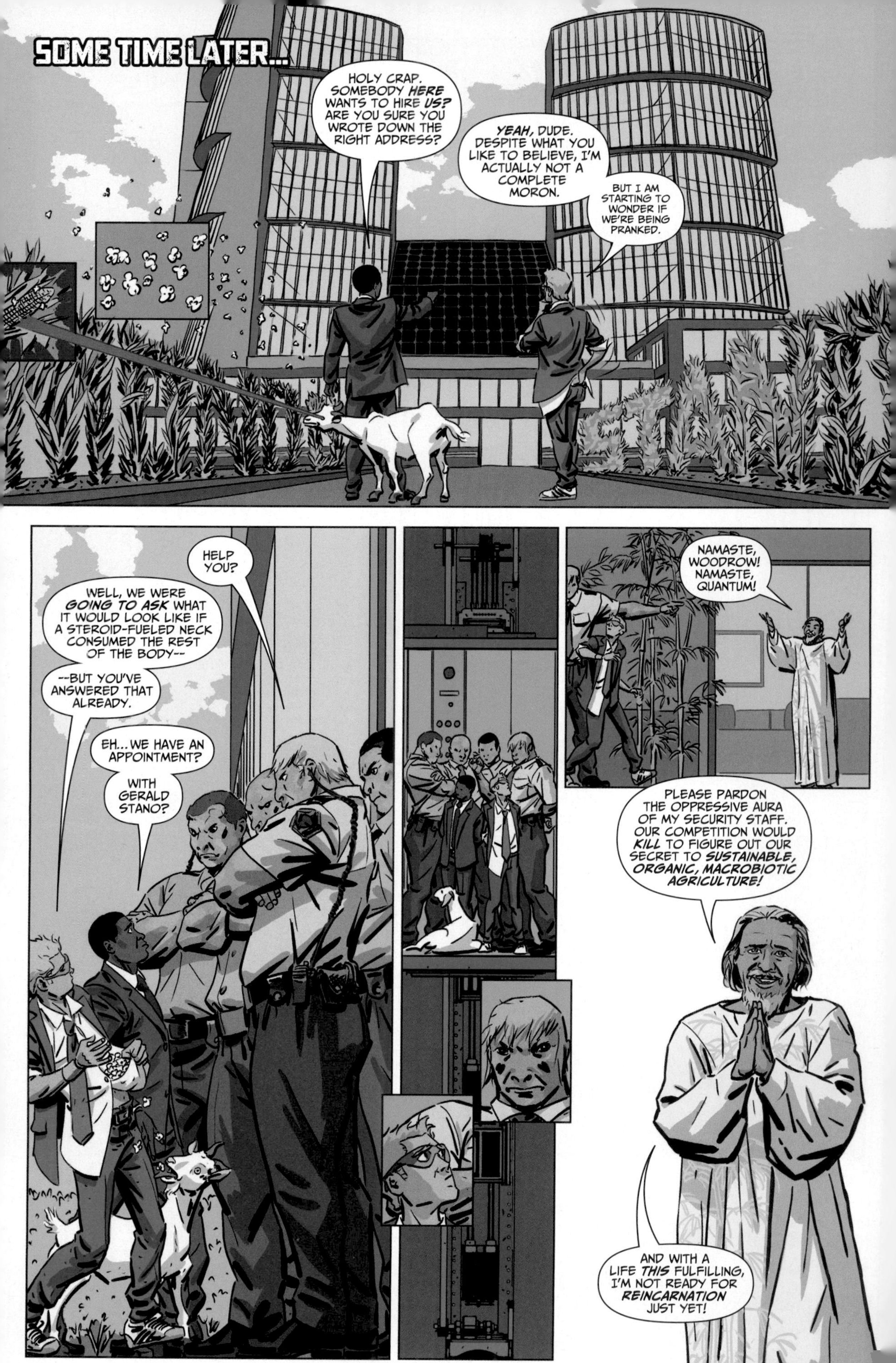
SOME TIME LATER...
HOLY CRAP. SOMEBODY HERE WANTS TO HIRE US? ARE YOU SURE YOU WROTE DOWN THE RIGHT ADDRESS?
YEAH, DUDE. DESPITE WHAT YOU LIKE TO BELIEVE, I'M ACTUALLY NOT A COMPLETE MORON.
BUT I AM STARTING TO WONDER IF WE'RE BEING PRANKED.
HELP YOU?
WELL, WE WERE GOING TO ASK WHAT IT WOULD LOOK LIKE IF A STEROID-FUELED NECK CONSUMED THE REST OF THE BODY--
--BUT YOU'VE ANSWERED THAT ALREADY.
EH...WE HAVE AN APPOINTMENT?
WITH GERALD STANO?
NAMASTE, WOODROW! NAMASTE, QUANTUM!
PLEASE PARDON THE OPPRESSIVE AURA OF MY SECURITY STAFF. OUR COMPETITION WOULD KILL TO FIGURE OUT OUR SECRET TO SUSTAINABLE, ORGANIC, MACROBIOTIC AGRICULTURE!
AND WITH A LIFE THIS FULFILLING, I'M NOT READY FOR REINCARNATION JUST YET!

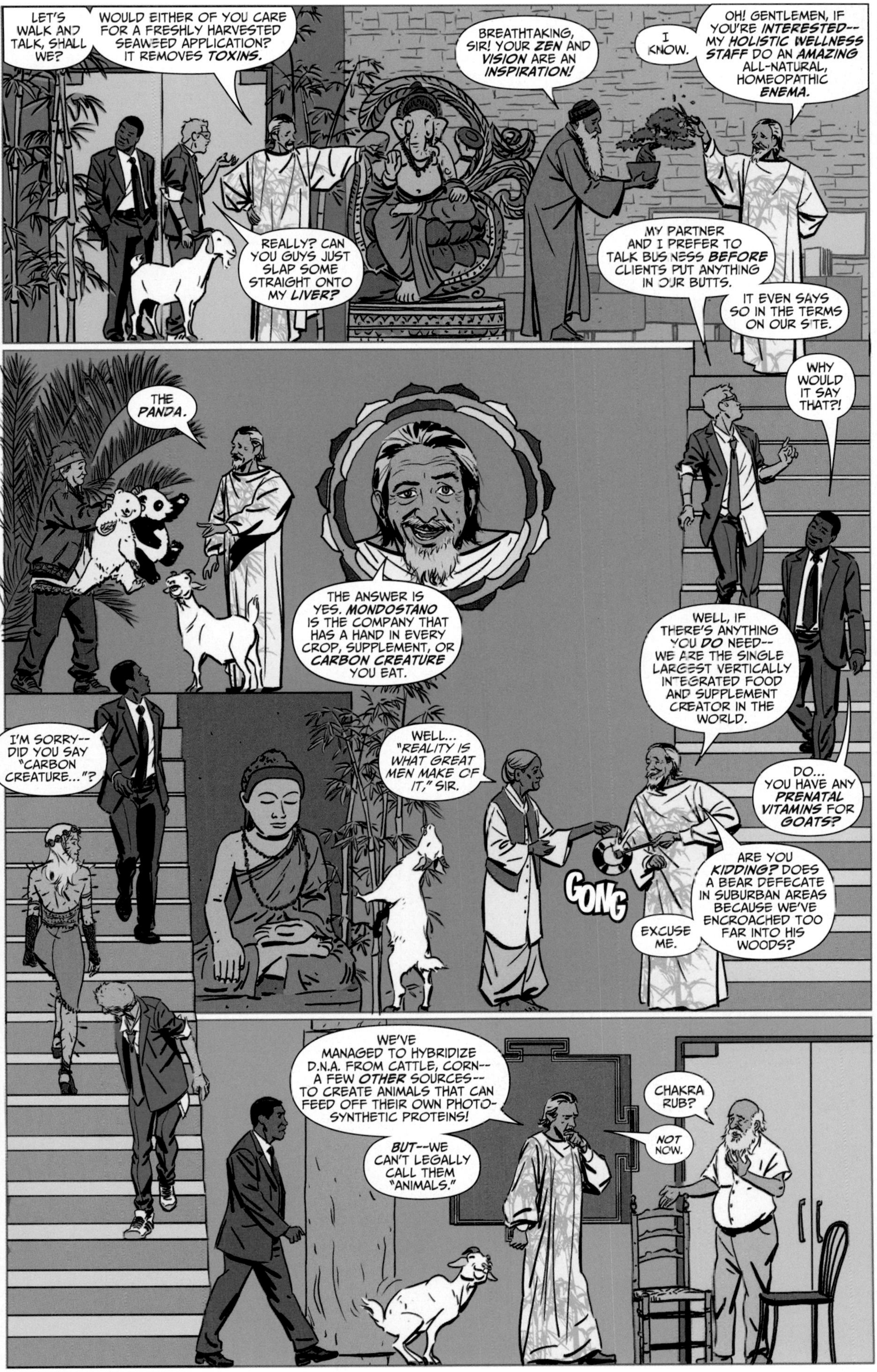

LET'S WALK AND TALK, SHALL WE?
WOULD EITHER OF YOU CARE FOR A FRESHLY HARVESTED SEAWEED APPLICATION? IT REMOVES TOXINS.
REALLY? CAN YOU GUYS JUST SLAP SOME STRAIGHT ONTO MY LIVER?
BREATHTAKING, SIR! YOUR ZEN AND VISION ARE AN INSPIRATION!
I KNOW.
OH! GENTLEMEN, IF YOU'RE INTERESTED-- MY HOLISTIC WELLNESS STAFF DO AN AMAZING ALL-NATURAL, HOMEOPATHIC ENEMA.
MY PARTNER AND I PREFER TO TALK BUSINESS BEFORE CLIENTS PUT ANYTHING IN OUR BUTTS.
IT EVEN SAYS SO IN THE TERMS ON OUR SITE.
WHY WOULD IT SAY THAT?!
THE PANDA.
THE ANSWER IS YES. MONDOSTANO IS THE COMPANY THAT HAS A HAND IN EVERY CROP, SUPPLEMENT, OR CARBON CREATURE YOU EAT.
WELL, IF THERE'S ANYTHING YOU DO NEED-- WE ARE THE SINGLE LARGEST VERTICALLY INTEGRATED FOOD AND SUPPLEMENT CREATOR IN THE WORLD.
I'M SORRY-- DID YOU SAY "CARBON CREATURE..."?
WELL... "REALITY IS WHAT GREAT MEN MAKE OF IT," SIR.
GONG
DO... YOU HAVE ANY PRENATAL VITAMINS FOR GOATS?
ARE YOU KIDDING? DOES A BEAR DEFECATE IN SUBURBAN AREAS BECAUSE WE'VE ENCROACHED TOO FAR INTO HIS WOODS?
EXCUSE ME.
WE'VE MANAGED TO HYBRIDIZE D.N.A. FROM CATTLE, CORN-- A FEW OTHER SOURCES-- TO CREATE ANIMALS THAT CAN FEED OFF THEIR OWN PHOTO-SYNTHETIC PROTEINS!
BUT--WE CAN'T LEGALLY CALL THEM "ANIMALS."
CHAKRA RUB?
NOT NOW.

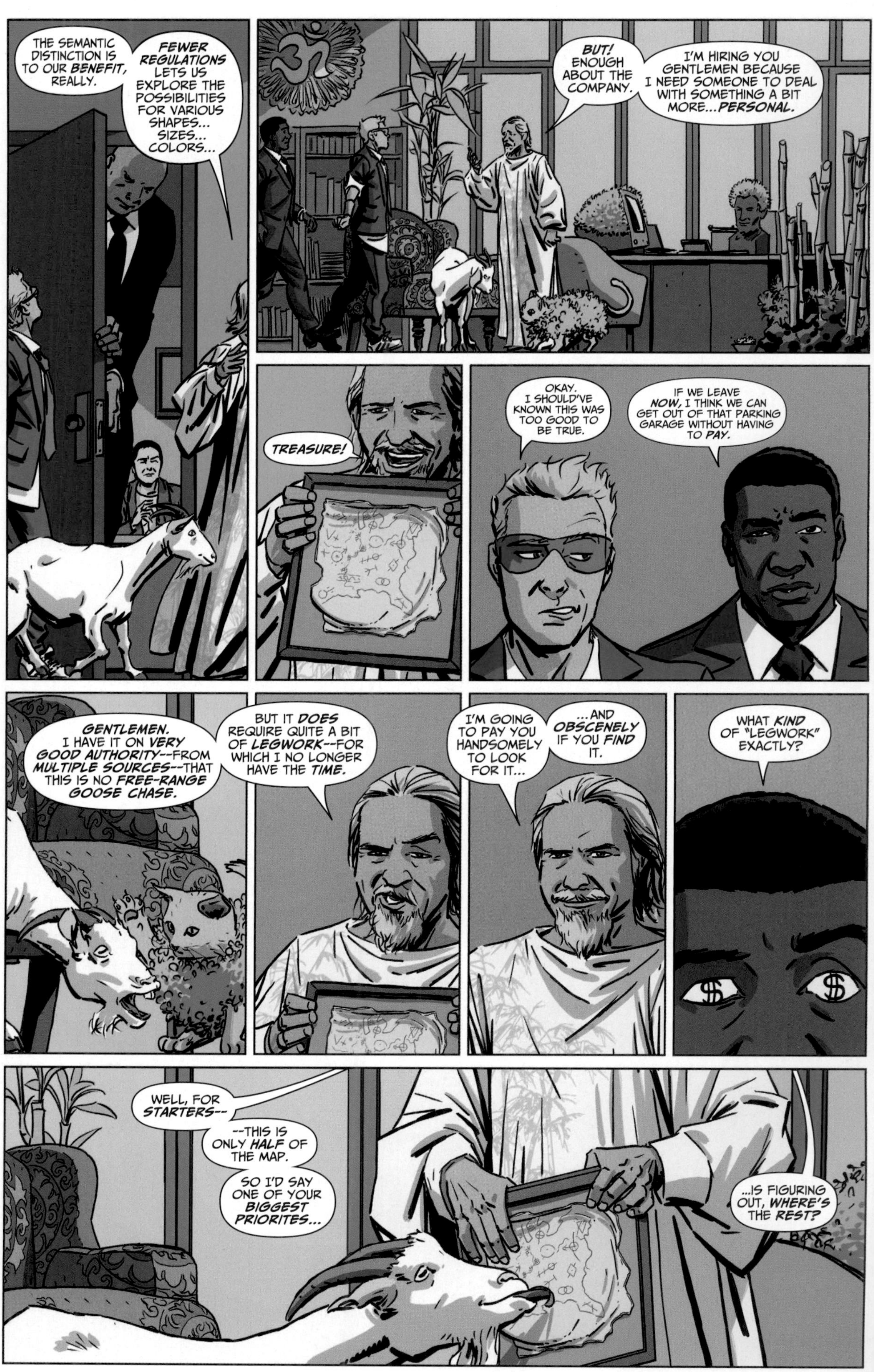
THE SEMANTIC DISTINCTION IS TO OUR BENEFIT, REALLY.
FEWER REGULATIONS LETS US EXPLORE THE POSSIBILITIES FOR VARIOUS SHAPES... SIZES... COLORS...
BUT! ENOUGH ABOUT THE COMPANY.
I'M HIRING YOU GENTLEMEN BECAUSE I NEED SOMEONE TO DEAL WITH SOMETHING A BIT MORE...PERSONAL.
TREASURE!
OKAY. I SHOULD'VE KNOWN THIS WAS TOO GOOD TO BE TRUE.
IF WE LEAVE NOW, I THINK WE CAN GET OUT OF THAT PARKING GARAGE WITHOUT HAVING TO PAY.
GENTLEMEN. I HAVE IT ON VERY GOOD AUTHORITY--FROM MULTIPLE SOURCES--THAT THIS IS NO FREE-RANGE GOOSE CHASE.
BUT IT DOES REQUIRE QUITE A BIT OF LEGWORK--FOR WHICH I NO LONGER HAVE THE TIME.
I'M GOING TO PAY YOU HANDSOMELY TO LOOK FOR IT...
...AND OBSCENELY IF YOU FIND IT.
WHAT KIND OF "LEGWORK" EXACTLY?
WELL, FOR STARTERS--
--THIS IS ONLY HALF OF THE MAP.
SO I'D SAY ONE OF YOUR BIGGEST PRIORITES...
...IS FIGURING OUT, WHERE'S THE REST?

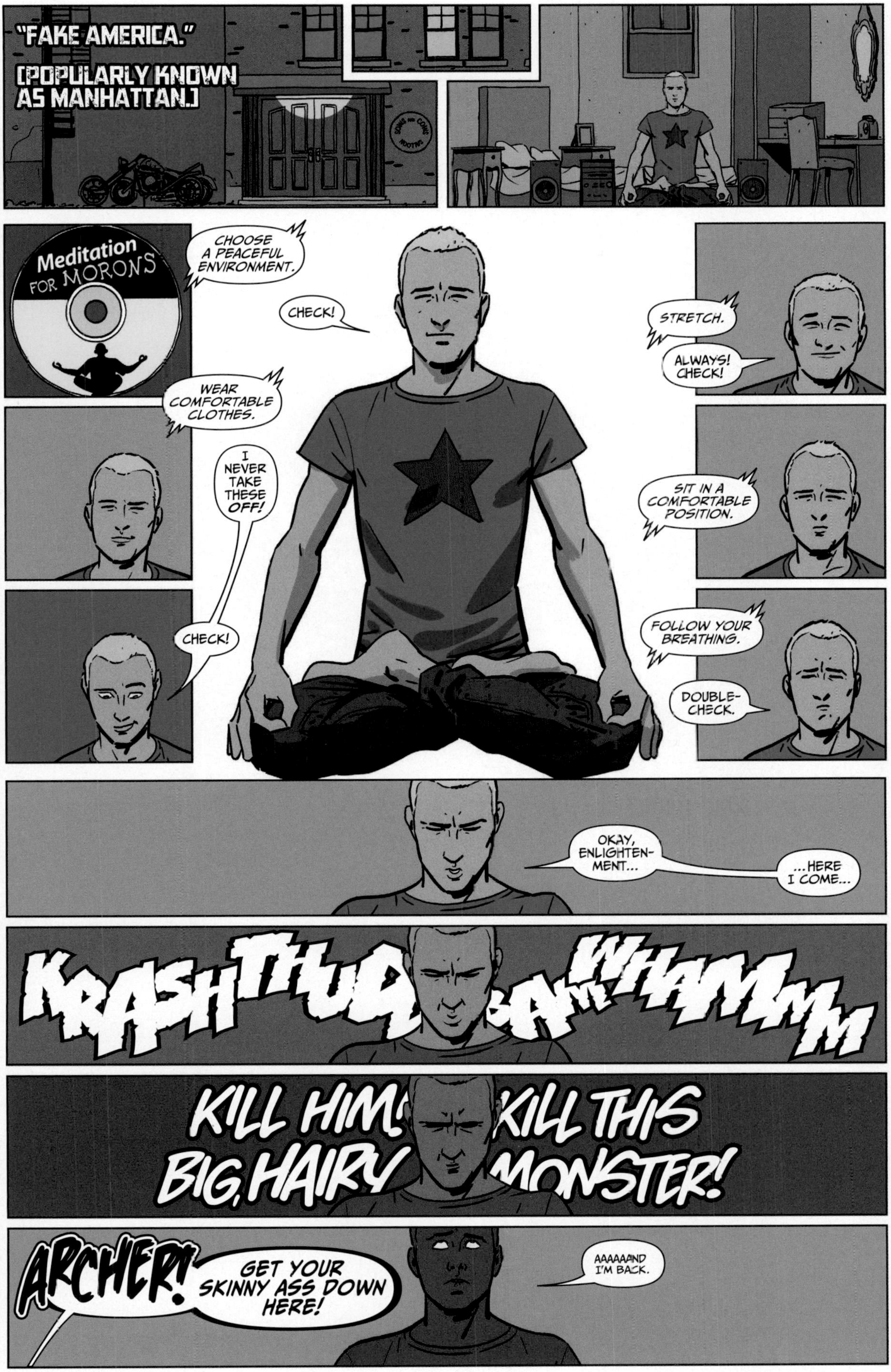
"FAKE AMERICA."
[POPULARLY KNOWN AS MANHATTAN.]
SONG AND COMIC BOOTING
Meditation FOR MORONS
CHOOSE A PEACEFUL ENVIRONMENT.
CHECK!
STRETCH.
ALWAYS! CHECK!
WEAR COMFORTABLE CLOTHES.
I NEVER TAKE THESE OFF!
CHECK!
SIT IN A COMFORTABLE POSITION.
FOLLOW YOUR BREATHING.
DOUBLE-CHECK.
OKAY, ENLIGHTEN-MENT...
...HERE I COME...
KRASH THUD BAM WHAMMM
KILL HIM! KILL THIS BIG, HAIRY MONSTER!
ARCHER! GET YOUR SKINNY ASS DOWN HERE!
AAAAAAND I'M BACK.

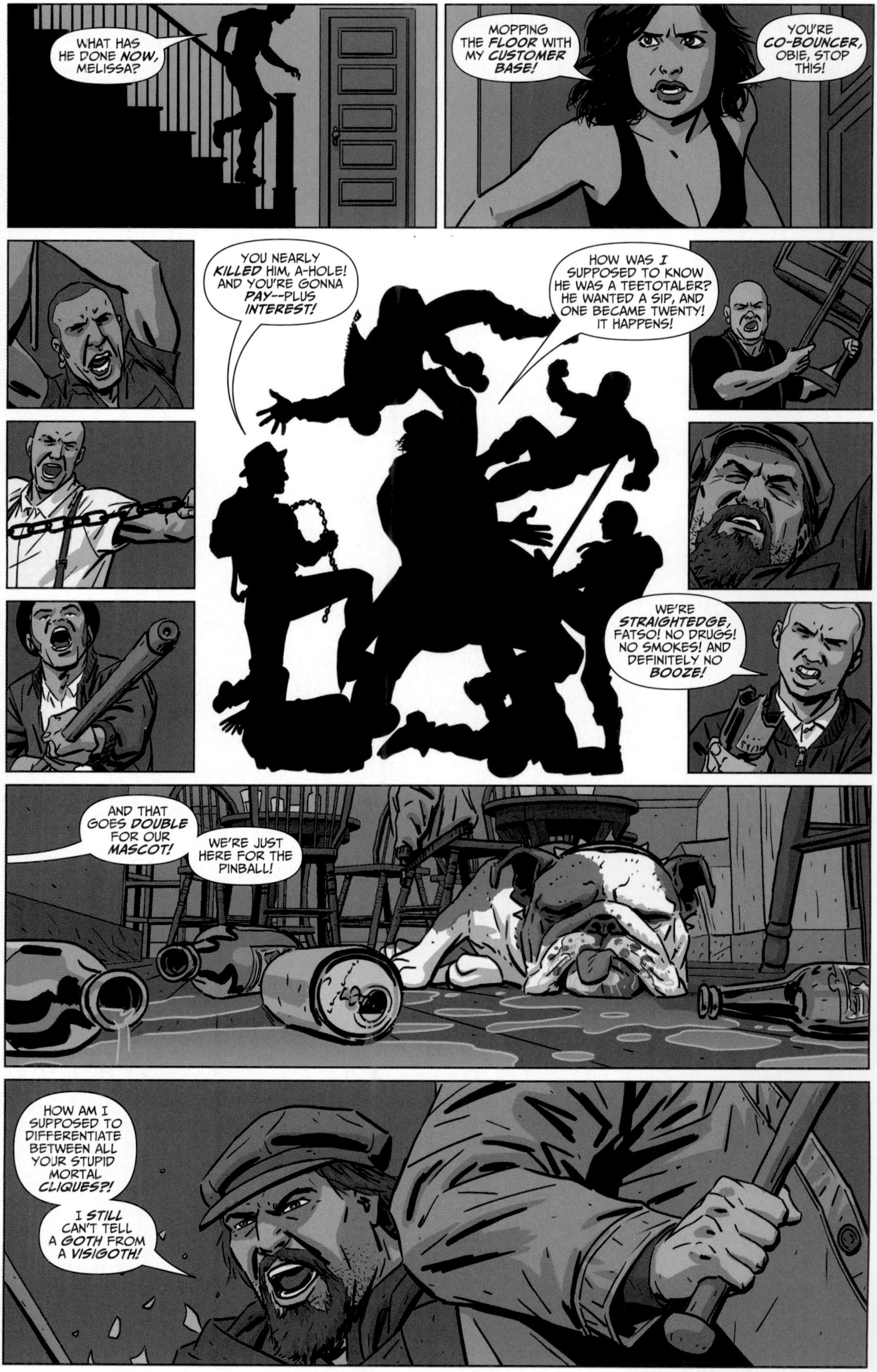
WHAT HAS HE DONE NOW, MELISSA?
MOPPING THE FLOOR WITH MY CUSTOMER BASE!
YOU'RE CO-BOUNCER, OBIE, STOP THIS!
YOU NEARLY KILLED HIM, A-HOLE! AND YOU'RE GONNA PAY--PLUS INTEREST!
HOW WAS I SUPPOSED TO KNOW HE WAS A TEETOTALER? HE WANTED A SIP, AND ONE BECAME TWENTY! IT HAPPENS!
WE'RE STRAIGHTEDGE, FATSO! NO DRUGS! NO SMOKES! AND DEFINITELY NO BOOZE!
AND THAT GOES DOUBLE FOR OUR MASCOT!
WE'RE JUST HERE FOR THE PINBALL!
HOW AM I SUPPOSED TO DIFFERENTIATE BETWEEN ALL YOUR STUPID MORTAL CLIQUES?!
I STILL CAN'T TELL A GOTH FROM A VISIGOTH!

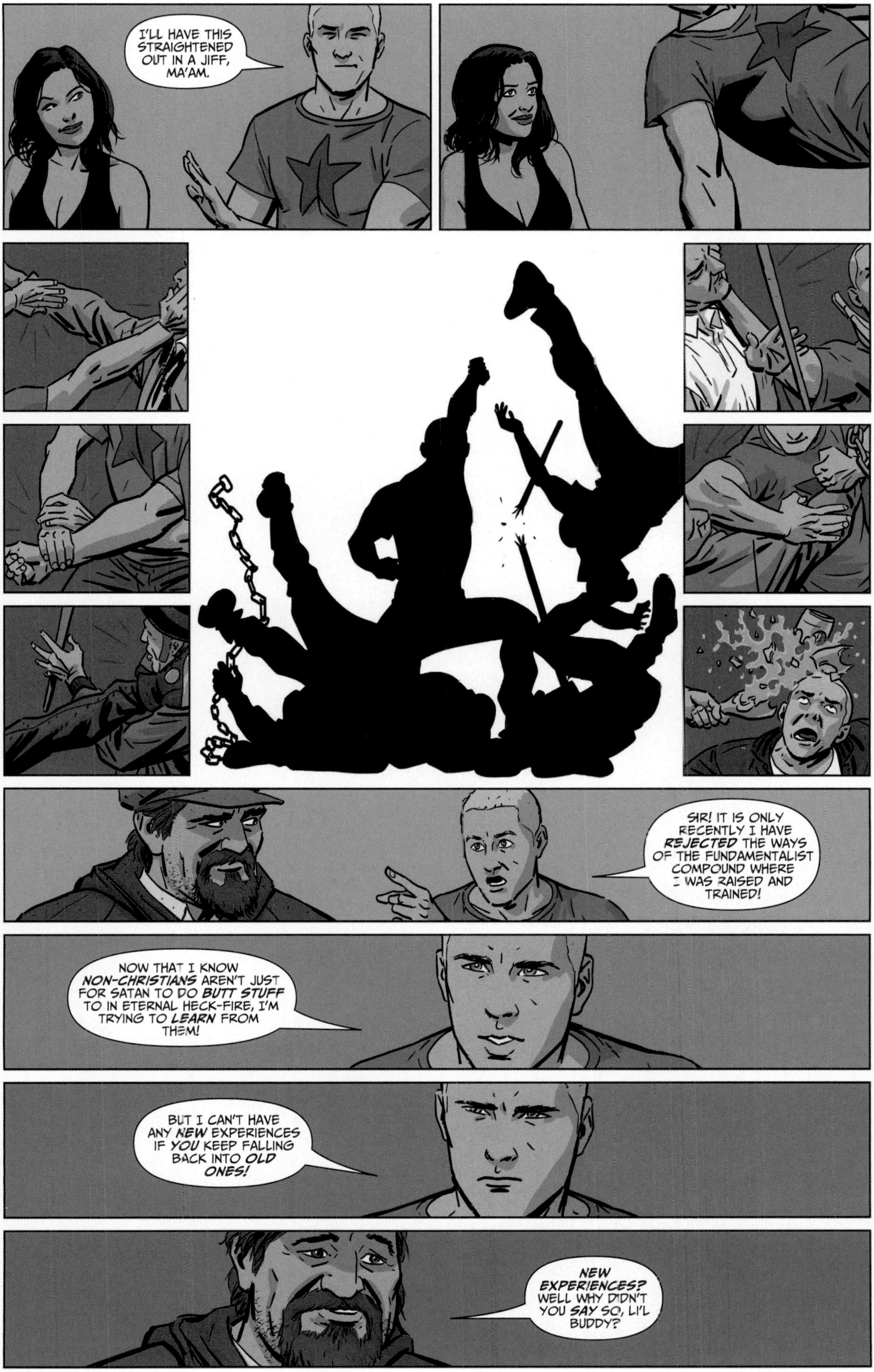
I'LL HAVE THIS STRAIGHTENED OUT IN A JIFF, MA'AM.
SIR! IT IS ONLY RECENTLY I HAVE REJECTED THE WAYS OF THE FUNDAMENTALIST COMPOUND WHERE I WAS RAISED AND TRAINED!
NOW THAT I KNOW NON-CHRISTIANS AREN'T JUST FOR SATAN TO DO BUTT STUFF TO IN ETERNAL HECK-FIRE, I'M TRYING TO LEARN FROM THEM!
BUT I CAN'T HAVE ANY NEW EXPERIENCES IF YOU KEEP FALLING BACK INTO OLD ONES!
NEW EXPERIENCES? WELL WHY DIDN'T YOU SAY SO, LI'L BUDDY?

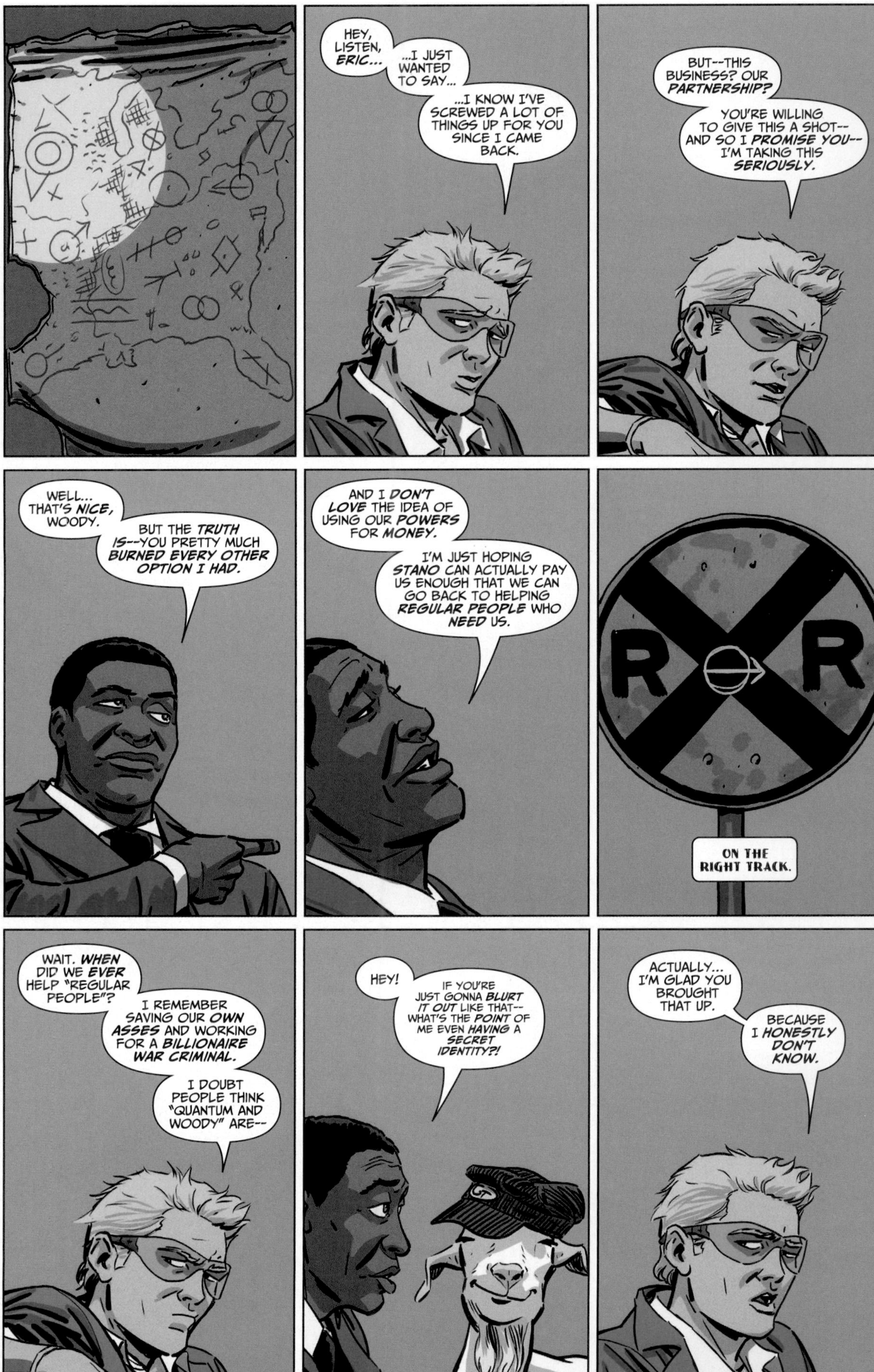
HEY, LISTEN, ERIC...
...I JUST WANTED TO SAY...
...I KNOW I'VE SCREWED A LOT OF THINGS UP FOR YOU SINCE I CAME BACK.
BUT--THIS BUSINESS? OUR PARTNERSHIP?
YOU'RE WILLING TO GIVE THIS A SHOT--AND SO I PROMISE YOU--I'M TAKING THIS SERIOUSLY.
WELL... THAT'S NICE, WOODY.
BUT THE TRUTH IS--YOU PRETTY MUCH BURNED EVERY OTHER OPTION I HAD.
AND I DON'T LOVE THE IDEA OF USING OUR POWERS FOR MONEY.
I'M JUST HOPING STANO CAN ACTUALLY PAY US ENOUGH THAT WE CAN GO BACK TO HELPING REGULAR PEOPLE WHO NEED US.
R
R
ON THE RIGHT TRACK.
WAIT. WHEN DID WE EVER HELP "REGULAR PEOPLE"?
I REMEMBER SAVING OUR OWN ASSES AND WORKING FOR A BILLIONAIRE WAR CRIMINAL.
I DOUBT PEOPLE THINK "QUANTUM AND WOODY" ARE--
HEY!
IF YOU'RE JUST GONNA BLURT IT OUT LIKE THAT--WHAT'S THE POINT OF ME EVEN HAVING A SECRET IDENTITY?!
ACTUALLY... I'M GLAD YOU BROUGHT THAT UP.
BECAUSE I HONESTLY DON'T KNOW.

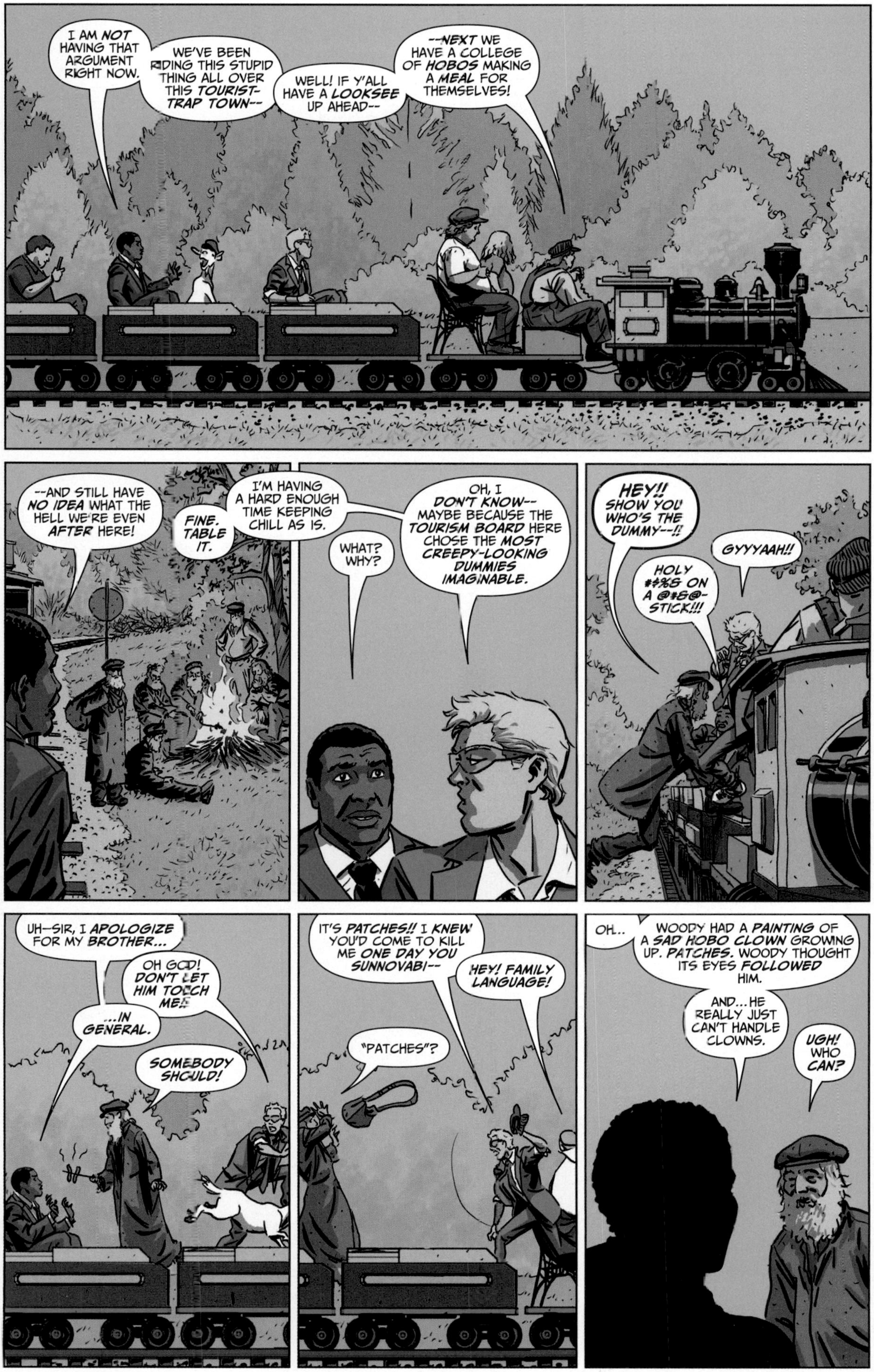
I AM NOT HAVING THAT ARGUMENT RIGHT NOW.
WE'VE BEEN RIDING THIS STUPID THING ALL OVER THIS TOURIST-TRAP TOWN--
WELL! IF Y'ALL HAVE A LOOKSEE UP AHEAD--
--NEXT WE HAVE A COLLEGE OF HOBOS MAKING A MEAL FOR THEMSELVES!
--AND STILL HAVE NO IDEA WHAT THE HELL WE'RE EVEN AFTER HERE!
I'M HAVING A HARD ENOUGH TIME KEEPING CHILL AS IS.
FINE. TABLE IT.
WHAT? WHY?
OH, I DON'T KNOW-- MAYBE BECAUSE THE TOURISM BOARD HERE CHOSE THE MOST CREEPY-LOOKING DUMMIES IMAGINABLE.
HEY!! SHOW YOU WHO'S THE DUMMY--!!
GYYYAAH!!
HOLY #$%S ON A @#&@-STICK!!!
UH--SIR, I APOLOGIZE FOR MY BROTHER...
OH GOD! DON'T LET HIM TOUCH ME!
...IN GENERAL.
SOMEBODY SHOULD!
IT'S PATCHES!! I KNEW YOU'D COME TO KILL ME ONE DAY YOU SUNNOVABI--
HEY! FAMILY LANGUAGE!
"PATCHES"?
OH...
WOODY HAD A PAINTING OF A SAD HOBO CLOWN GROWING UP. PATCHES. WOODY THOUGHT ITS EYES FOLLOWED HIM.
AND... HE REALLY JUST CAN'T HANDLE CLOWNS.
UGH! WHO CAN?

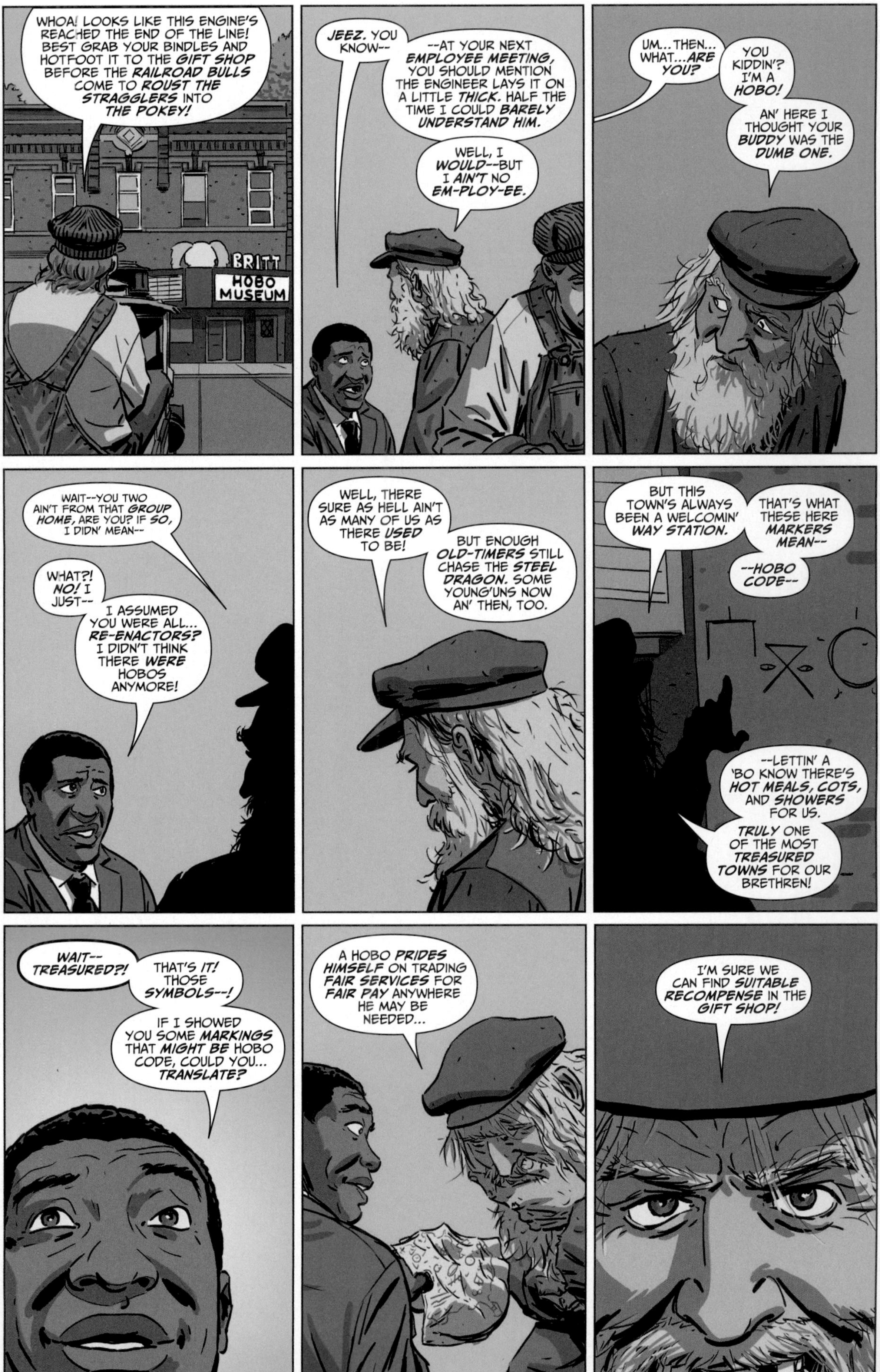
WHOA! LOOKS LIKE THIS ENGINE'S REACHED THE END OF THE LINE! BEST GRAB YOUR BINDLES AND HOTFOOT IT TO THE GIFT SHOP BEFORE THE RAILROAD BULLS COME TO ROUST THE STRAGGLERS INTO THE POKEY!
BRITT
HOBO MUSEUM
JEEZ. YOU KNOW--
--AT YOUR NEXT EMPLOYEE MEETING, YOU SHOULD MENTION THE ENGINEER LAYS IT ON A LITTLE THICK. HALF THE TIME I COULD BARELY UNDERSTAND HIM.
WELL, I WOULD--BUT I AIN'T NO EM-PLOY-EE.
UM...THEN... WHAT...ARE YOU?
YOU KIDDIN'? I'M A HOBO!
AN' HERE I THOUGHT YOUR BUDDY WAS THE DUMB ONE.
WAIT--YOU TWO AIN'T FROM THAT GROUP HOME, ARE YOU? IF SO, I DIDN' MEAN--
WHAT?! NO! I JUST--
I ASSUMED YOU WERE ALL... RE-ENACTORS? I DIDN'T THINK THERE WERE HOBOS ANYMORE!
WELL, THERE SURE AS HELL AIN'T AS MANY OF US AS THERE USED TO BE!
BUT ENOUGH OLD-TIMERS STILL CHASE THE STEEL DRAGON. SOME YOUNG'UNS NOW AN' THEN, TOO.
BUT THIS TOWN'S ALWAYS BEEN A WELCOMIN' WAY STATION.
THAT'S WHAT THESE HERE MARKERS MEAN--
--HOBO CODE--
--LETTIN' A 'BO KNOW THERE'S HOT MEALS, COTS, AND SHOWERS FOR US.
TRULY ONE OF THE MOST TREASURED TOWNS FOR OUR BRETHREN!
WAIT-- TREASURED?!
THAT'S IT! THOSE SYMBOLS--!
IF I SHOWED YOU SOME MARKINGS THAT MIGHT BE HOBO CODE, COULD YOU... TRANSLATE?
A HOBO PRIDES HIMSELF ON TRADING FAIR SERVICES FOR FAIR PAY ANYWHERE HE MAY BE NEEDED...
I'M SURE WE CAN FIND SUITABLE RECOMPENSE IN THE GIFT SHOP!

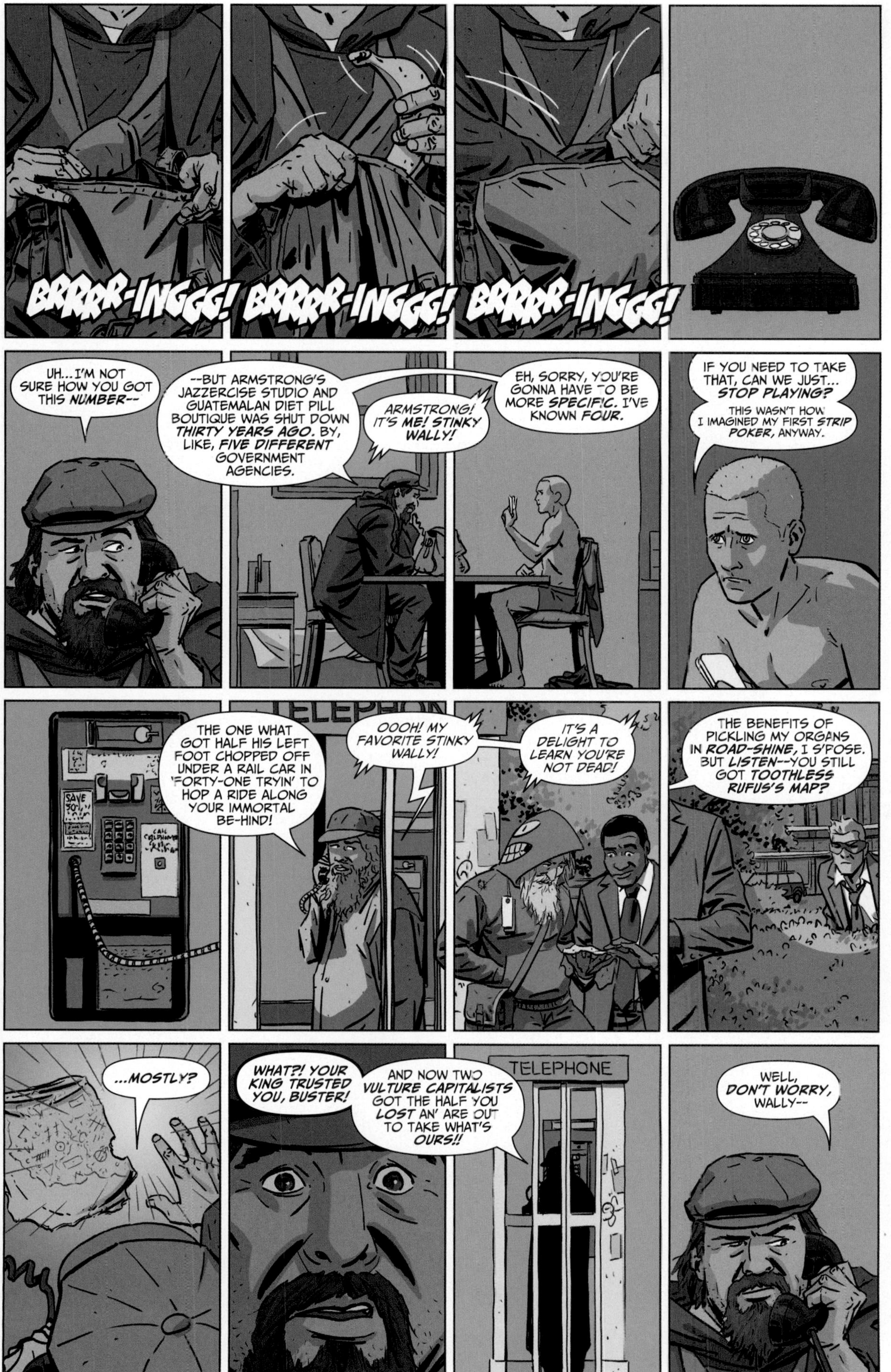
BRRRR-INGGG! BRRRR-INGGG! BRRRR-INGGG!
UH... I'M NOT SURE HOW YOU GOT THIS NUMBER--
--BUT ARMSTRONG'S JAZZERCISE STUDIO AND GUATEMALAN DIET PILL BOUTIQUE WAS SHUT DOWN THIRTY YEARS AGO. BY, LIKE, FIVE DIFFERENT GOVERNMENT AGENCIES.
ARMSTRONG! IT'S ME! STINKY WALLY!
EH, SORRY, YOU'RE GONNA HAVE TO BE MORE SPECIFIC. I'VE KNOWN FOUR.
IF YOU NEED TO TAKE THAT, CAN WE JUST... STOP PLAYING?
THIS WASN'T HOW I IMAGINED MY FIRST STRIP POKER, ANYWAY.
THE ONE WHAT GOT HALF HIS LEFT FOOT CHOPPED OFF UNDER A RAIL CAR IN 'FORTY-ONE TRYIN' TO HOP A RIDE ALONG YOUR IMMORTAL BE-HIND!
OOOH! MY FAVORITE STINKY WALLY!
IT'S A DELIGHT TO LEARN YOU'RE NOT DEAD!
THE BENEFITS OF PICKLING MY ORGANS IN ROAD-SHINE, I S'POSE. BUT LISTEN--YOU STILL GOT TOOTHLESS RUFUS'S MAP?
...MOSTLY?
WHAT?! YOUR KING TRUSTED YOU, BUSTER!
AND NOW TWO VULTURE CAPITALISTS GOT THE HALF YOU LOST AN' ARE OUT TO TAKE WHAT'S OURS!!
TELEPHONE
WELL, DON'T WORRY, WALLY--

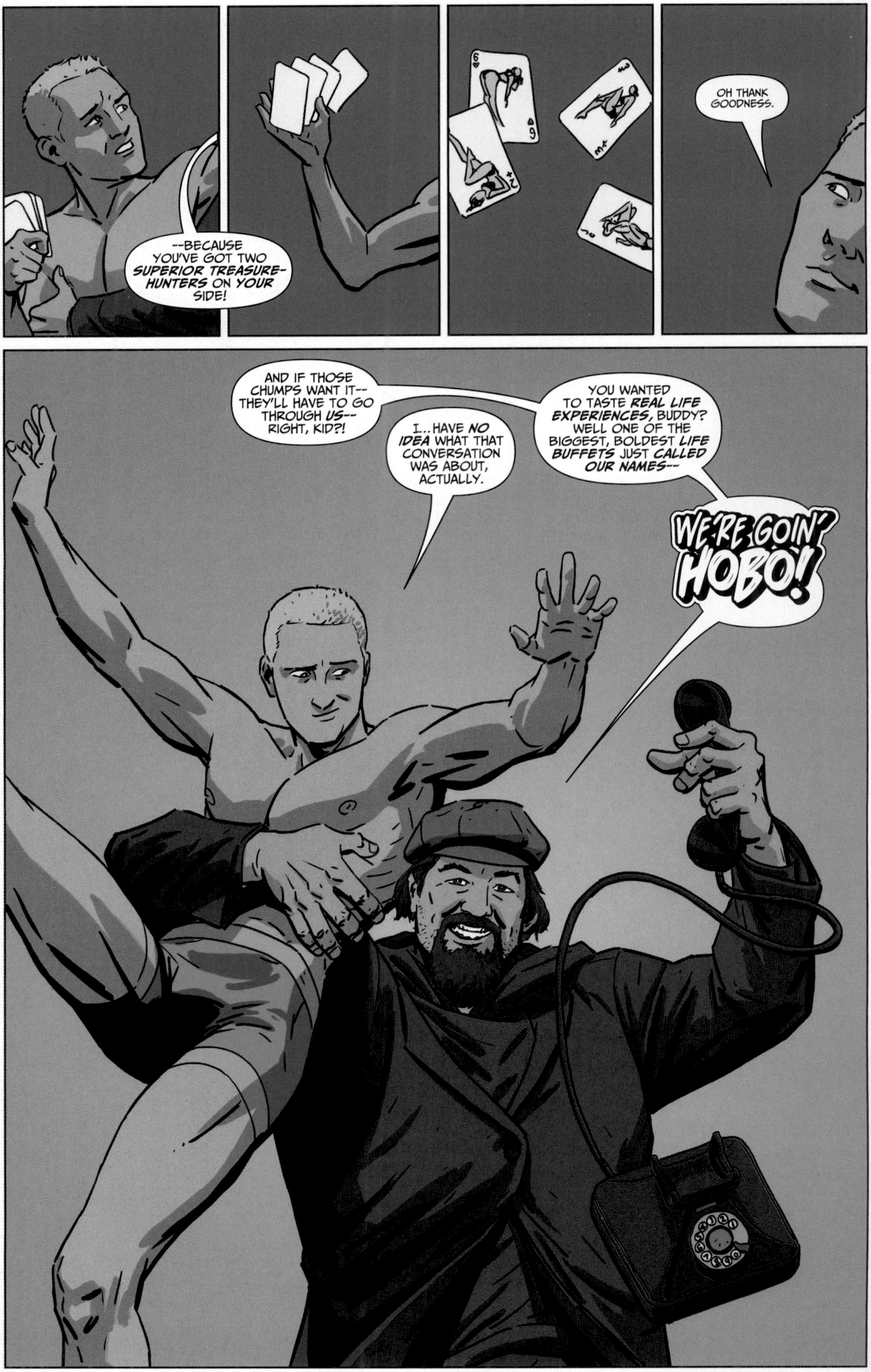
--BECAUSE YOU'VE GOT TWO *SUPERIOR TREASURE-HUNTERS* ON *YOUR* SIDE!
OH THANK GOODNESS.
AND IF THOSE CHUMPS WANT IT-- THEY'LL HAVE TO GO THROUGH *US*-- RIGHT, KID?!
I...HAVE *NO IDEA* WHAT THAT CONVERSATION WAS ABOUT, ACTUALLY.
YOU WANTED TO TASTE *REAL LIFE EXPERIENCES,* BUDDY? WELL ONE OF THE BIGGEST, BOLDEST *LIFE BUFFETS* JUST *CALLED OUR NAMES*--
WE'RE GOIN' HOBO!

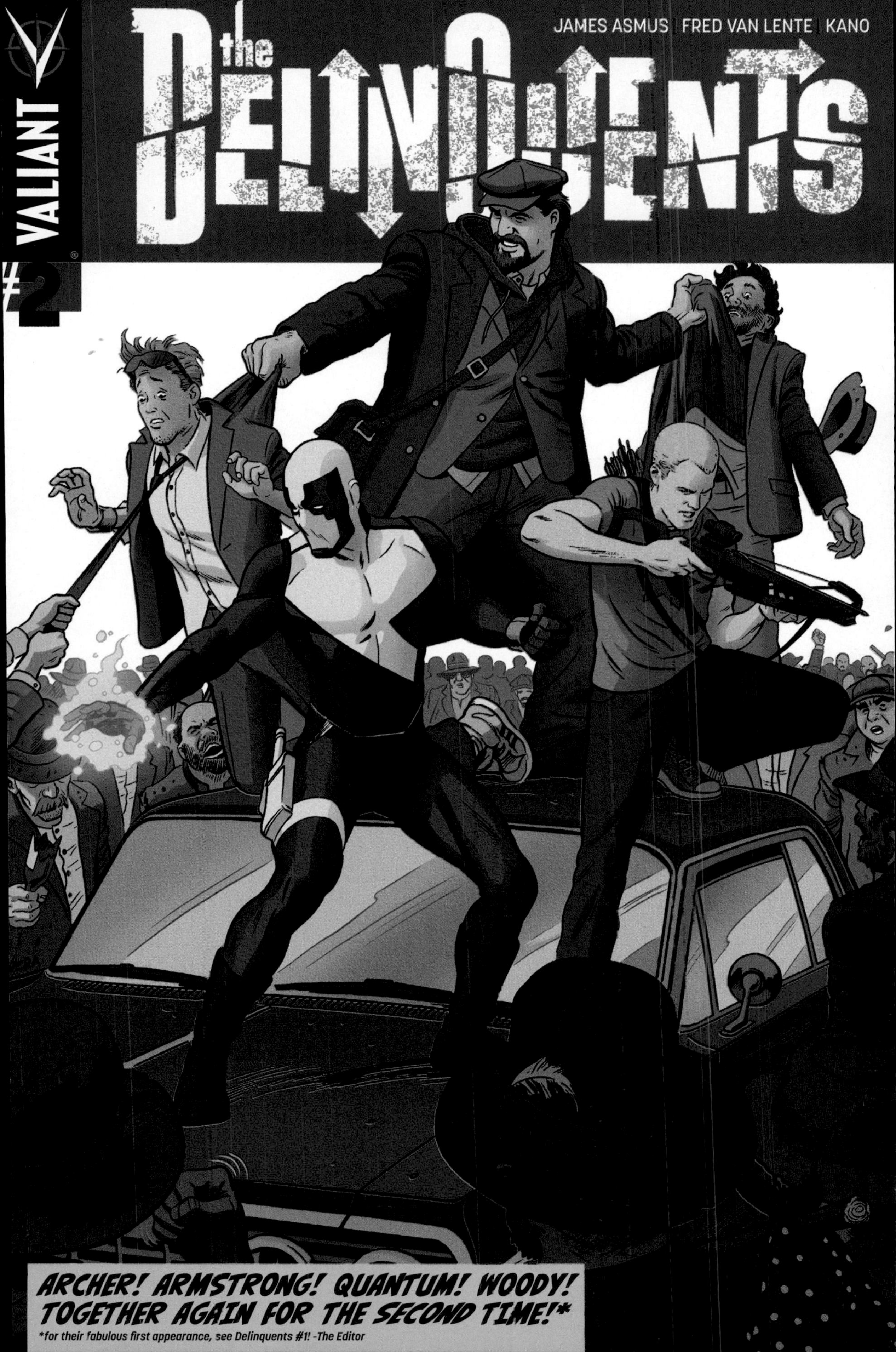
VALIANT
#2
JAMES ASMUS | FRED VAN LENTE | KANO
the DELINQUENTS
ARCHER! ARMSTRONG! QUANTUM! WOODY!
TOGETHER AGAIN FOR THE SECOND TIME!*
*for their fabulous first appearance, see Delinquents #1! -The Editor

WANTED

OBADIAH ARCHER

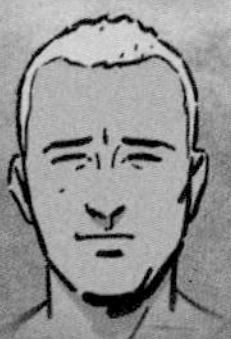

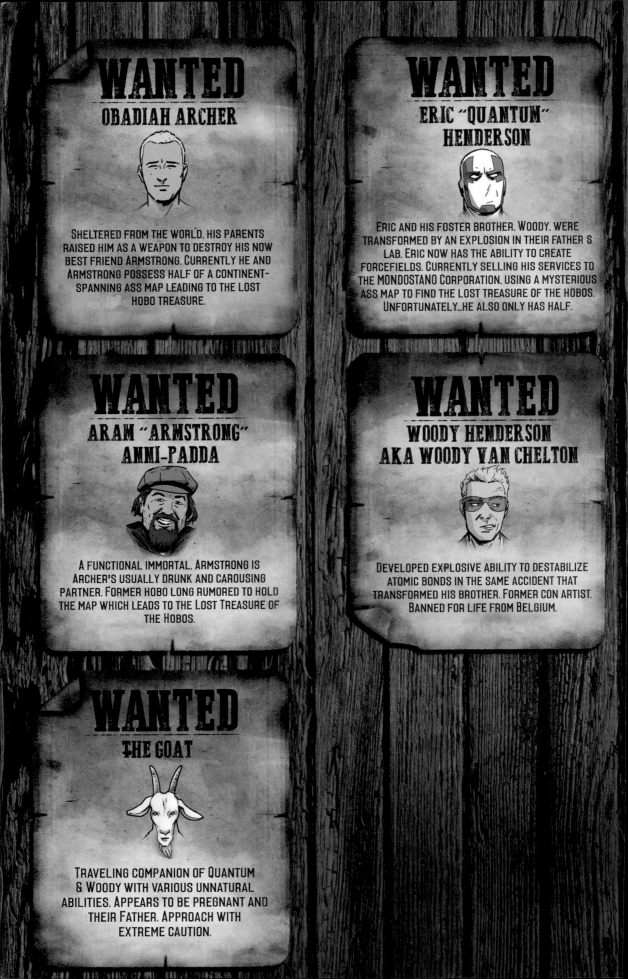

Sheltered from the world, his parents raised him as a weapon to destroy his now best friend Armstrong. Currently he and Armstrong possess half of a continent-spanning ass map leading to the lost hobo treasure.

WANTED

ERIC "QUANTUM" HENDERSON

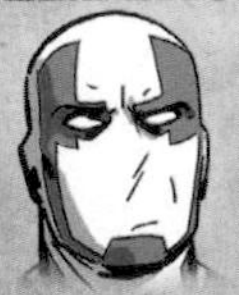

Eric and his foster brother, Woody, were transformed by an explosion in their father s lab. Eric now has the ability to create forcefields. Currently selling his services to the Mondostano Corporation, using a mysterious ass map to find the lost treasure of the hobos. Unfortunately...he also only has half.

WANTED

ARAM "ARMSTRONG" ANNI-PADDA

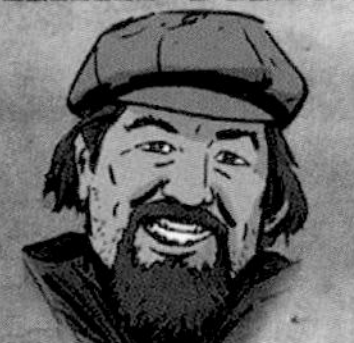

A functional immortal, Armstrong is Archer's usually drunk and carousing partner. Former hobo long rumored to hold the map which leads to the Lost Treasure of the Hobos.

WANTED

WOODY HENDERSON AKA WOODY VAN CHELTON

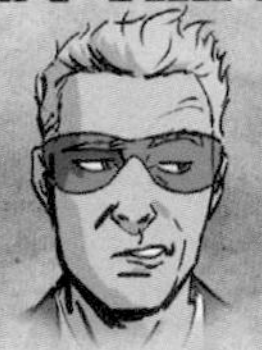

Developed explosive ability to destabilize atomic bonds in the same accident that transformed his brother. Former con artist. Banned for life from Belgium.

WANTED

THE GOAT

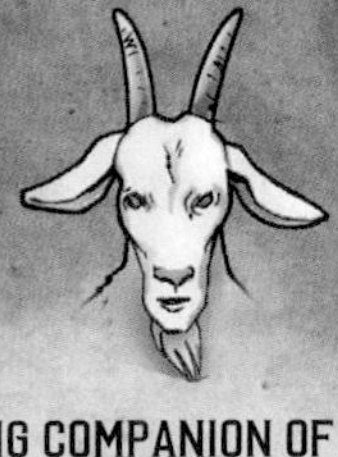

Traveling companion of Quantum & Woody with various unnatural abilities. Appears to be pregnant and their Father. Approach with extreme caution.

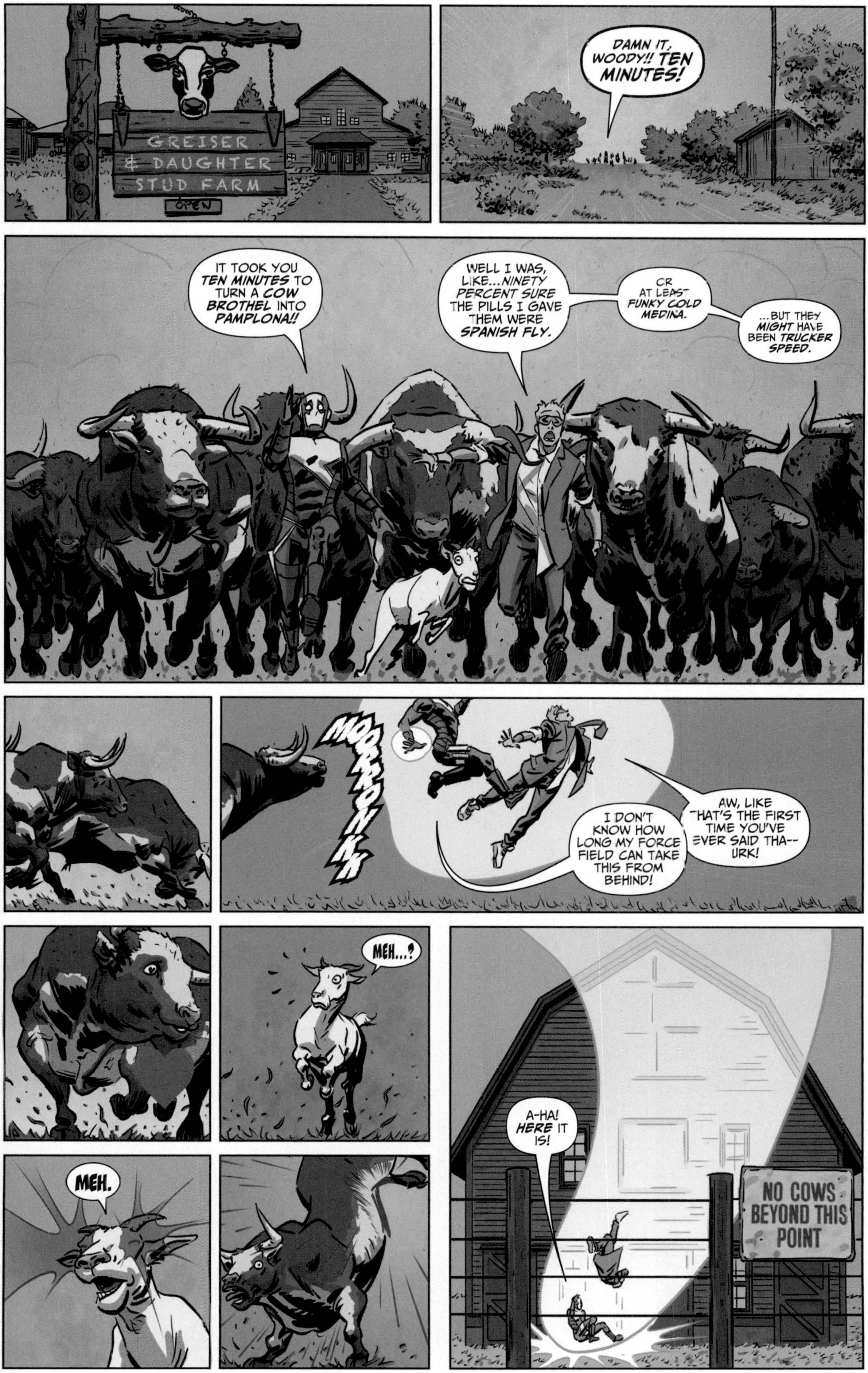
GREISER & DAUGHTER STUD FARM
OPEN
DAMN IT, WOODY!! TEN MINUTES!
IT TOOK YOU TEN MINUTES TO TURN A COW BROTHEL INTO PAMPLONA!!
WELL I WAS, LIKE...NINETY PERCENT SURE THE PILLS I GAVE THEM WERE SPANISH FLY.
OR AT LEAST FUNKY COLD MEDINA.
...BUT THEY MIGHT HAVE BEEN TRUCKER SPEED.
MOOOONK
I DON'T KNOW HOW LONG MY FORCE FIELD CAN TAKE THIS FROM BEHIND!
AW, LIKE THAT'S THE FIRST TIME YOU'VE EVER SAID THA-- URK!
MEH...?
MEH.
A-HA! HERE IT IS!
NO COWS BEYOND THIS POINT

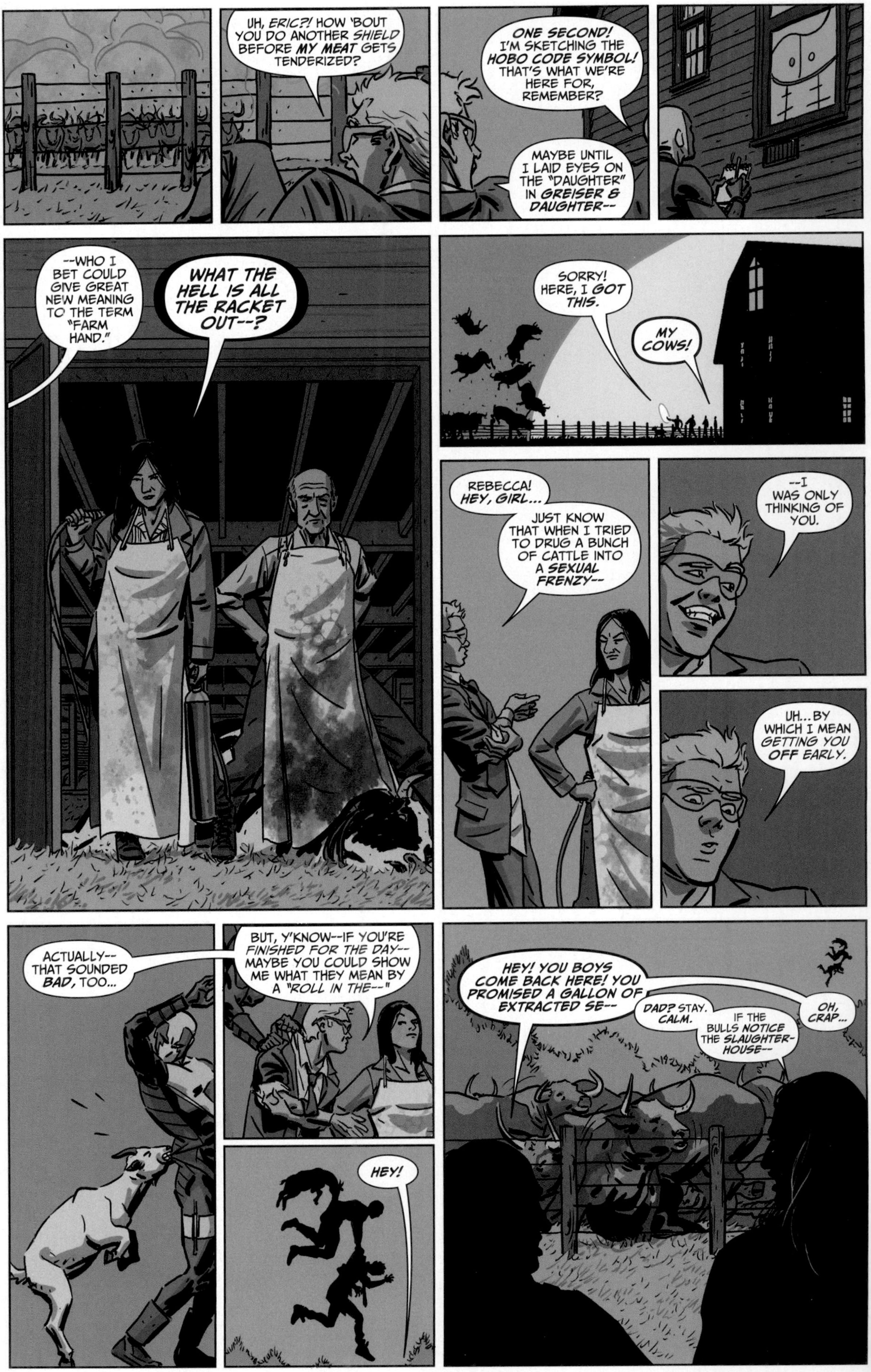
UH, ERIC?! HOW 'BOUT YOU DO ANOTHER SHIELD BEFORE MY MEAT GETS TENDERIZED?
ONE SECOND! I'M SKETCHING THE HOBO CODE SYMBOL! THAT'S WHAT WE'RE HERE FOR, REMEMBER?
MAYBE UNTIL I LAID EYES ON THE "DAUGHTER" IN GREISER & DAUGHTER--
--WHO I BET COULD GIVE GREAT NEW MEANING TO THE TERM "FARM HAND."
WHAT THE HELL IS ALL THE RACKET OUT--?
SORRY! HERE, I GOT THIS.
MY COWS!
REBECCA! HEY, GIRL...
JUST KNOW THAT WHEN I TRIED TO DRUG A BUNCH OF CATTLE INTO A SEXUAL FRENZY--
--I WAS ONLY THINKING OF YOU.
UH...BY WHICH I MEAN GETTING YOU OFF EARLY.
ACTUALLY-- THAT SOUNDED BAD, TOO...
BUT, Y'KNOW--IF YOU'RE FINISHED FOR THE DAY--MAYBE YOU COULD SHOW ME WHAT THEY MEAN BY A "ROLL IN THE--"
HEY!
HEY! YOU BOYS COME BACK HERE! YOU PROMISED A GALLON OF EXTRACTED SE--
DAD? STAY. CALM.
IF THE BULLS NOTICE THE SLAUGHTER-HOUSE--
OH, CRAP...

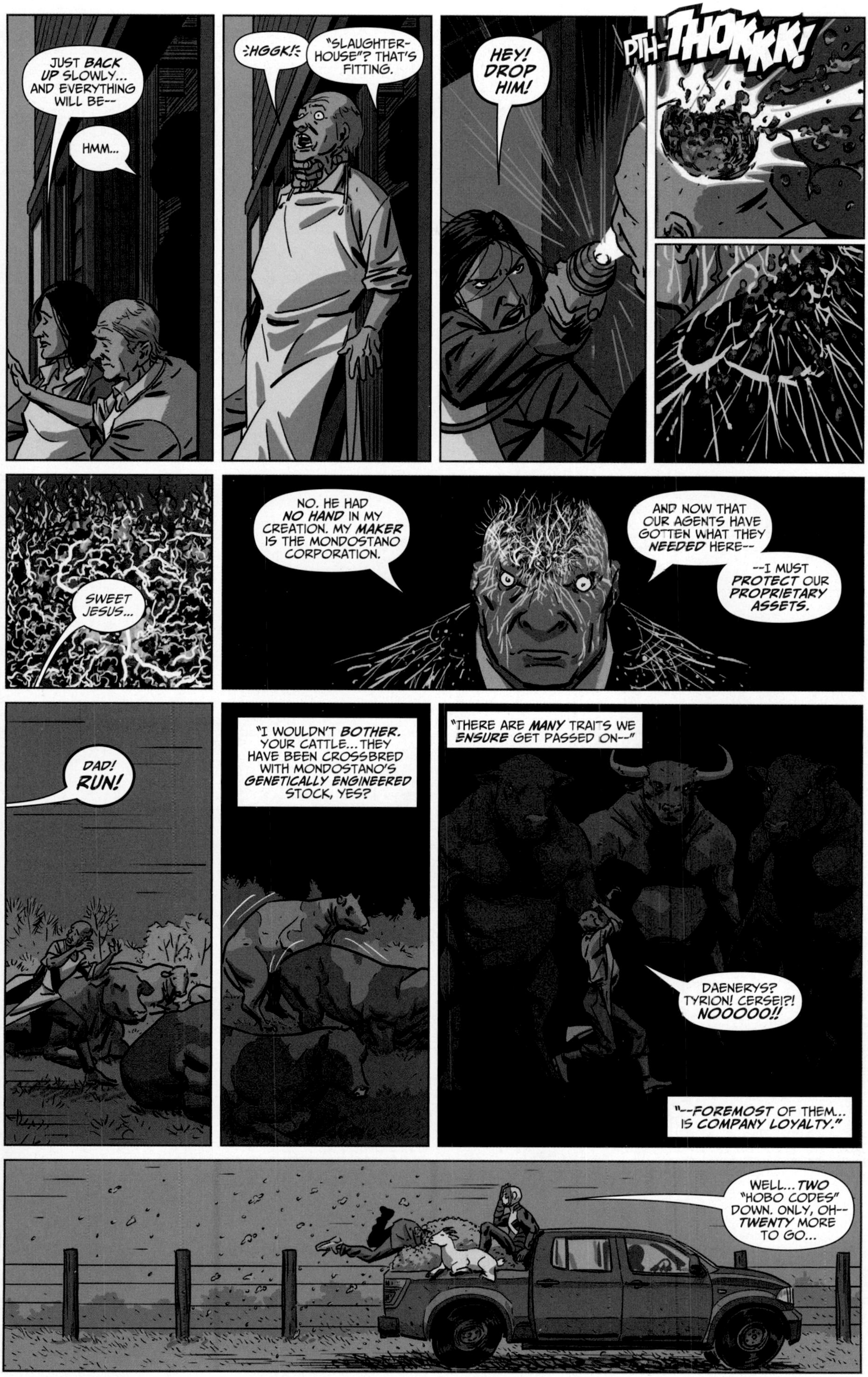
JUST BACK UP SLOWLY... AND EVERYTHING WILL BE--
HMM...
HGGK!
"SLAUGHTER-HOUSE"? THAT'S FITTING.
HEY! DROP HIM!
PTH-THOKKK!
NO. HE HAD NO HAND IN MY CREATION. MY MAKER IS THE MONDOSTANO CORPORATION.
SWEET JESUS...
AND NOW THAT OUR AGENTS HAVE GOTTEN WHAT THEY NEEDED HERE--
--I MUST PROTECT OUR PROPRIETARY ASSETS.
DAD! RUN!
"I WOULDN'T BOTHER. YOUR CATTLE... THEY HAVE BEEN CROSSBRED WITH MONDOSTANO'S GENETICALLY ENGINEERED STOCK, YES?
"THERE ARE MANY TRAITS WE ENSURE GET PASSED ON--"
DAENERYS? TYRION! CERSEI?! NOOOOO!!
"--FOREMOST OF THEM... IS COMPANY LOYALTY."
WELL... TWO "HOBO CODES" DOWN. ONLY, OH-- TWENTY MORE TO GO...

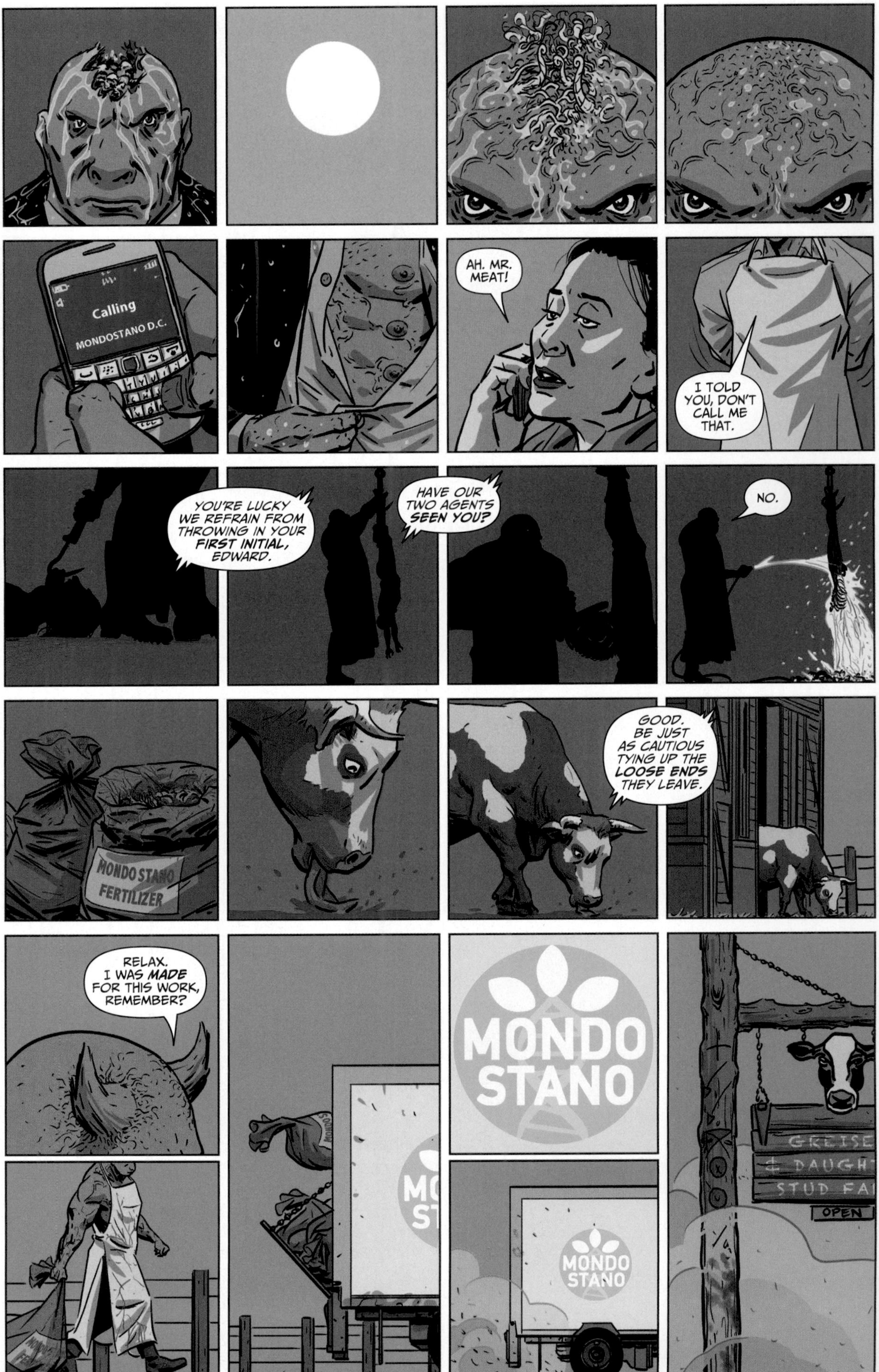

Calling
MONDOSTANO D.C.
AH. MR. MEAT!
I TOLD YOU, DON'T CALL ME THAT.
YOU'RE LUCKY WE REFRAIN FROM THROWING IN YOUR FIRST INITIAL, EDWARD.
HAVE OUR TWO AGENTS SEEN YOU?
NO.
MONDO STANO FERTILIZER
GOOD. BE JUST AS CAUTIOUS TYING UP THE LOOSE ENDS THEY LEAVE.
RELAX. I WAS MADE FOR THIS WORK, REMEMBER?
MONDO STANO
MONDO STANO
OPEN

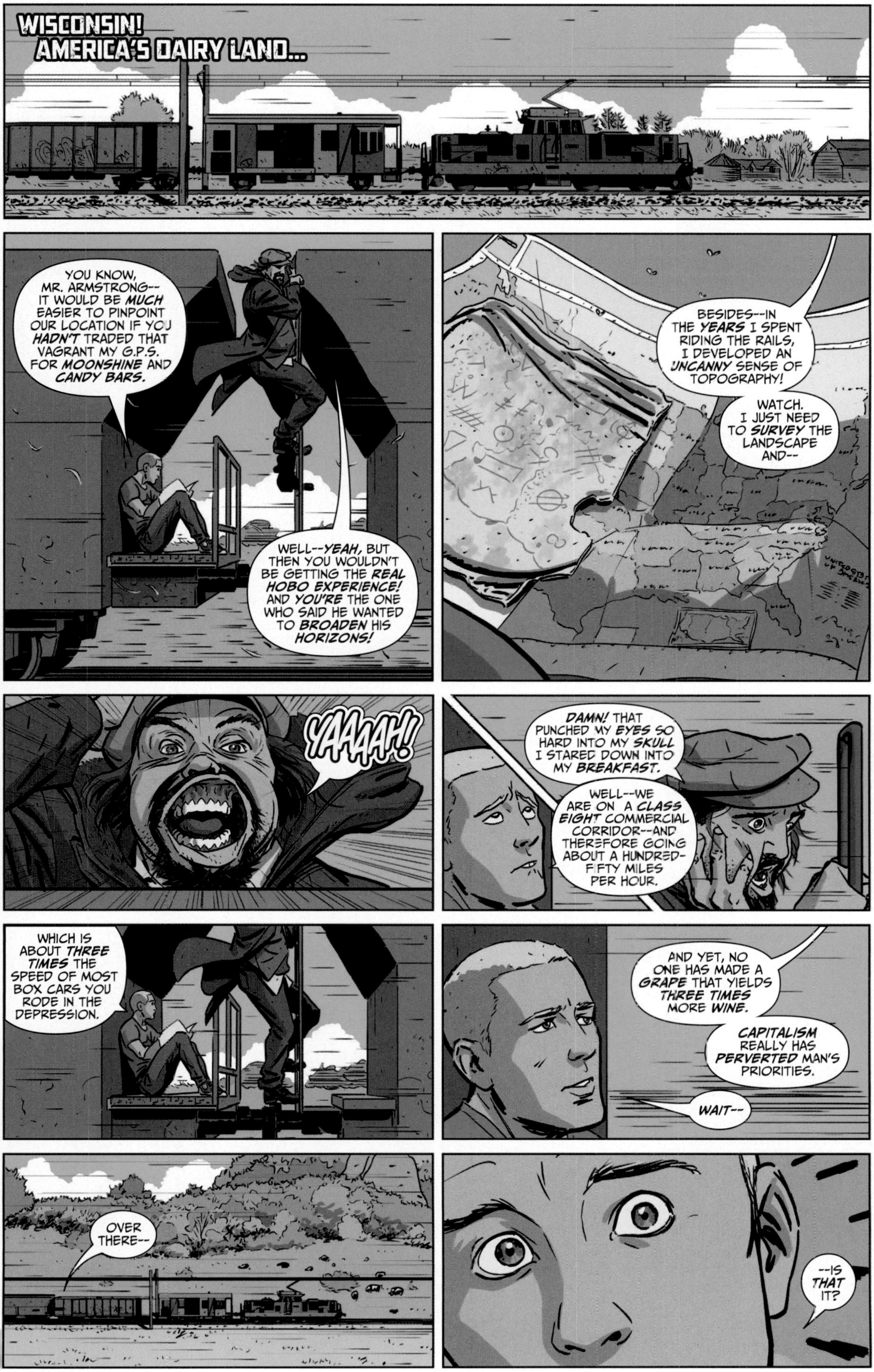
WISCONSIN! AMERICA'S DAIRY LAND...
YOU KNOW, MR. ARMSTRONG-- IT WOULD BE MUCH EASIER TO PINPOINT OUR LOCATION IF YOU HADN'T TRADED THAT VAGRANT MY G.P.S. FOR MOONSHINE AND CANDY BARS.
WELL--YEAH, BUT THEN YOU WOULDN'T BE GETTING THE REAL HOBO EXPERIENCE! AND YOU'RE THE ONE WHO SAID HE WANTED TO BROADEN HIS HORIZONS!
BESIDES--IN THE YEARS I SPENT RIDING THE RAILS, I DEVELOPED AN UNCANNY SENSE OF TOPOGRAPHY!
WATCH. I JUST NEED TO SURVEY THE LANDSCAPE AND--
YAAAAH!
DAMN! THAT PUNCHED MY EYES SO HARD INTO MY SKULL I STARED DOWN INTO MY BREAKFAST.
WELL--WE ARE ON A CLASS EIGHT COMMERCIAL CORRIDOR--AND THEREFORE GOING ABOUT A HUNDRED-FIFTY MILES PER HOUR.
WHICH IS ABOUT THREE TIMES THE SPEED OF MOST BOX CARS YOU RODE IN THE DEPRESSION.
AND YET, NO ONE HAS MADE A GRAPE THAT YIELDS THREE TIMES MORE WINE.
CAPITALISM REALLY HAS PERVERTED MAN'S PRIORITIES.
WAIT--
OVER THERE--
--IS THAT IT?

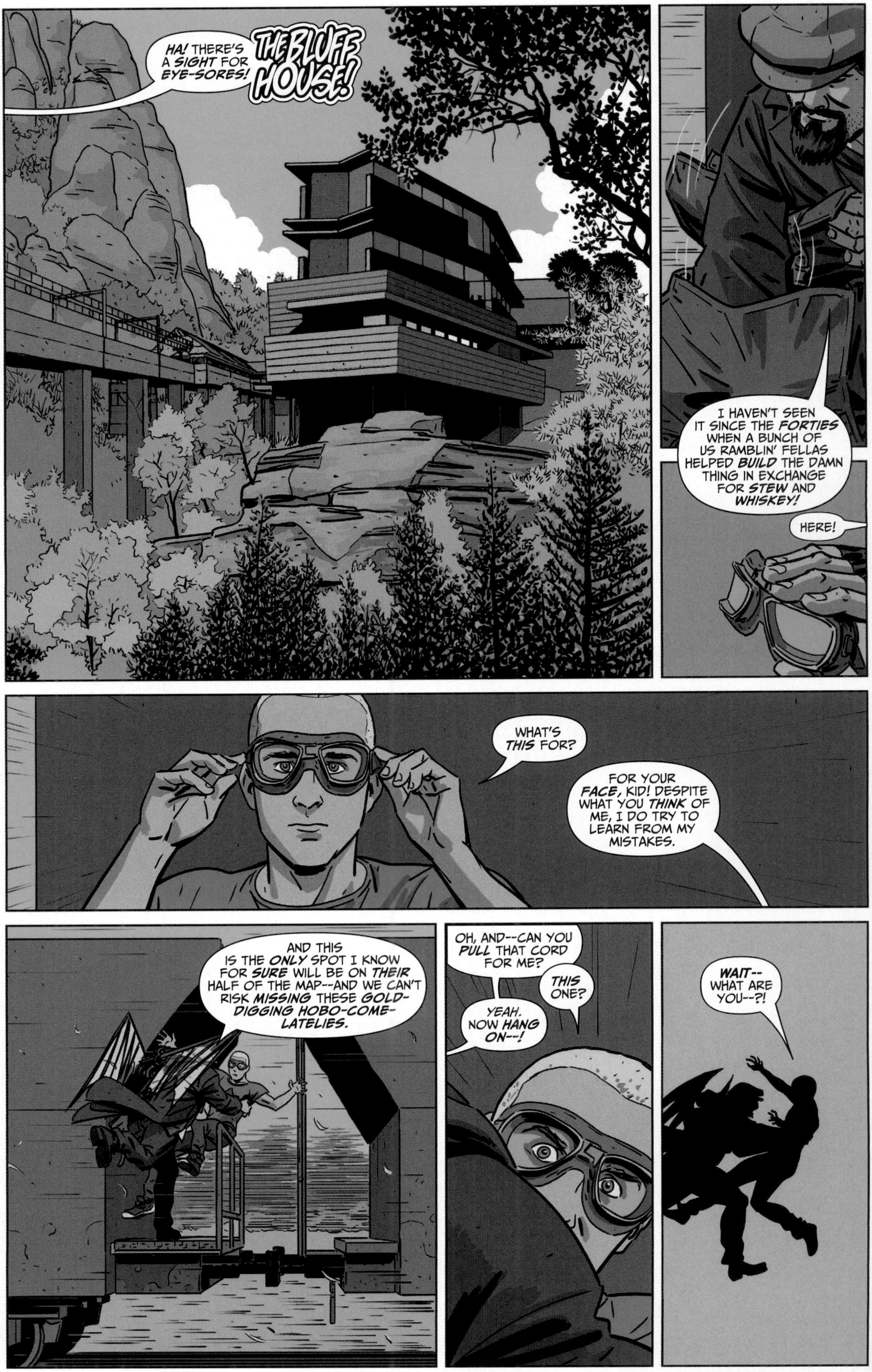
HA! THERE'S A SIGHT FOR EYE-SORES!
THE BLUFF HOUSE!
I HAVEN'T SEEN IT SINCE THE FORTIES WHEN A BUNCH OF US RAMBLIN' FELLAS HELPED BUILD THE DAMN THING IN EXCHANGE FOR STEW AND WHISKEY!
HERE!
WHAT'S THIS FOR?
FOR YOUR FACE, KID! DESPITE WHAT YOU THINK OF ME, I DO TRY TO LEARN FROM MY MISTAKES.
AND THIS IS THE ONLY SPOT I KNOW FOR SURE WILL BE ON THEIR HALF OF THE MAP--AND WE CAN'T RISK MISSING THESE GOLD-DIGGING HOBO-COME-LATELIES.
OH, AND--CAN YOU PULL THAT CORD FOR ME?
THIS ONE?
YEAH. NOW HANG ON--!
WAIT-- WHAT ARE YOU--?!

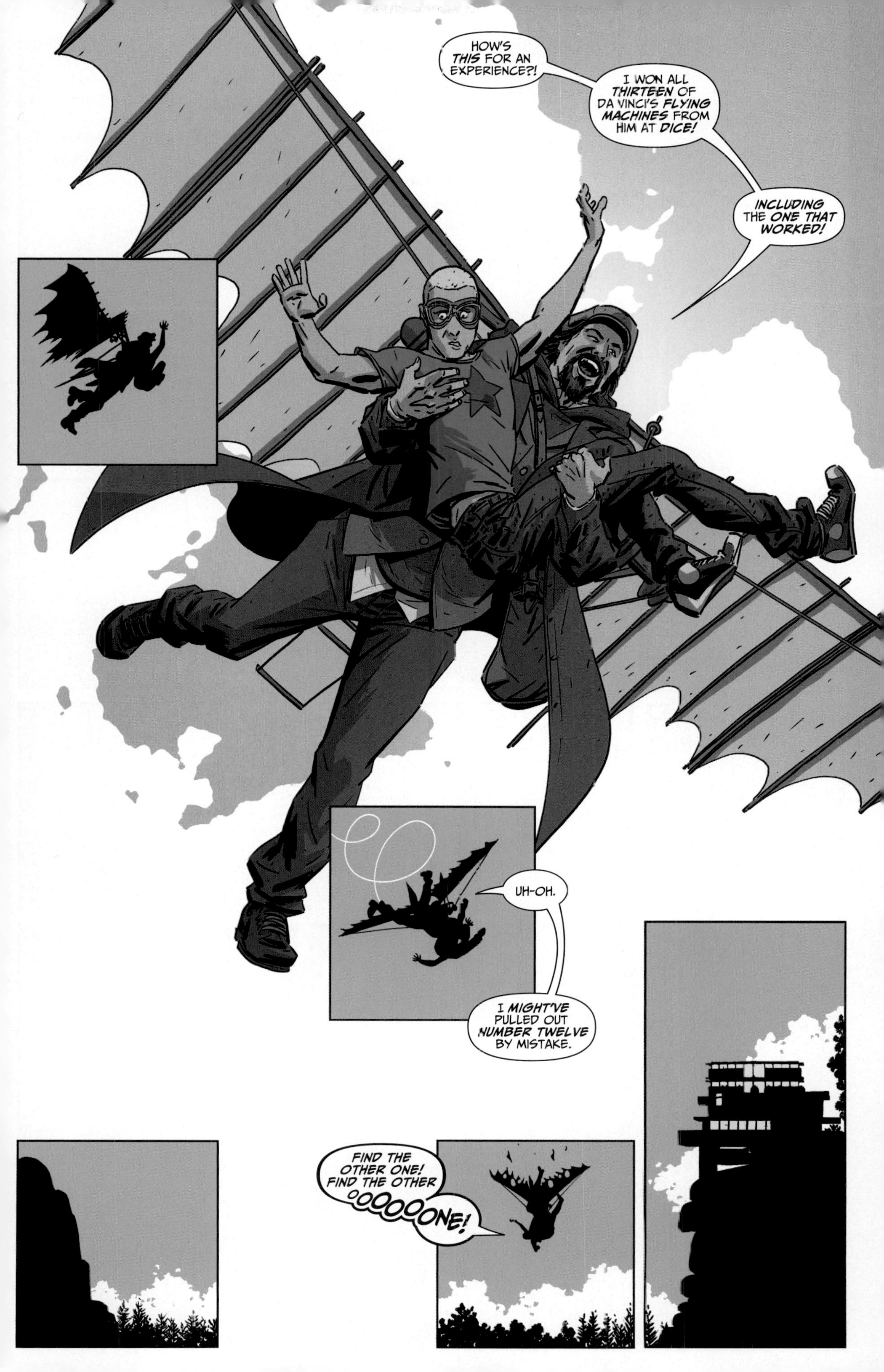
HOW'S THIS FOR AN EXPERIENCE?!
I WON ALL THIRTEEN OF DA VINCI'S FLYING MACHINES FROM HIM AT DICE!
INCLUDING THE ONE THAT WORKED!
UH-OH.
I MIGHT'VE PULLED OUT NUMBER TWELVE BY MISTAKE.
FIND THE OTHER ONE! FIND THE OTHER OOOOOONE!

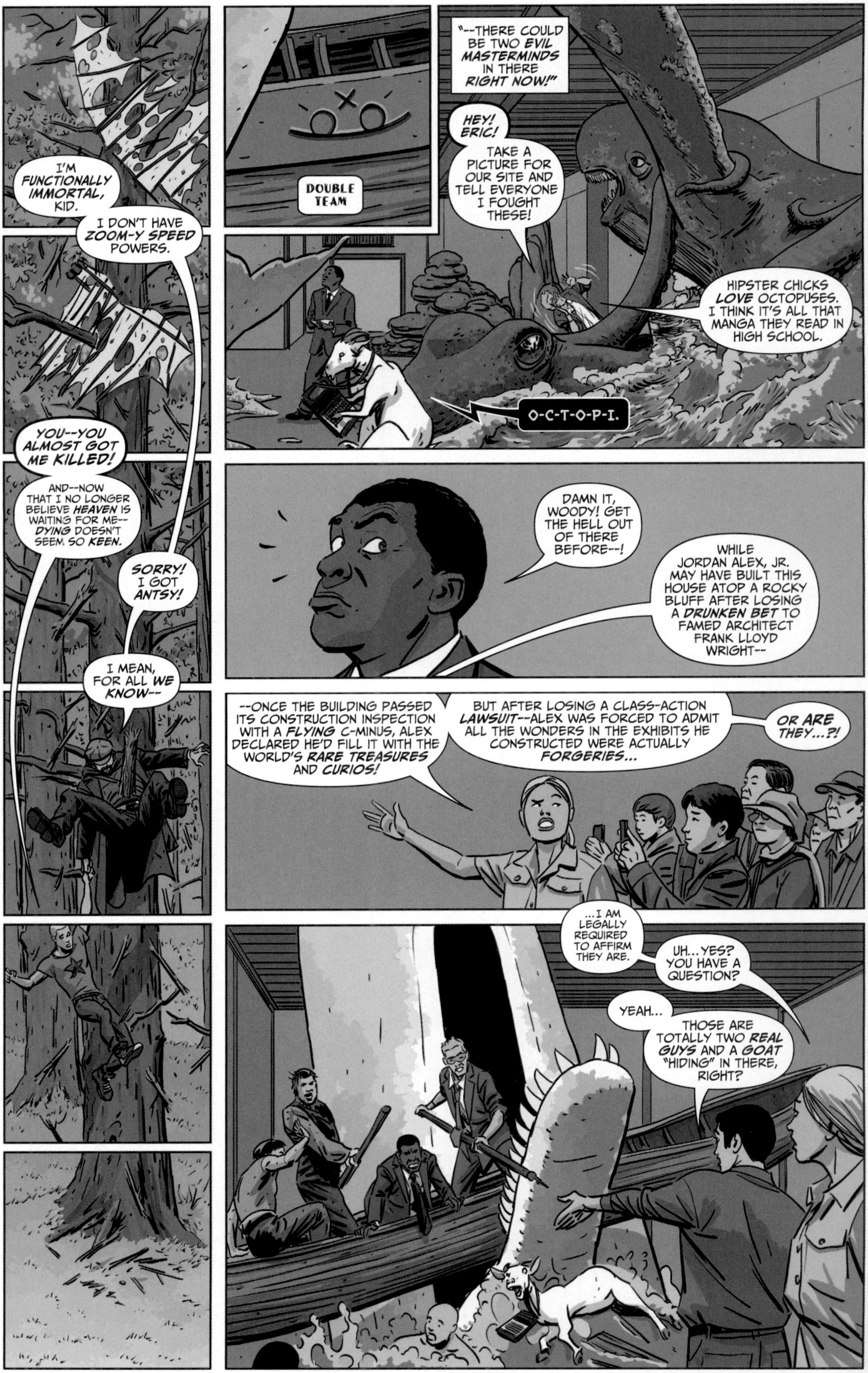

I'M FUNCTIONALLY IMMORTAL, KID.
I DON'T HAVE ZOOM-Y SPEED POWERS.
DOUBLE TEAM
"--THERE COULD BE TWO EVIL MASTERMINDS IN THERE RIGHT NOW!"
HEY! ERIC!
TAKE A PICTURE FOR OUR SITE AND TELL EVERYONE I FOUGHT THESE!
HIPSTER CHICKS LOVE OCTOPUSES. I THINK IT'S ALL THAT MANGA THEY READ IN HIGH SCHOOL.
O-C-T-O-P-I.
YOU--YOU ALMOST GOT ME KILLED!
AND--NOW THAT I NO LONGER BELIEVE HEAVEN IS WAITING FOR ME--DYING DOESN'T SEEM SO KEEN.
DAMN IT, WOODY! GET THE HELL OUT OF THERE BEFORE--!
WHILE JORDAN ALEX, JR. MAY HAVE BUILT THIS HOUSE ATOP A ROCKY BLUFF AFTER LOSING A DRUNKEN BET TO FAMED ARCHITECT FRANK LLOYD WRIGHT--
SORRY! I GOT ANTSY!
I MEAN, FOR ALL WE KNOW--
--ONCE THE BUILDING PASSED ITS CONSTRUCTION INSPECTION WITH A FLYING C-MINUS, ALEX DECLARED HE'D FILL IT WITH THE WORLD'S RARE TREASURES AND CURIOS!
BUT AFTER LOSING A CLASS-ACTION LAWSUIT--ALEX WAS FORCED TO ADMIT ALL THE WONDERS IN THE EXHIBITS HE CONSTRUCTED WERE ACTUALLY FORGERIES...
OR ARE THEY...?!
...I AM LEGALLY REQUIRED TO AFFIRM THEY ARE.
UH...YES? YOU HAVE A QUESTION?
YEAH...
THOSE ARE TOTALLY TWO REAL GUYS AND A GOAT "HIDING" IN THERE, RIGHT?

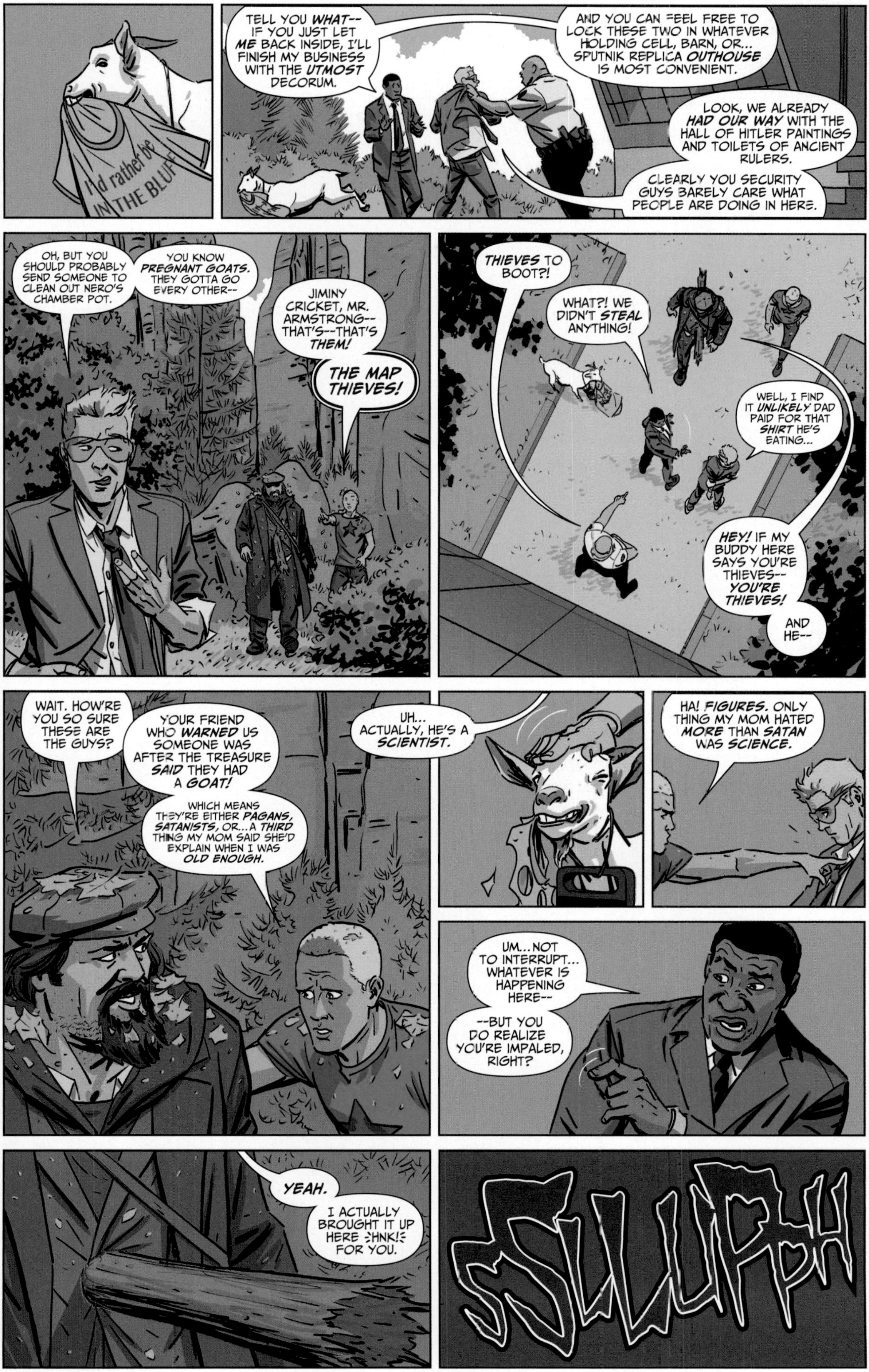
I'd rather be IN THE BLUFF
TELL YOU WHAT-- IF YOU JUST LET ME BACK INSIDE, I'LL FINISH MY BUSINESS WITH THE UTMOST DECORUM.
AND YOU CAN FEEL FREE TO LOCK THESE TWO IN WHATEVER HOLDING CELL, BARN, OR... SPUTNIK REPLICA OUTHOUSE IS MOST CONVENIENT.
LOOK, WE ALREADY HAD OUR WAY WITH THE HALL OF HITLER PAINTINGS AND TOILETS OF ANCIENT RULERS.
CLEARLY YOU SECURITY GUYS BARELY CARE WHAT PEOPLE ARE DOING IN HERE.
OH, BUT YOU SHOULD PROBABLY SEND SOMEONE TO CLEAN OUT NERO'S CHAMBER POT.
YOU KNOW PREGNANT GOATS. THEY GOTTA GO EVERY OTHER--
JIMINY CRICKET, MR. ARMSTRONG-- THAT'S--THAT'S THEM!
THE MAP THIEVES!
THIEVES TO BOOT?!
WHAT?! WE DIDN'T STEAL ANYTHING!
WELL, I FIND IT UNLIKELY DAD PAID FOR THAT SHIRT HE'S EATING...
HEY! IF MY BUDDY HERE SAYS YOU'RE THIEVES-- YOU'RE THIEVES!
AND HE--
WAIT. HOW'RE YOU SO SURE THESE ARE THE GUYS?
YOUR FRIEND WHO WARNED US SOMEONE WAS AFTER THE TREASURE SAID THEY HAD A GOAT!
WHICH MEANS THEY'RE EITHER PAGANS, SATANISTS, OR...A THIRD THING MY MOM SAID SHE'D EXPLAIN WHEN I WAS OLD ENOUGH.
UH... ACTUALLY, HE'S A SCIENTIST.
HA! FIGURES. ONLY THING MY MOM HATED MORE THAN SATAN WAS SCIENCE.
UM...NOT TO INTERRUPT... WHATEVER IS HAPPENING HERE--
--BUT YOU DO REALIZE YOU'RE IMPALED, RIGHT?
YEAH.
I ACTUALLY BROUGHT IT UP HERE :HNK!: FOR YOU.
SSLUPPH

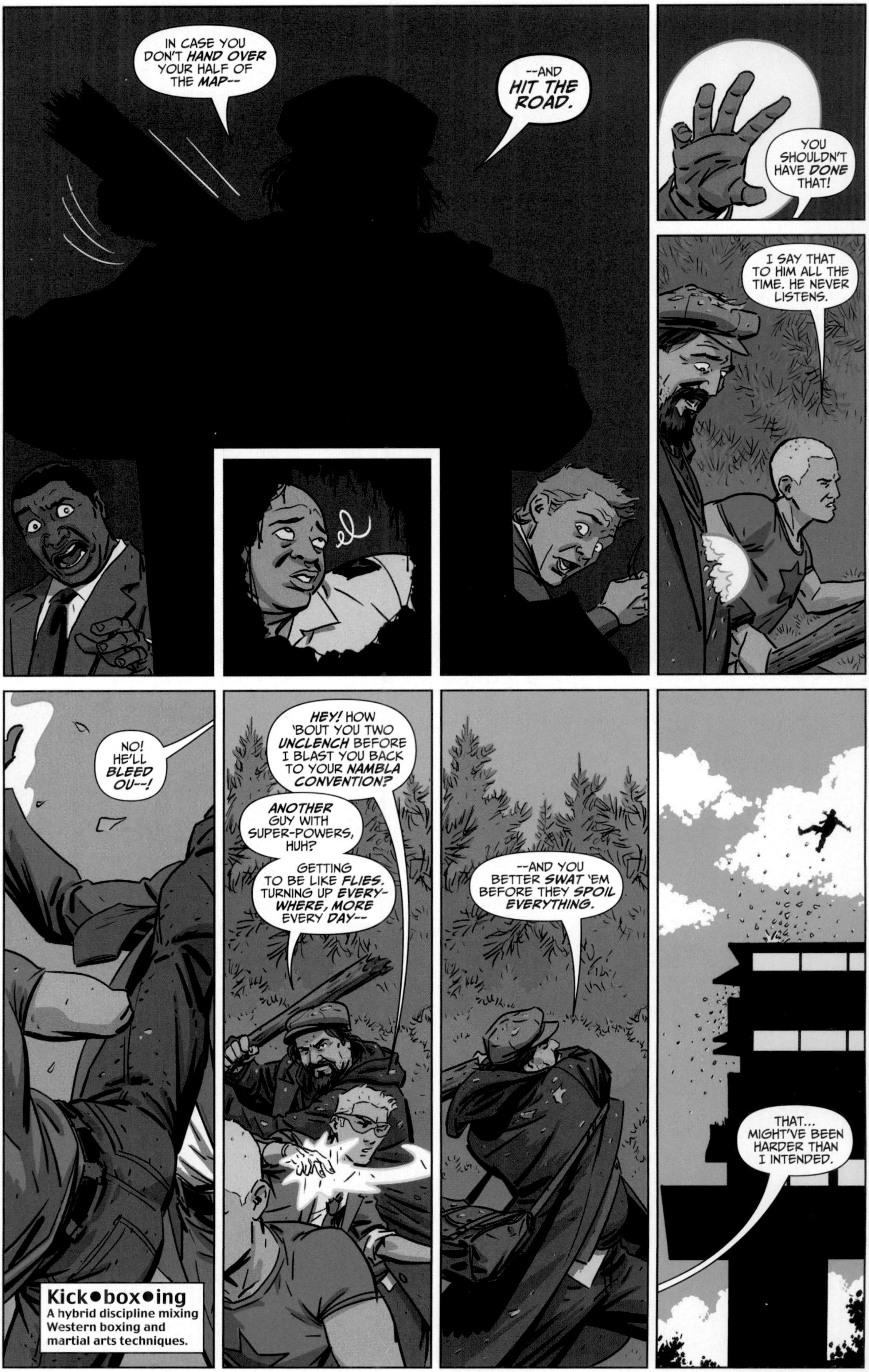
IN CASE YOU DON'T HAND OVER YOUR HALF OF THE MAP--
--AND HIT THE ROAD.
YOU SHOULDN'T HAVE DONE THAT!
I SAY THAT TO HIM ALL THE TIME. HE NEVER LISTENS.
NO! HE'LL BLEED OU--!
HEY! HOW 'BOUT YOU TWO UNCLENCH BEFORE I BLAST YOU BACK TO YOUR NAMBLA CONVENTION?
ANOTHER GUY WITH SUPER-POWERS, HUH?
GETTING TO BE LIKE FLIES. TURNING UP EVERY-WHERE, MORE EVERY DAY--
--AND YOU BETTER SWAT 'EM BEFORE THEY SPOIL EVERYTHING.
THAT... MIGHT'VE BEEN HARDER THAN I INTENDED.
Kick•box•ing
A hybrid discipline mixing Western boxing and martial arts techniques.

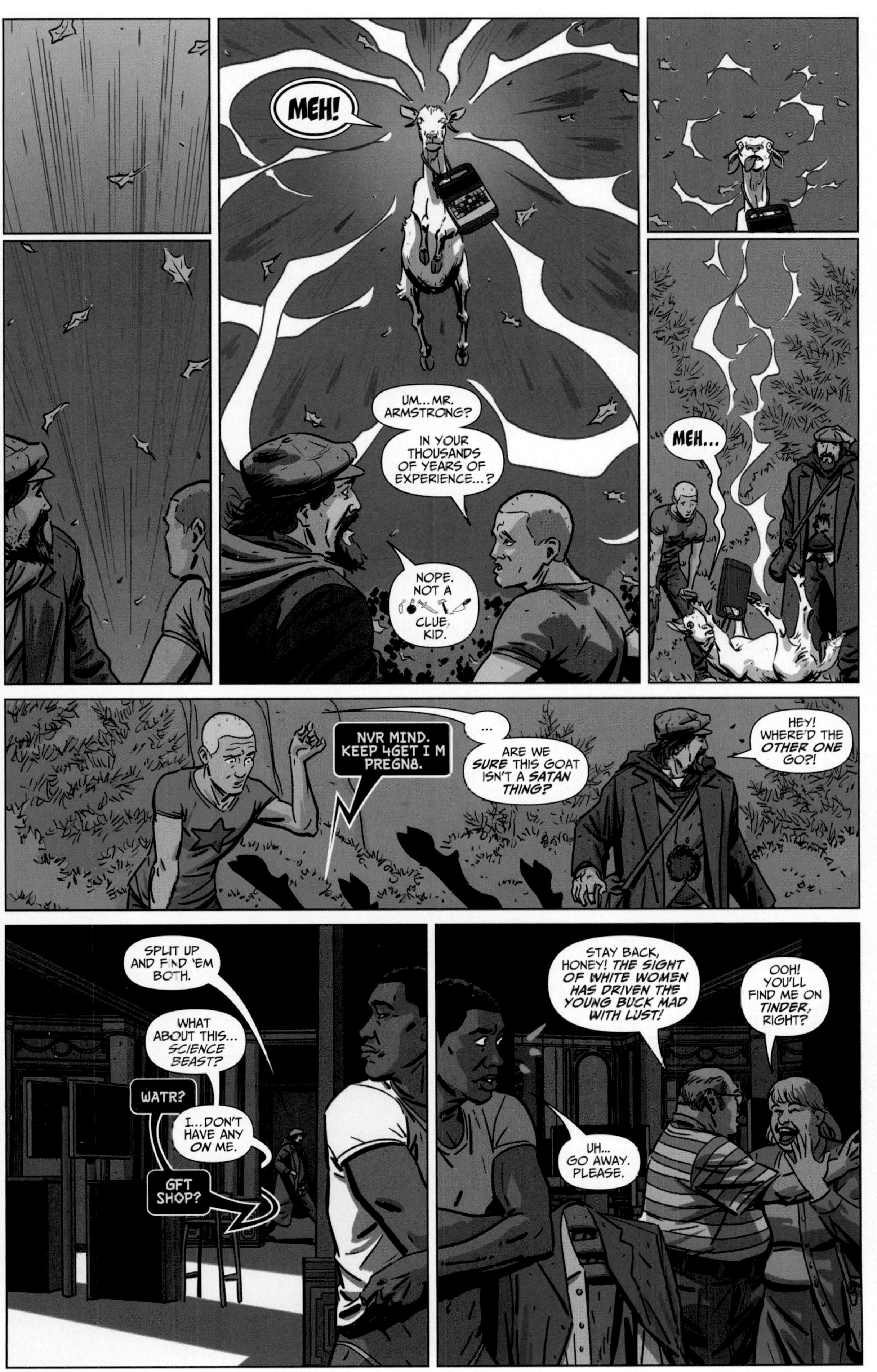
MEH!
UM...MR. ARMSTRONG?
IN YOUR THOUSANDS OF YEARS OF EXPERIENCE...?
NOPE. NOT A CLUE, KID.
MEH...
NVR MIND. KEEP 4GET I M PREGN8.
...
ARE WE SURE THIS GOAT ISN'T A SATAN THING?
HEY! WHERE'D THE OTHER ONE GO?!
SPLIT UP AND FIND 'EM BOTH.
WHAT ABOUT THIS... SCIENCE BEAST?
WATR?
I...DON'T HAVE ANY ON ME.
GFT SHOP?
STAY BACK, HONEY! THE SIGHT OF WHITE WOMEN HAS DRIVEN THE YOUNG BUCK MAD WITH LUST!
OOH! YOU'LL FIND ME ON TINDER, RIGHT?
UH... GO AWAY. PLEASE.

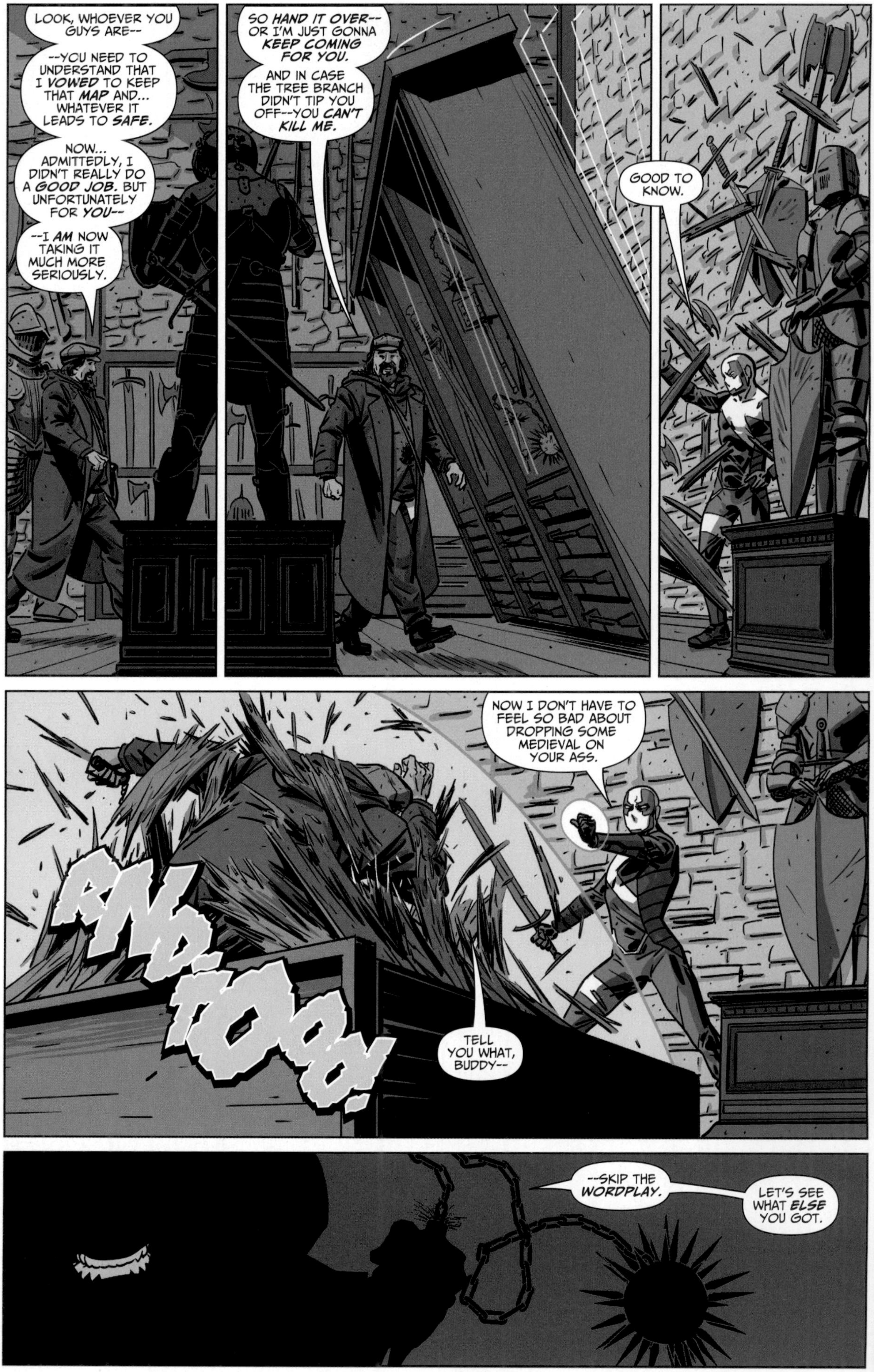
LOOK, WHOEVER YOU GUYS ARE--
--YOU NEED TO UNDERSTAND THAT I VOWED TO KEEP THAT MAP AND... WHATEVER IT LEADS TO SAFE.
NOW... ADMITTEDLY, I DIDN'T REALLY DO A GOOD JOB. BUT UNFORTUNATELY FOR YOU--
--I AM NOW TAKING IT MUCH MORE SERIOUSLY.
SO HAND IT OVER-- OR I'M JUST GONNA KEEP COMING FOR YOU.
AND IN CASE THE TREE BRANCH DIDN'T TIP YOU OFF--YOU CAN'T KILL ME.
GOOD TO KNOW.
NOW I DON'T HAVE TO FEEL SO BAD ABOUT DROPPING SOME MEDIEVAL ON YOUR ASS.
TELL YOU WHAT, BUDDY--
--SKIP THE WORDPLAY.
LET'S SEE WHAT ELSE YOU GOT.

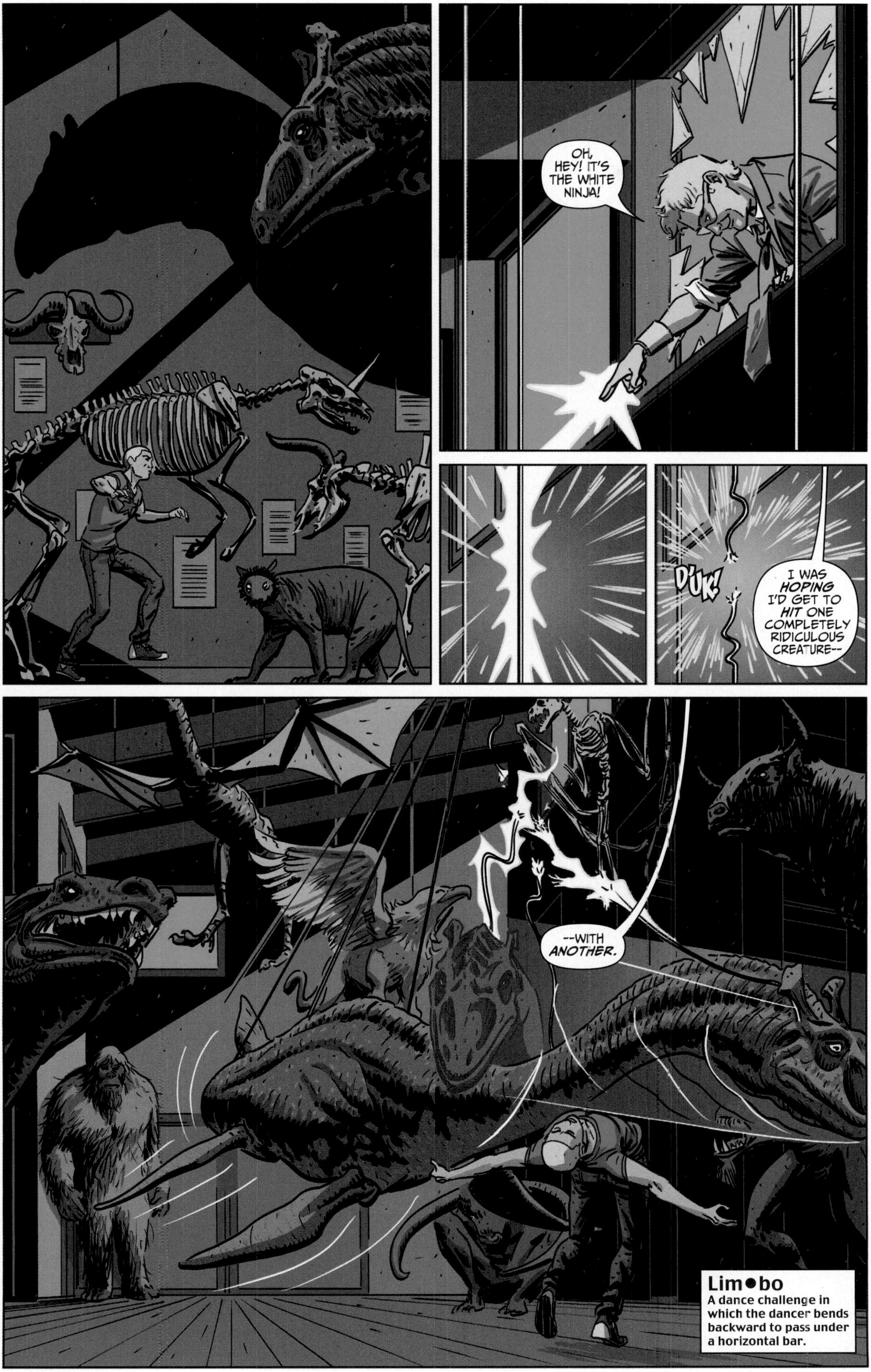
OH, HEY! IT'S THE WHITE NINJA!
D'UK!
I WAS HOPING I'D GET TO HIT ONE COMPLETELY RIDICULOUS CREATURE--
--WITH ANOTHER.
Lim●bo
A dance challenge in which the dancer bends backward to pass under a horizontal bar.

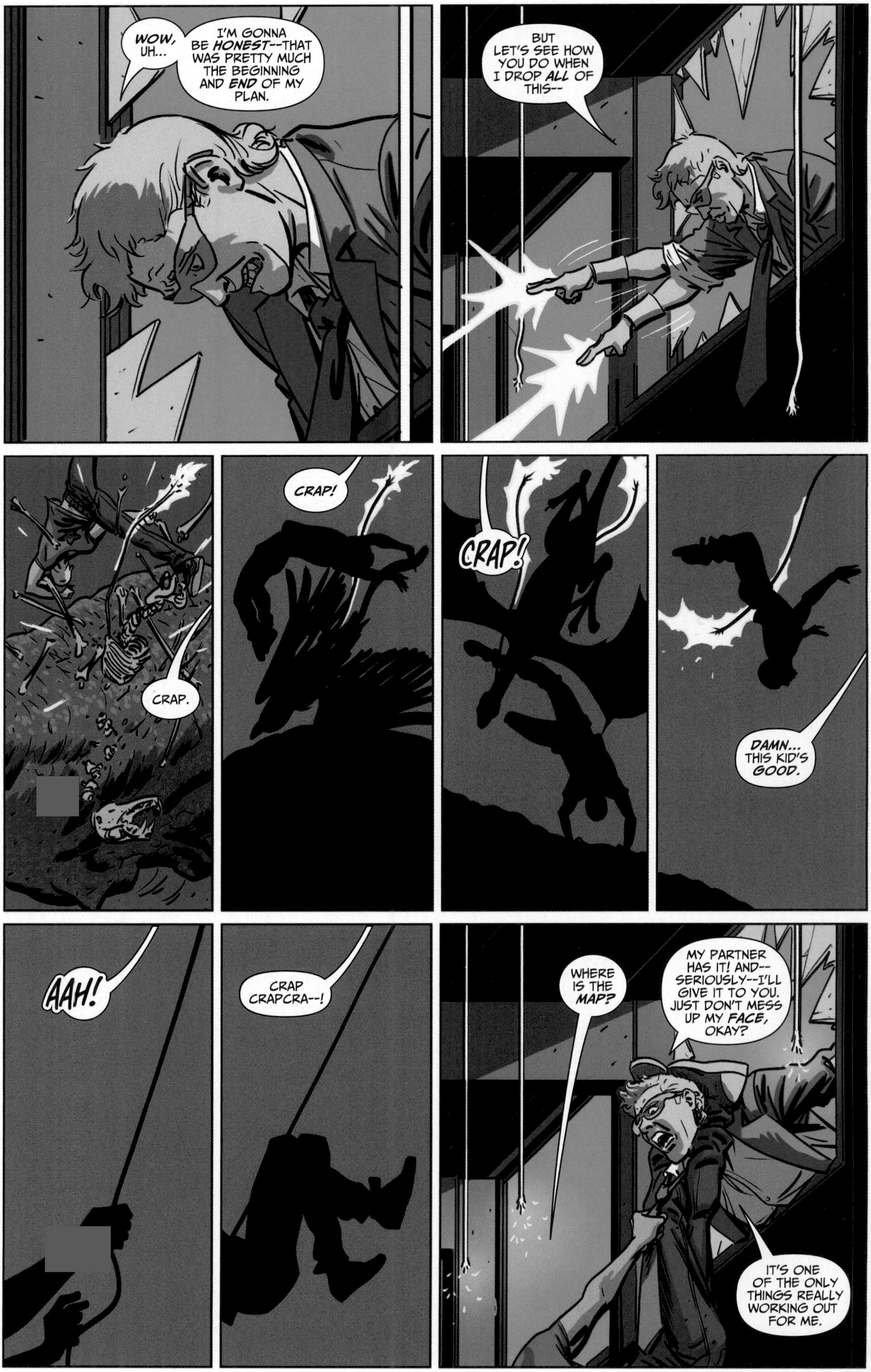
WOW, UH...
I'M GONNA BE HONEST--THAT WAS PRETTY MUCH THE BEGINNING AND END OF MY PLAN.
BUT LET'S SEE HOW YOU DO WHEN I DROP ALL OF THIS--
CRAP.
CRAP!
CRAP!
DAMN... THIS KID'S GOOD.
AAH!
CRAP CRAPCRA--!
WHERE IS THE MAP?
MY PARTNER HAS IT! AND--SERIOUSLY--I'LL GIVE IT TO YOU. JUST DON'T MESS UP MY FACE, OKAY?
IT'S ONE OF THE ONLY THINGS REALLY WORKING OUT FOR ME.

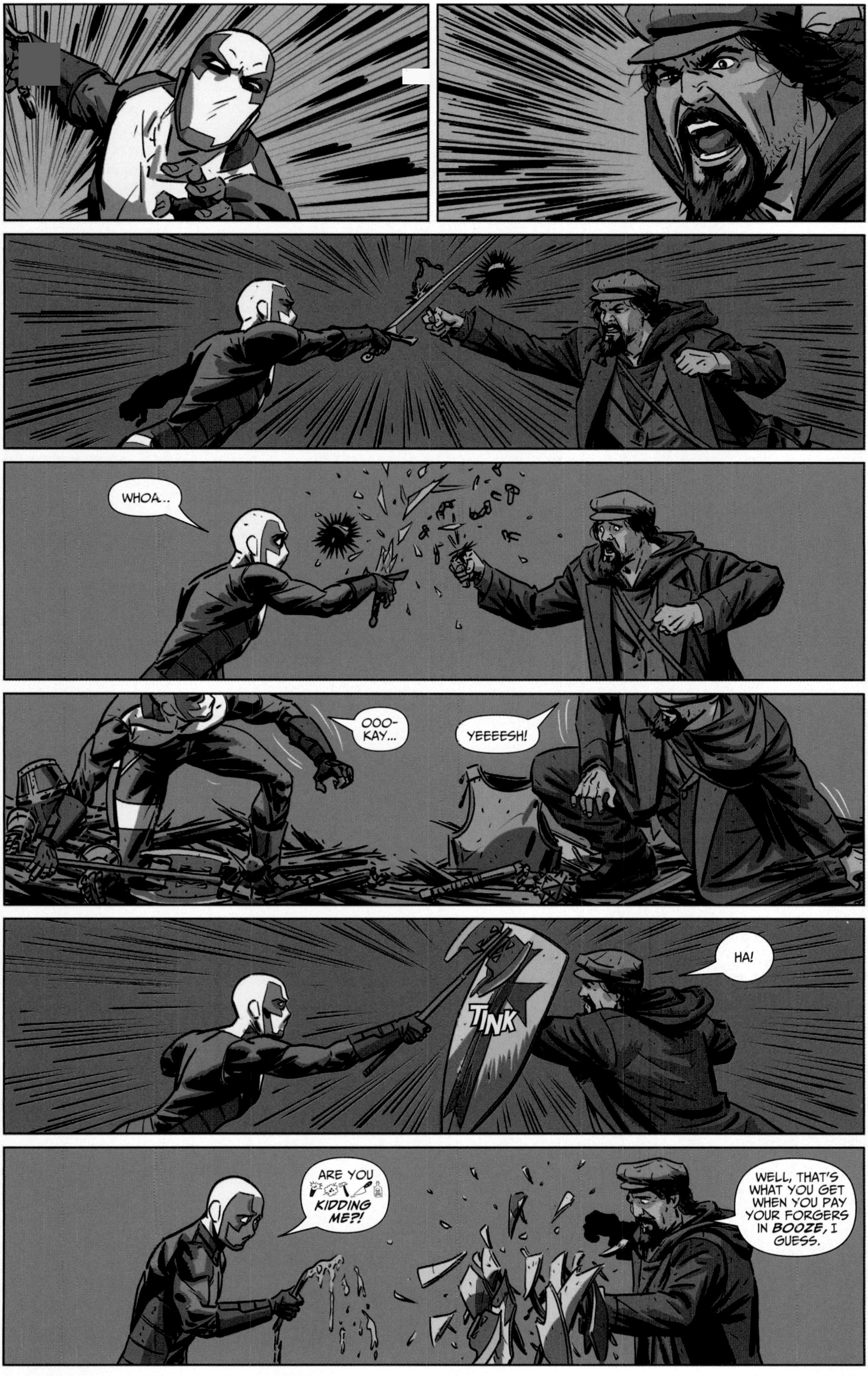
WHOA...
OOO-KAY...
YEEEESH!
TINK
HA!
ARE YOU KIDDING ME?!
WELL, THAT'S WHAT YOU GET WHEN YOU PAY YOUR FORGERS IN BOOZE, I GUESS.

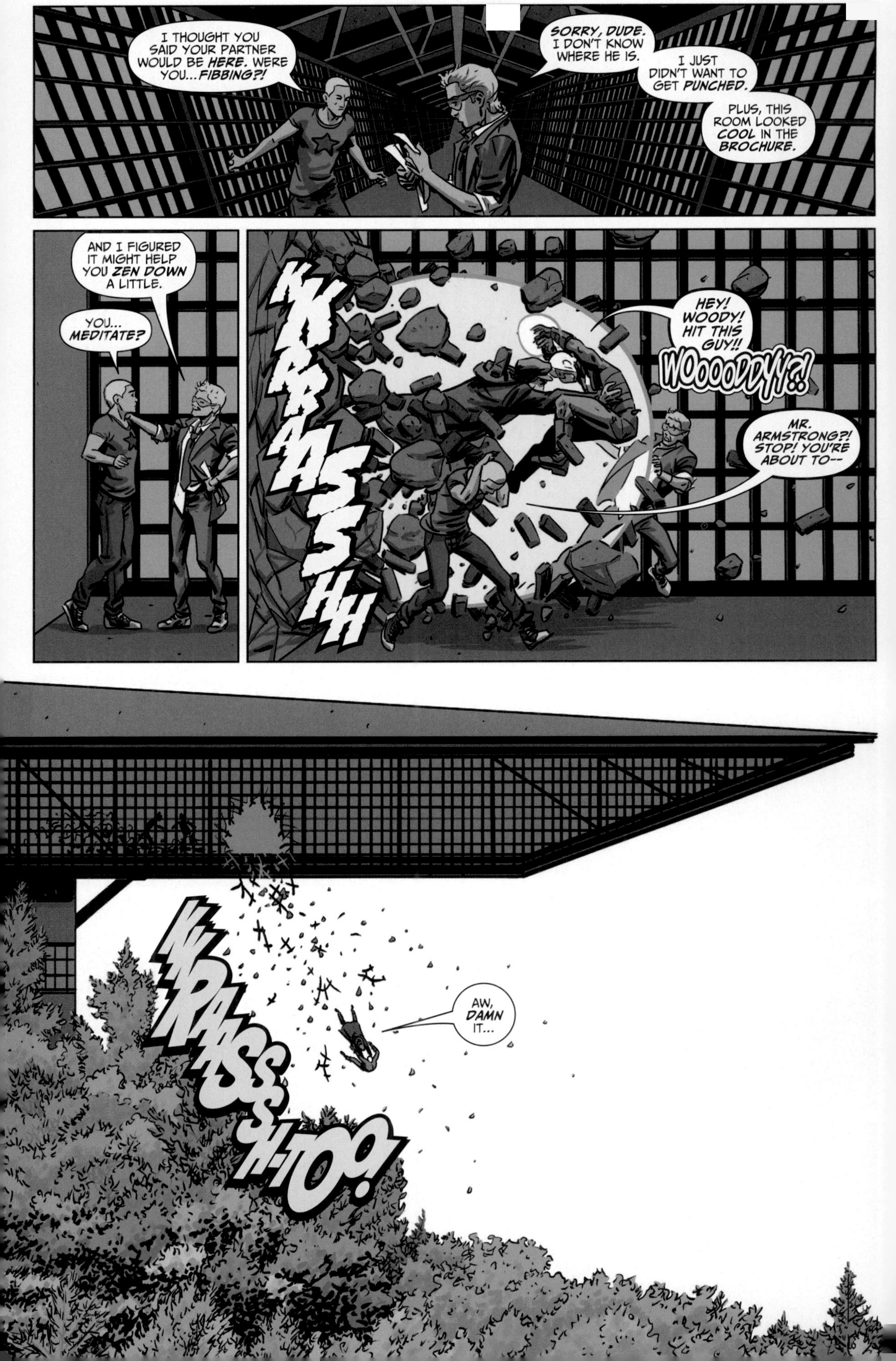
I THOUGHT YOU SAID YOUR PARTNER WOULD BE HERE. WERE YOU... FIBBING?!
SORRY, DUDE. I DON'T KNOW WHERE HE IS.
I JUST DIDN'T WANT TO GET PUNCHED.
PLUS, THIS ROOM LOOKED COOL IN THE BROCHURE.
AND I FIGURED IT MIGHT HELP YOU ZEN DOWN A LITTLE.
YOU... MEDITATE?
KKRRAASSHH
HEY! WOODY! HIT THIS GUY!!
WOOOODDYY?!
MR. ARMSTRONG?! STOP! YOU'RE ABOUT TO--
KRASSSH-TOO!
AW, DAMN IT...

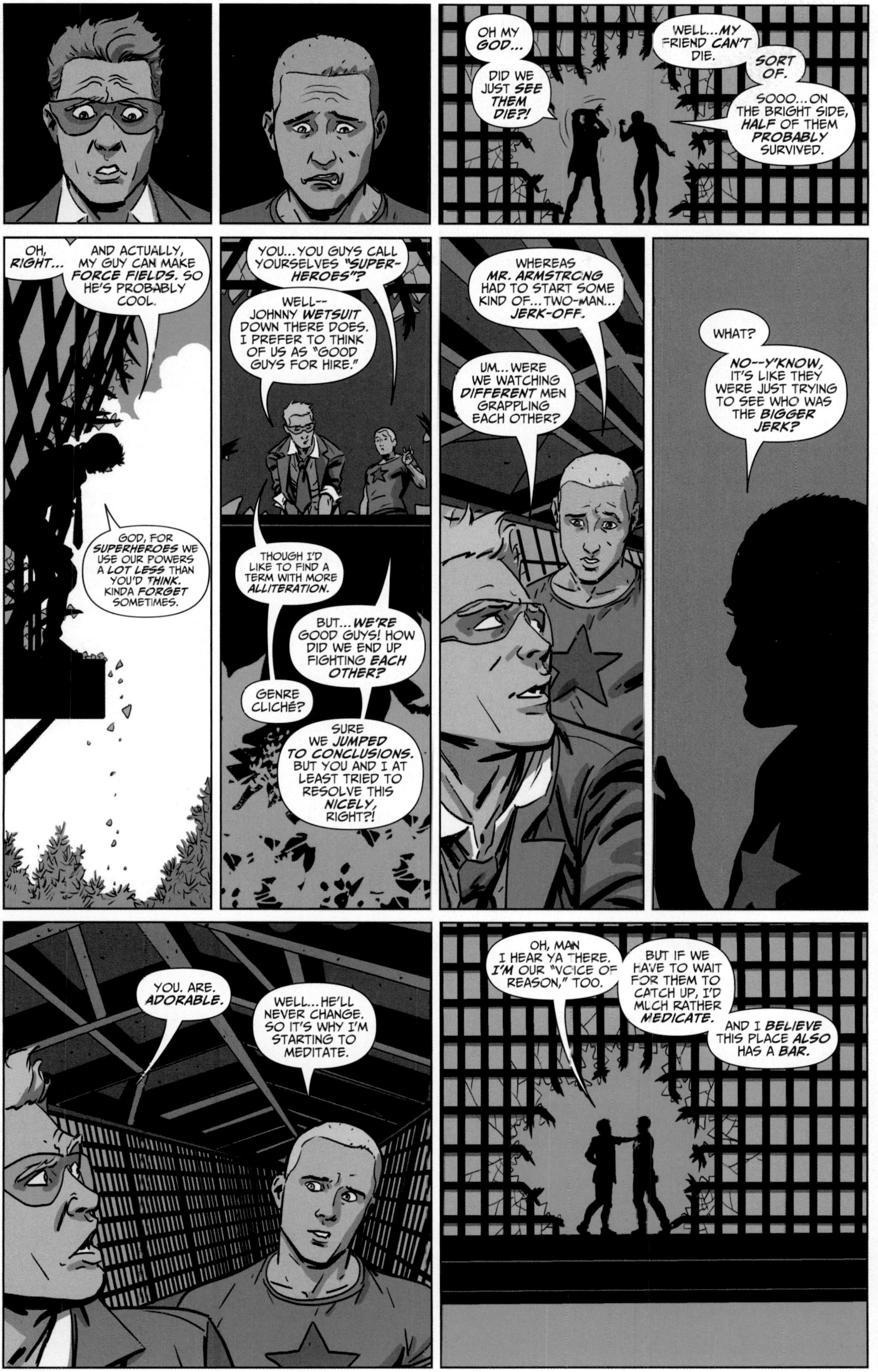
OH MY GOD...
DID WE JUST SEE THEM DIE?!
WELL...MY FRIEND CAN'T DIE.
SORT OF.
SOOO...ON THE BRIGHT SIDE, HALF OF THEM PROBABLY SURVIVED.
OH, RIGHT...
AND ACTUALLY, MY GUY CAN MAKE FORCE FIELDS. SO HE'S PROBABLY COOL.
GOD, FOR SUPERHEROES WE USE OUR POWERS A LOT LESS THAN YOU'D THINK. KINDA FORGET SOMETIMES.
YOU...YOU GUYS CALL YOURSELVES "SUPER-HEROES"?
WELL-- JOHNNY WETSUIT DOWN THERE DOES. I PREFER TO THINK OF US AS "GOOD GUYS FOR HIRE."
THOUGH I'D LIKE TO FIND A TERM WITH MORE ALLITERATION.
BUT...WE'RE GOOD GUYS! HOW DID WE END UP FIGHTING EACH OTHER?
GENRE CLICHÉ?
SURE WE JUMPED TO CONCLUSIONS. BUT YOU AND I AT LEAST TRIED TO RESOLVE THIS NICELY, RIGHT?!
WHEREAS MR. ARMSTRONG HAD TO START SOME KIND OF...TWO-MAN... JERK-OFF.
UM...WERE WE WATCHING DIFFERENT MEN GRAPPLING EACH OTHER?
WHAT?
NO--Y'KNOW, IT'S LIKE THEY WERE JUST TRYING TO SEE WHO WAS THE BIGGER JERK?
YOU. ARE. ADORABLE.
WELL...HE'LL NEVER CHANGE. SO IT'S WHY I'M STARTING TO MEDITATE.
OH, MAN I HEAR YA THERE. I'M OUR "VOICE OF REASON," TOO.
BUT IF WE HAVE TO WAIT FOR THEM TO CATCH UP, I'D MUCH RATHER MEDICATE.
AND I BELIEVE THIS PLACE ALSO HAS A BAR.

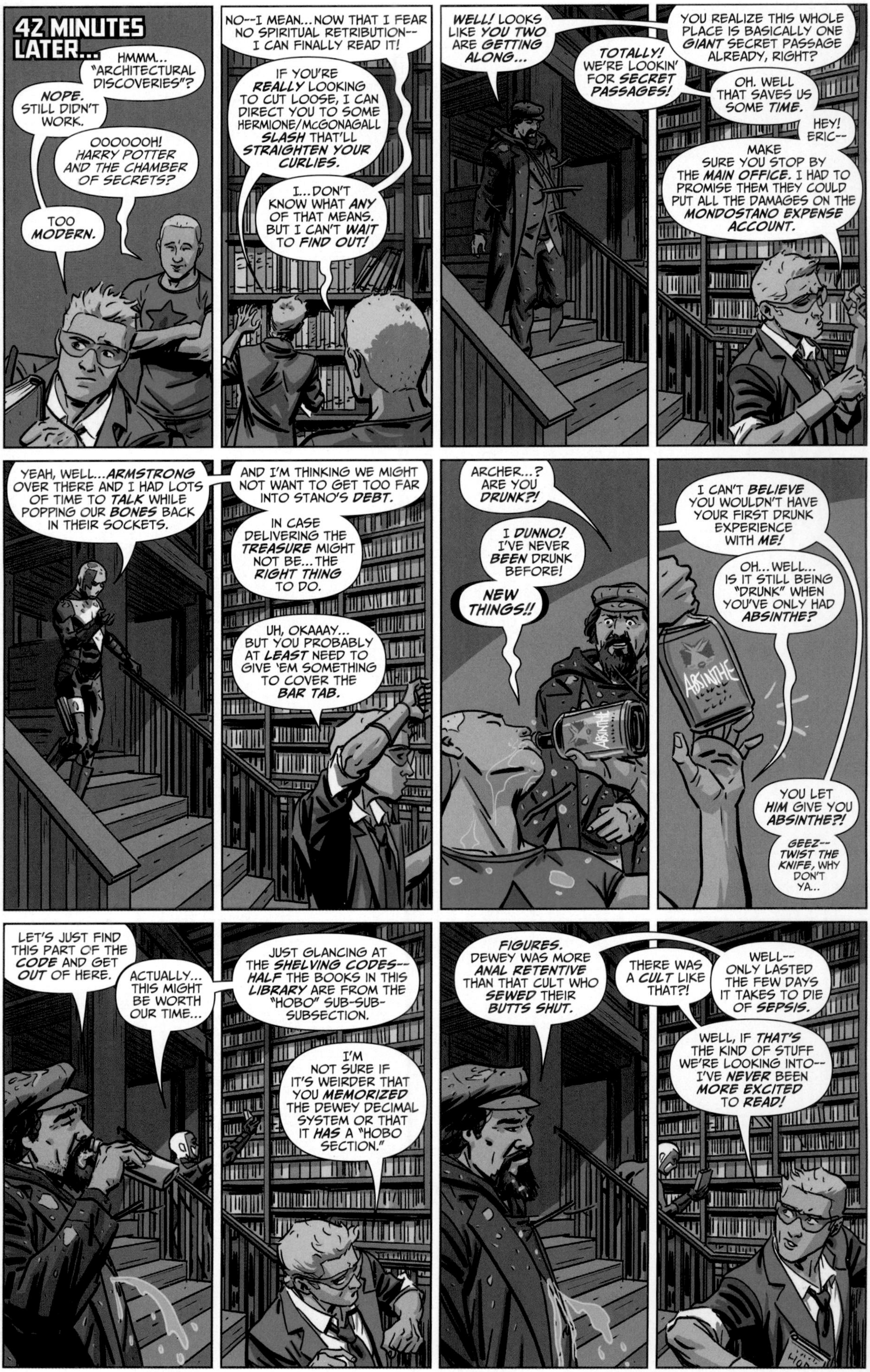

42 MINUTES LATER...
HMMM... "ARCHITECTURAL DISCOVERIES"?
NOPE. STILL DIDN'T WORK.
OOOOOOH! HARRY POTTER AND THE CHAMBER OF SECRETS?
TOO MODERN.
NO--I MEAN...NOW THAT I FEAR NO SPIRITUAL RETRIBUTION-- I CAN FINALLY READ IT!
IF YOU'RE REALLY LOOKING TO CUT LOOSE, I CAN DIRECT YOU TO SOME HERMIONE/MCGONAGALL SLASH THAT'LL STRAIGHTEN YOUR CURLIES.
I...DON'T KNOW WHAT ANY OF THAT MEANS. BUT I CAN'T WAIT TO FIND OUT!
WELL! LOOKS LIKE YOU TWO ARE GETTING ALONG...
YOU REALIZE THIS WHOLE PLACE IS BASICALLY ONE GIANT SECRET PASSAGE ALREADY, RIGHT?
TOTALLY! WE'RE LOOKIN' FOR SECRET PASSAGES!
OH. WELL THAT SAVES US SOME TIME.
HEY! ERIC--
MAKE SURE YOU STOP BY THE MAIN OFFICE. I HAD TO PROMISE THEM THEY COULD PUT ALL THE DAMAGES ON THE MONDOSTANO EXPENSE ACCOUNT.
YEAH, WELL...ARMSTRONG OVER THERE AND I HAD LOTS OF TIME TO TALK WHILE POPPING OUR BONES BACK IN THEIR SOCKETS.
AND I'M THINKING WE MIGHT NOT WANT TO GET TOO FAR INTO STANO'S DEBT.
IN CASE DELIVERING THE TREASURE MIGHT NOT BE...THE RIGHT THING TO DO.
UH, OKAAAY... BUT YOU PROBABLY AT LEAST NEED TO GIVE 'EM SOMETHING TO COVER THE BAR TAB.
ARCHER...? ARE YOU DRUNK?!
I DUNNO! I'VE NEVER BEEN DRUNK BEFORE!
NEW THINGS!!
ABSINTHE
ABSINTHE
I CAN'T BELIEVE YOU WOULDN'T HAVE YOUR FIRST DRUNK EXPERIENCE WITH ME!
OH...WELL... IS IT STILL BEING "DRUNK" WHEN YOU'VE ONLY HAD ABSINTHE?
YOU LET HIM GIVE YOU ABSINTHE?!
GEEZ-- TWIST THE KNIFE, WHY DON'T YA...
LET'S JUST FIND THIS PART OF THE CODE AND GET OUT OF HERE.
ACTUALLY... THIS MIGHT BE WORTH OUR TIME...
JUST GLANCING AT THE SHELVING CODES-- HALF THE BOOKS IN THIS LIBRARY ARE FROM THE "HOBO" SUB-SUB-SUBSECTION.
I'M NOT SURE IF IT'S WEIRDER THAT YOU MEMORIZED THE DEWEY DECIMAL SYSTEM OR THAT IT HAS A "HOBO SECTION."
FIGURES. DEWEY WAS MORE ANAL RETENTIVE THAN THAT CULT WHO SEWED THEIR BUTTS SHUT.
THERE WAS A CULT LIKE THAT?!
WELL-- ONLY LASTED THE FEW DAYS IT TAKES TO DIE OF SEPSIS.
WELL, IF THAT'S THE KIND OF STUFF WE'RE LOOKING INTO-- I'VE NEVER BEEN MORE EXCITED TO READ!

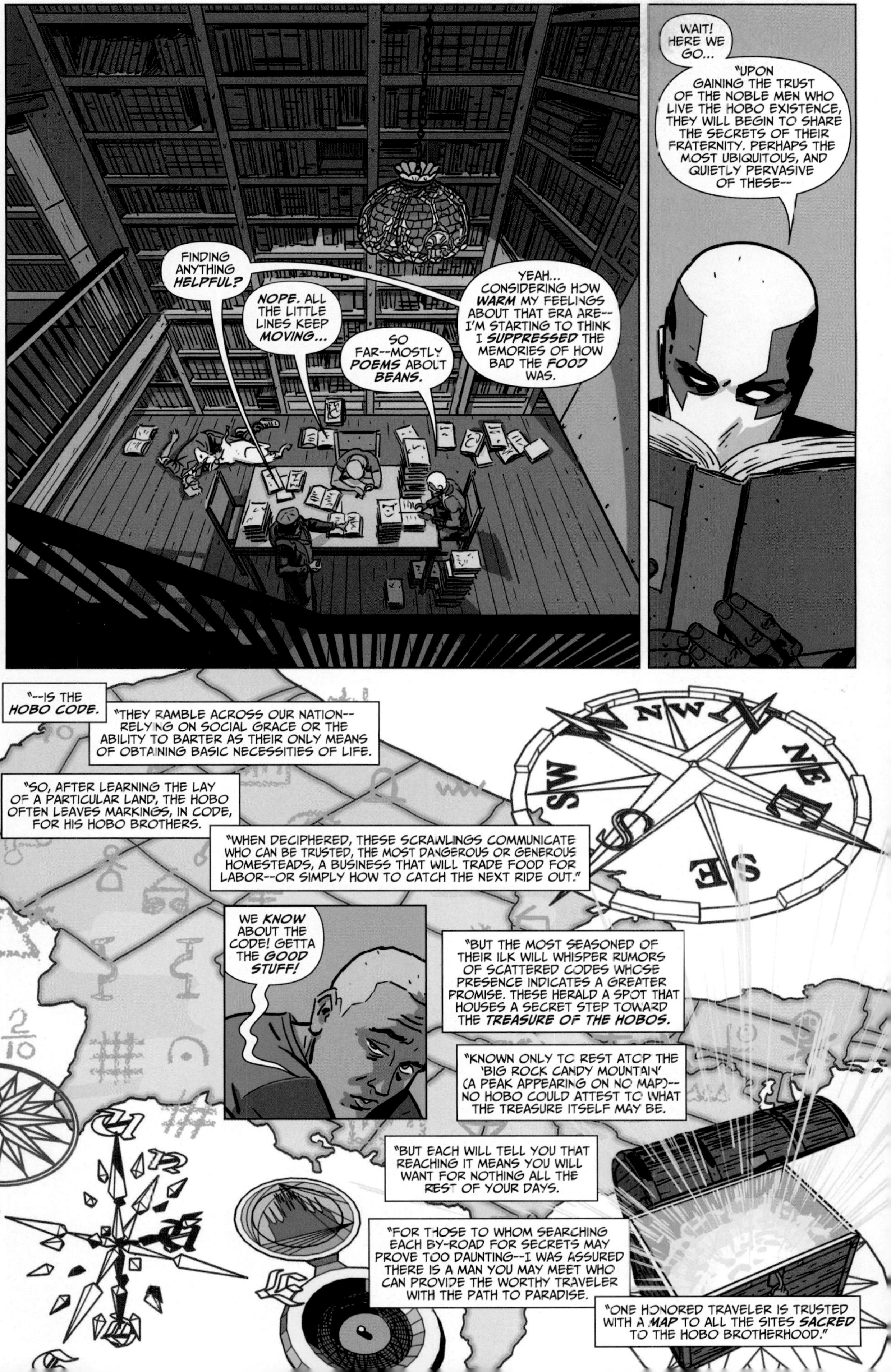
FINDING ANYTHING HELPFUL?
NOPE. ALL THE LITTLE LINES KEEP MOVING...
SO FAR--MOSTLY POEMS ABOUT BEANS.
YEAH... CONSIDERING HOW WARM MY FEELINGS ABOUT THAT ERA ARE-- I'M STARTING TO THINK I SUPPRESSED THE MEMORIES OF HOW BAD THE FOOD WAS.
WAIT! HERE WE GO...
"UPON GAINING THE TRUST OF THE NOBLE MEN WHO LIVE THE HOBO EXISTENCE, THEY WILL BEGIN TO SHARE THE SECRETS OF THEIR FRATERNITY. PERHAPS THE MOST UBIQUITOUS, AND QUIETLY PERVASIVE OF THESE--
"--IS THE HOBO CODE.
"THEY RAMBLE ACROSS OUR NATION-- RELYING ON SOCIAL GRACE OR THE ABILITY TO BARTER AS THEIR ONLY MEANS OF OBTAINING BASIC NECESSITIES OF LIFE.
"SO, AFTER LEARNING THE LAY OF A PARTICULAR LAND, THE HOBO OFTEN LEAVES MARKINGS, IN CODE, FOR HIS HOBO BROTHERS.
"WHEN DECIPHERED, THESE SCRAWLINGS COMMUNICATE WHO CAN BE TRUSTED, THE MOST DANGEROUS OR GENEROUS HOMESTEADS, A BUSINESS THAT WILL TRADE FOOD FOR LABOR--OR SIMPLY HOW TO CATCH THE NEXT RIDE OUT."
WE KNOW ABOUT THE CODE! GETTA THE GOOD STUFF!
"BUT THE MOST SEASONED OF THEIR ILK WILL WHISPER RUMORS OF SCATTERED CODES WHOSE PRESENCE INDICATES A GREATER PROMISE. THESE HERALD A SPOT THAT HOUSES A SECRET STEP TOWARD THE TREASURE OF THE HOBOS.
"KNOWN ONLY TO REST ATOP THE 'BIG ROCK CANDY MOUNTAIN' (A PEAK APPEARING ON NO MAP)-- NO HOBO COULD ATTEST TO WHAT THE TREASURE ITSELF MAY BE.
"BUT EACH WILL TELL YOU THAT REACHING IT MEANS YOU WILL WANT FOR NOTHING ALL THE REST OF YOUR DAYS.
"FOR THOSE TO WHOM SEARCHING EACH BY-ROAD FOR SECRETS MAY PROVE TOO DAUNTING--I WAS ASSURED THERE IS A MAN YOU MAY MEET WHO CAN PROVIDE THE WORTHY TRAVELER WITH THE PATH TO PARADISE.
"ONE HONORED TRAVELER IS TRUSTED WITH A MAP TO ALL THE SITES SACRED TO THE HOBO BROTHERHOOD."

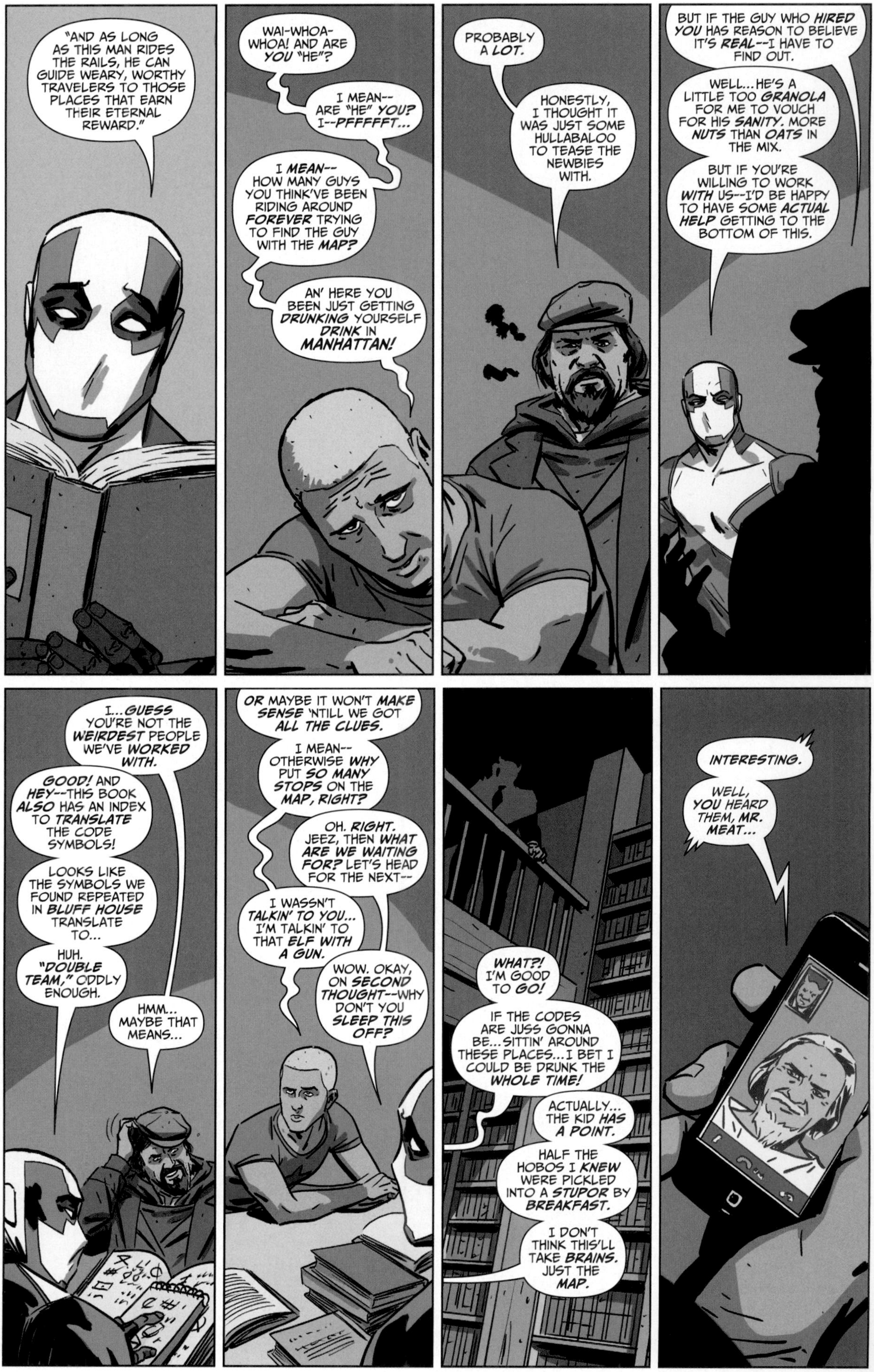
"AND AS LONG AS THIS MAN RIDES THE RAILS, HE CAN GUIDE WEARY, WORTHY TRAVELERS TO THOSE PLACES THAT EARN THEIR ETERNAL REWARD."
WAI-WHOA-WHOA! AND ARE YOU "HE"?
I MEAN-- ARE "HE" YOU? I--PFFFFFT...
I MEAN-- HOW MANY GUYS YOU THINK'VE BEEN RIDING AROUND FOREVER TRYING TO FIND THE GUY WITH THE MAP?
AN' HERE YOU BEEN JUST GETTING DRUNKING YOURSELF DRINK IN MANHATTAN!
PROBABLY A LOT.
HONESTLY, I THOUGHT IT WAS JUST SOME HULLABALOO TO TEASE THE NEWBIES WITH.
BUT IF THE GUY WHO HIRED YOU HAS REASON TO BELIEVE IT'S REAL--I HAVE TO FIND OUT.
WELL... HE'S A LITTLE TOO GRANOLA FOR ME TO VOUCH FOR HIS SANITY. MORE NUTS THAN OATS IN THE MIX.
BUT IF YOU'RE WILLING TO WORK WITH US--I'D BE HAPPY TO HAVE SOME ACTUAL HELP GETTING TO THE BOTTOM OF THIS.
I...GUESS YOU'RE NOT THE WEIRDEST PEOPLE WE'VE WORKED WITH.
GOOD! AND HEY--THIS BOOK ALSO HAS AN INDEX TO TRANSLATE THE CODE SYMBOLS!
LOOKS LIKE THE SYMBOLS WE FOUND REPEATED IN BLUFF HOUSE TRANSLATE TO...
HUH. "DOUBLE TEAM," ODDLY ENOUGH.
HMM... MAYBE THAT MEANS...
OR MAYBE IT WON'T MAKE SENSE 'NTILL WE GOT ALL THE CLUES.
I MEAN-- OTHERWISE WHY PUT SO MANY STOPS ON THE MAP, RIGHT?
OH. RIGHT. JEEZ, THEN WHAT ARE WE WAITING FOR? LET'S HEAD FOR THE NEXT--
I WASSN'T TALKIN' TO YOU... I'M TALKIN' TO THAT ELF WITH A GUN.
WOW. OKAY, ON SECOND THOUGHT--WHY DON'T YOU SLEEP THIS OFF?
WHAT?! I'M GOOD TO GO!
IF THE CODES ARE JUSS GONNA BE...SITTIN' AROUND THESE PLACES...I BET I COULD BE DRUNK THE WHOLE TIME!
ACTUALLY... THE KID HAS A POINT.
HALF THE HOBOS I KNEW WERE PICKLED INTO A STUPOR BY BREAKFAST.
I DON'T THINK THIS'LL TAKE BRAINS. JUST THE MAP.
INTERESTING.
WELL, YOU HEARD THEM, MR. MEAT...

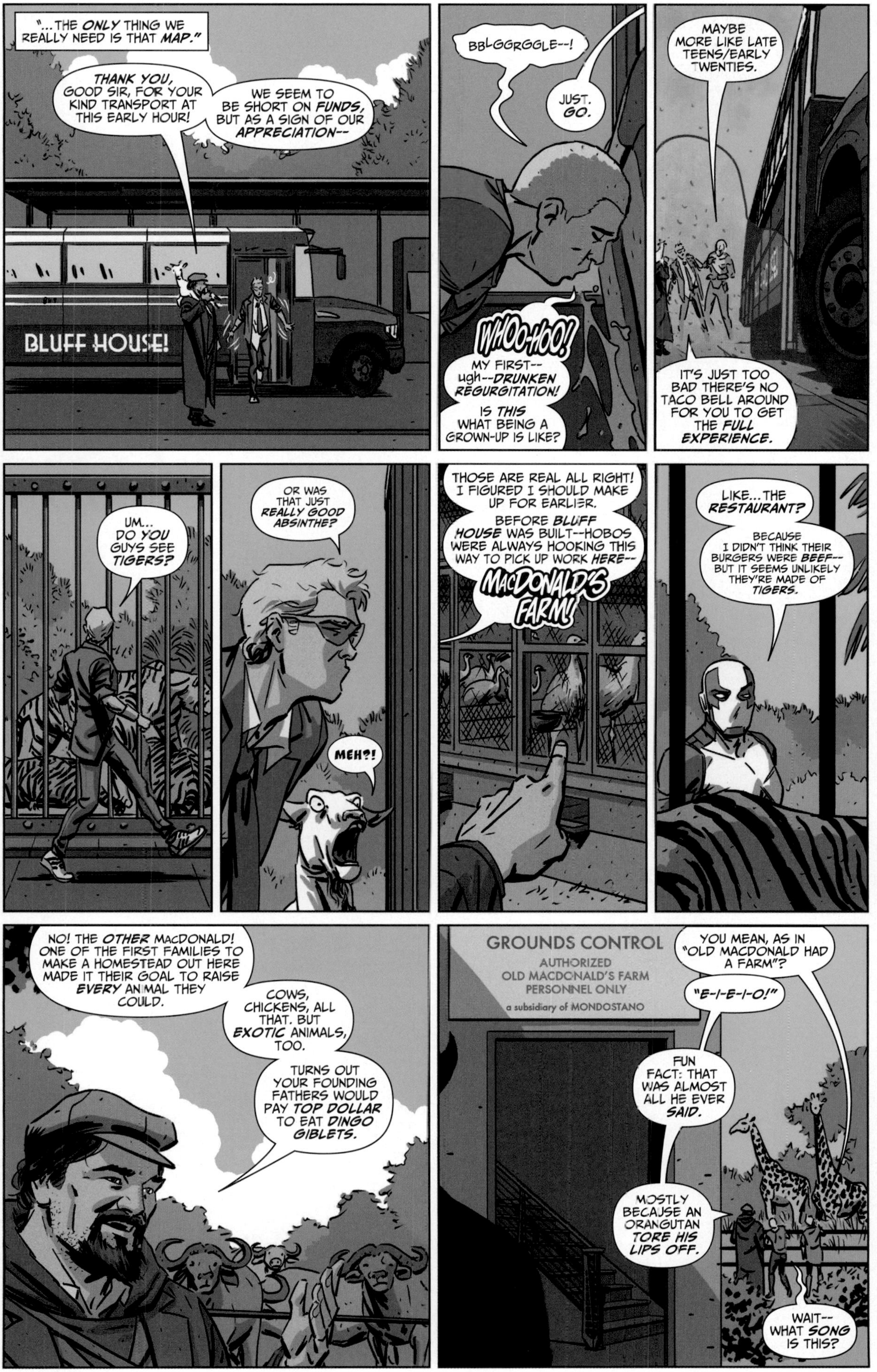

"...THE ONLY THING WE REALLY NEED IS THAT MAP."
THANK YOU, GOOD SIR, FOR YOUR KIND TRANSPORT AT THIS EARLY HOUR!
WE SEEM TO BE SHORT ON FUNDS, BUT AS A SIGN OF OUR APPRECIATION--
BLUFF HOUSE!
BBLGGRGGLE--!
JUST. GO.
WHOO-HOO!
MY FIRST--ugh--DRUNKEN REGURGITATION!
IS THIS WHAT BEING A GROWN-UP IS LIKE?
MAYBE MORE LIKE LATE TEENS/EARLY TWENTIES.
IT'S JUST TOO BAD THERE'S NO TACO BELL AROUND FOR YOU TO GET THE FULL EXPERIENCE.
UM... DO YOU GUYS SEE TIGERS?
OR WAS THAT JUST REALLY GOOD ABSINTHE?
MEH?!
THOSE ARE REAL ALL RIGHT! I FIGURED I SHOULD MAKE UP FOR EARLIER.
BEFORE BLUFF HOUSE WAS BUILT--HOBOS WERE ALWAYS HOOKING THIS WAY TO PICK UP WORK HERE--
MacDONALD'S FARM!
LIKE...THE RESTAURANT?
BECAUSE I DIDN'T THINK THEIR BURGERS WERE BEEF--BUT IT SEEMS UNLIKELY THEY'RE MADE OF TIGERS.
NO! THE OTHER MacDONALD! ONE OF THE FIRST FAMILIES TO MAKE A HOMESTEAD OUT HERE MADE IT THEIR GOAL TO RAISE EVERY ANIMAL THEY COULD.
COWS, CHICKENS, ALL THAT. BUT EXOTIC ANIMALS, TOO.
TURNS OUT YOUR FOUNDING FATHERS WOULD PAY TOP DOLLAR TO EAT DINGO GIBLETS.
GROUNDS CONTROL
AUTHORIZED
OLD MACDONALD'S FARM
PERSONNEL ONLY
a subsidiary of MONDOSTANO
YOU MEAN, AS IN "OLD MACDONALD HAD A FARM"?
"E-I-E-I-O!"
FUN FACT: THAT WAS ALMOST ALL HE EVER SAID.
MOSTLY BECAUSE AN ORANGUTAN TORE HIS LIPS OFF.
WAIT--WHAT SONG IS THIS?

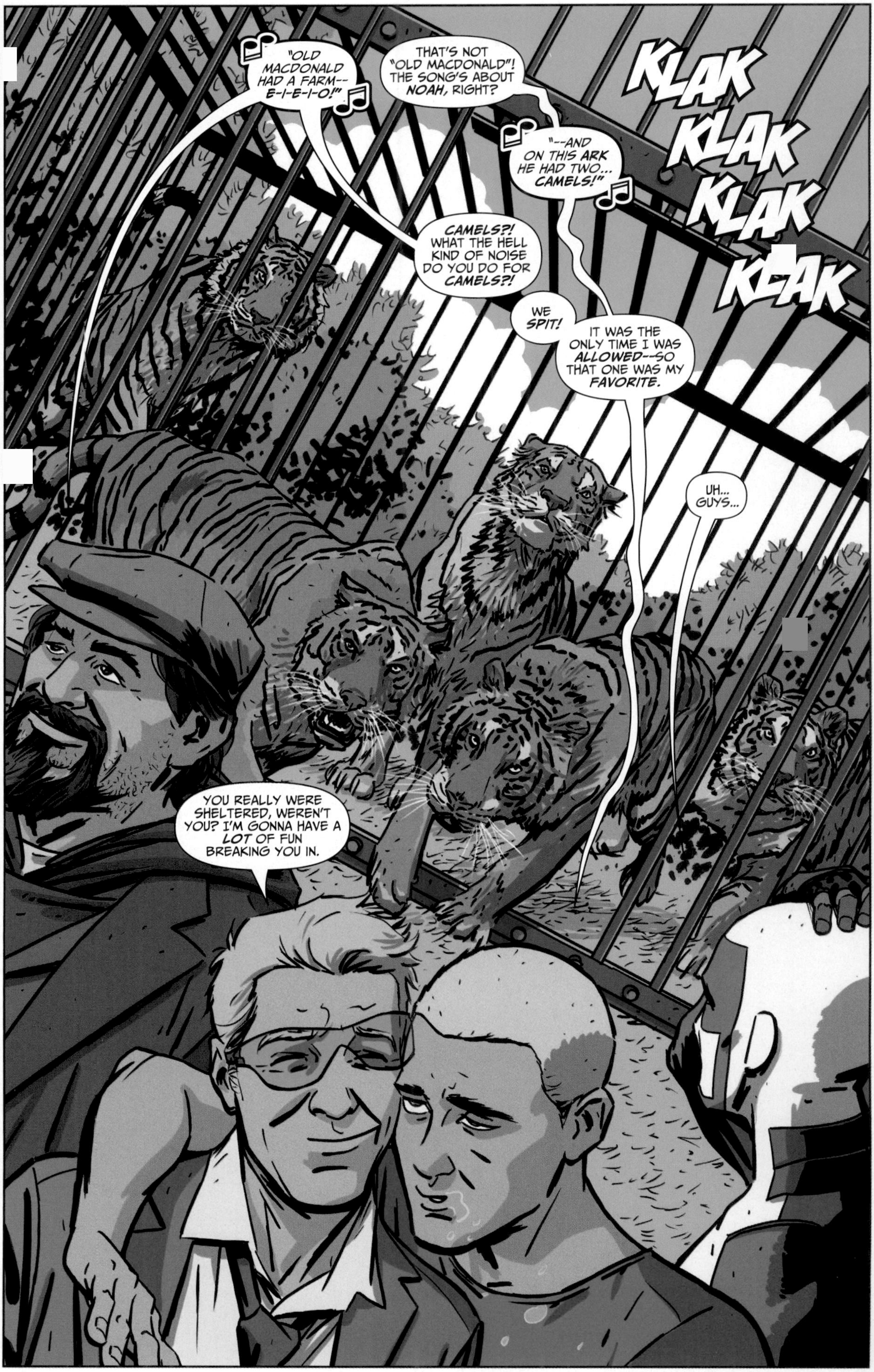
"OLD MACDONALD HAD A FARM-- E-I-E-I-O!"
THAT'S NOT "OLD MACDONALD"! THE SONG'S ABOUT NOAH, RIGHT?
"--AND ON THIS ARK HE HAD TWO... CAMELS!"
CAMELS?! WHAT THE HELL KIND OF NOISE DO YOU DO FOR CAMELS?!
WE SPIT!
IT WAS THE ONLY TIME I WAS ALLOWED--SO THAT ONE WAS MY FAVORITE.
KLAK KLAK KLAK KLAK
UH... GUYS...
YOU REALLY WERE SHELTERED, WEREN'T YOU? I'M GONNA HAVE A LOT OF FUN BREAKING YOU IN.

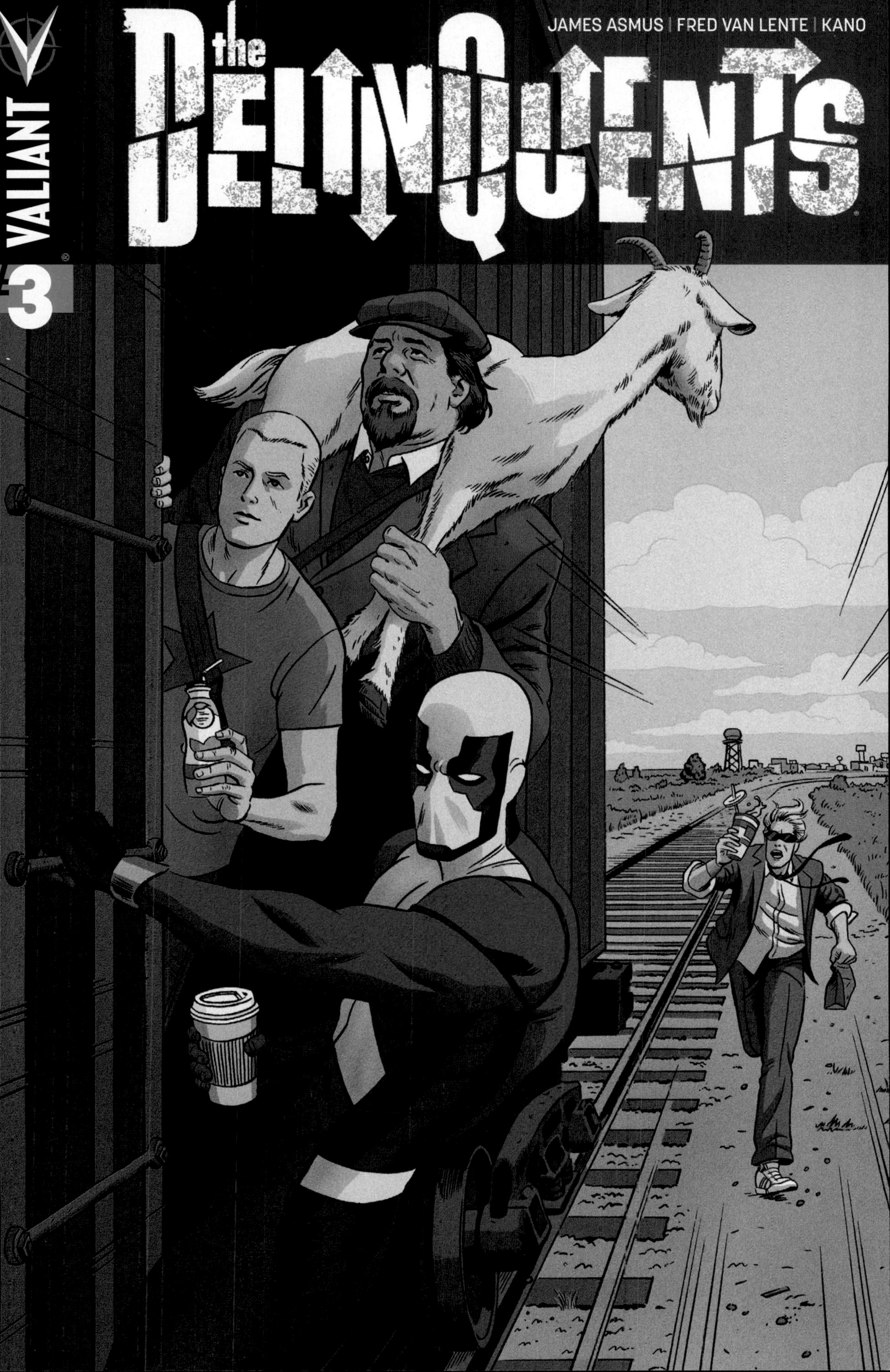
JAMES ASMUS | FRED VAN LENTE | KANO
the DELINQUENTS
VALIANT
3

delinquents

Quantum

Eric and his foster brother, Woody, were transformed by an explosion in their father's lab. Eric became Quantum, and acquired the ability to create force fields. As a hero for gainful employment, he is currently selling his services to the Mondostano Corporation, using a mysterious ass map to find the lost treasure of the hobos. Unfortunately...he only has half the map.

Archer

Sheltered from the world, Obadiah Archer's parents raised him as a weapon to destroy Armstrong—who is now his best friend. Archer and Armstrong now possess the other half of a continent-spanning ass map leading to the lost treasure of the hobos.

Armstrong

Effectively immortal, Armstrong is Archer's usually drunk and carousing partner, and a former hobo tasked with guarding the map to the lost treasure of the hobos.

Woody

Trapped in the same lab accident that turned his brother into Quantum, this guy developed the ability to shoot glowy energy blasts from his hands. Former con artist. Banned for life from Belgium.

The Goat

This old girl is the traveling companion of Quantum and Woody, mysteriously imbued with various unnatural superpowers, as well as the mind of their late father. She's also in a delicate condition (pregnant). Approach with extreme caution.

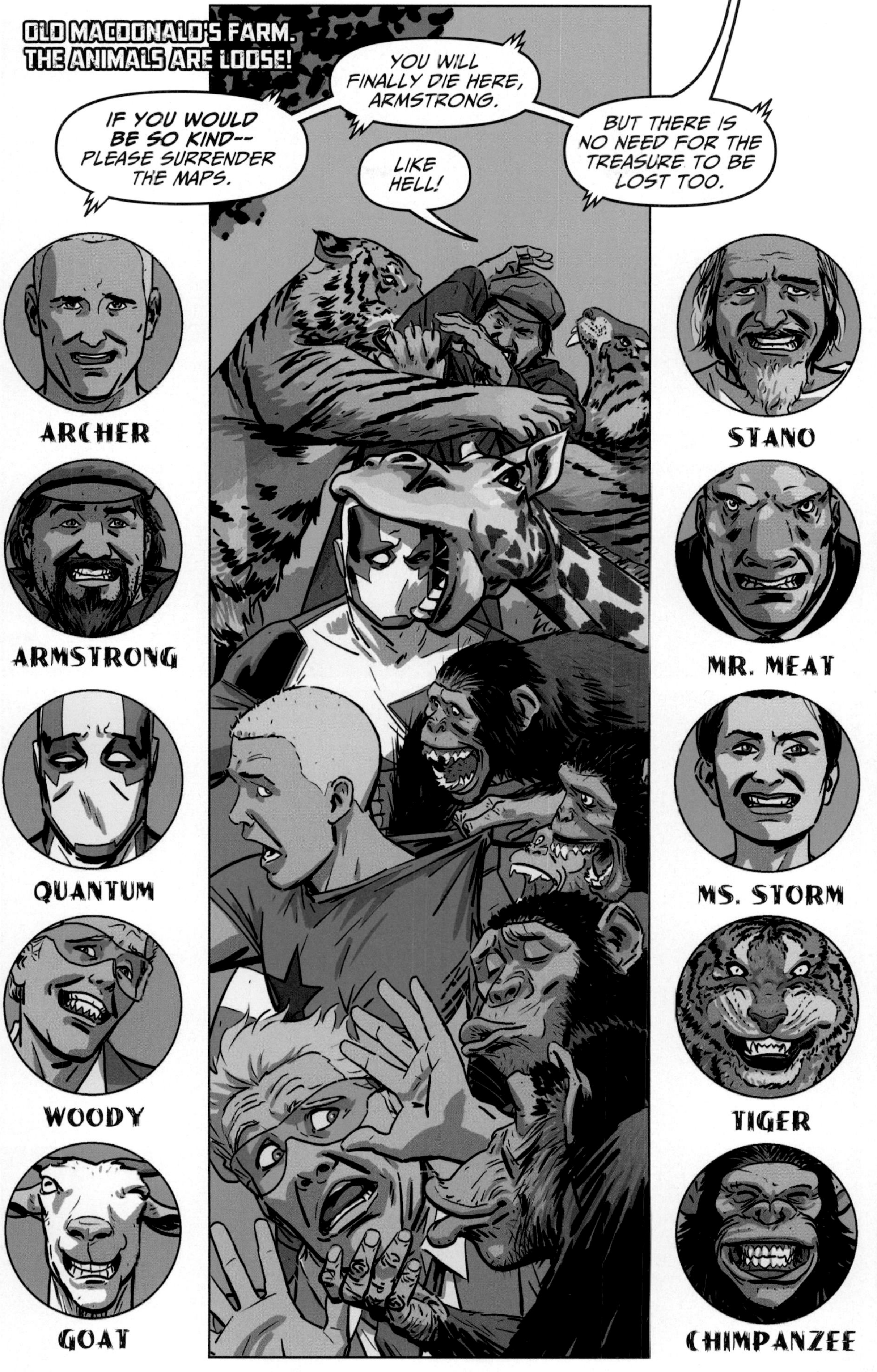
OLD MACDONALD'S FARM. THE ANIMALS ARE LOOSE!
IF YOU WOULD BE SO KIND-- PLEASE SURRENDER THE MAPS.
YOU WILL FINALLY DIE HERE, ARMSTRONG.
LIKE HELL!
BUT THERE IS NO NEED FOR THE TREASURE TO BE LOST TOO.
ARCHER
ARMSTRONG
QUANTUM
WOODY
GOAT
STANO
MR. MEAT
MS. STORM
TIGER
CHIMPANZEE

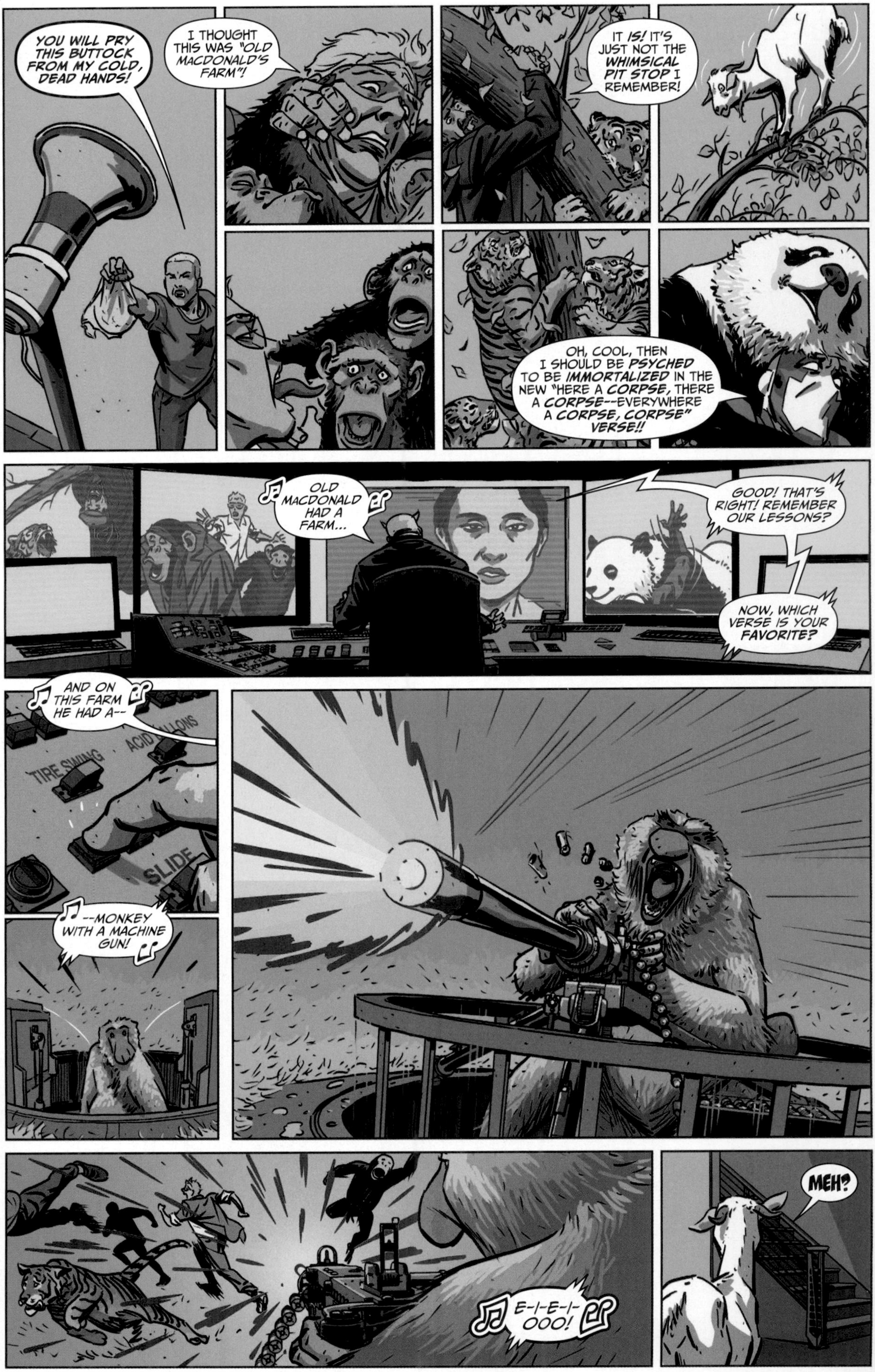

YOU WILL PRY THIS BUTTOCK FROM MY COLD, DEAD HANDS!
I THOUGHT THIS WAS "OLD MACDONALD'S FARM"!
IT IS! IT'S JUST NOT THE WHIMSICAL PIT STOP I REMEMBER!
OH, COOL, THEN I SHOULD BE PSYCHED TO BE IMMORTALIZED IN THE NEW "HERE A CORPSE, THERE A CORPSE--EVERYWHERE A CORPSE, CORPSE" VERSE!!
OLD MACDONALD HAD A FARM...
GOOD! THAT'S RIGHT! REMEMBER OUR LESSONS?
NOW, WHICH VERSE IS YOUR FAVORITE?
AND ON THIS FARM HE HAD A--
TIRE SWING
ACID
SLIDE
--MONKEY WITH A MACHINE GUN!
E-I-E-I-OOO!
MEH?

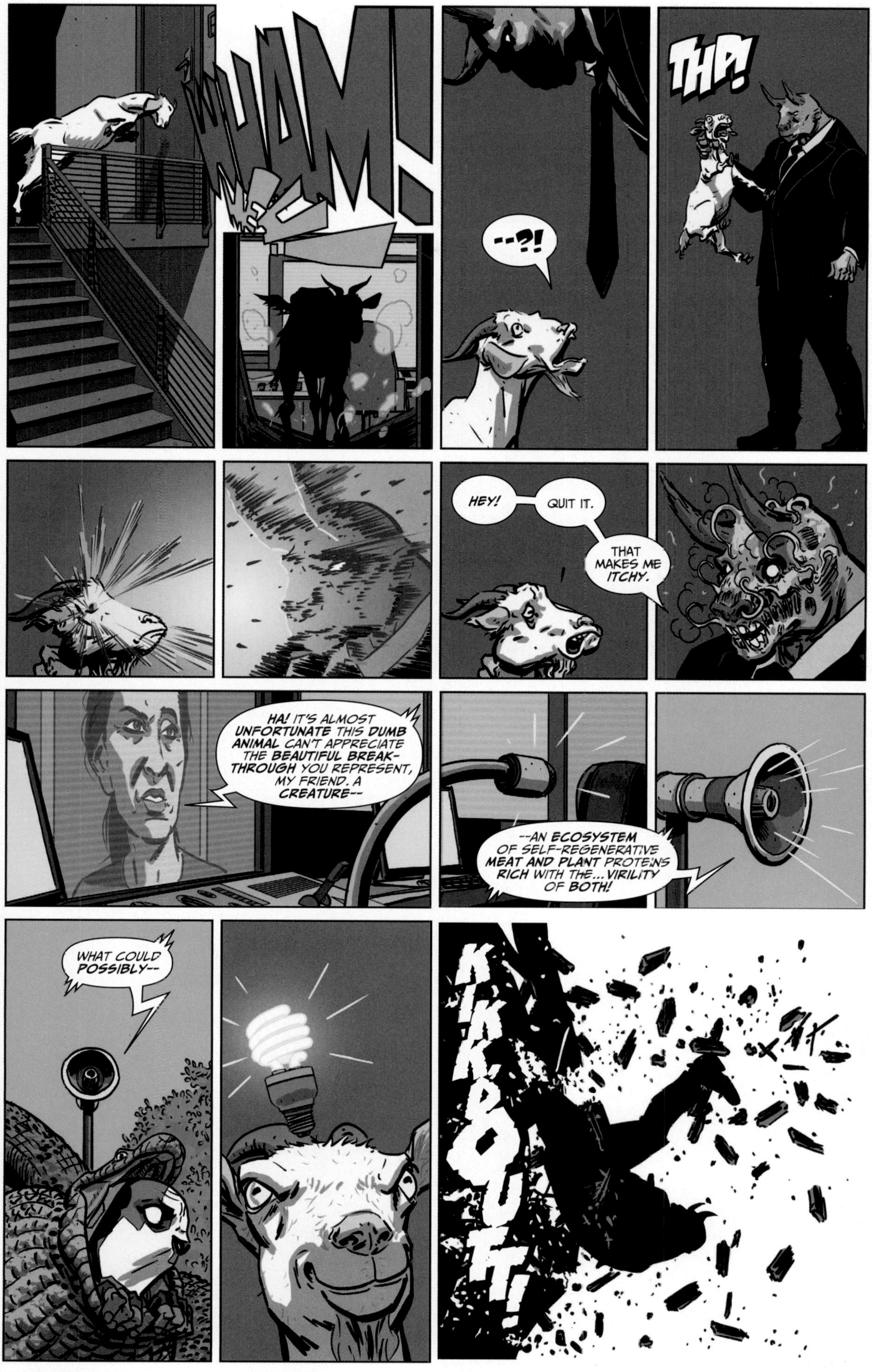

WHAM!
--?!
THP!
HEY!
QUIT IT.
THAT MAKES ME ITCHY.
HA! IT'S ALMOST UNFORTUNATE THIS DUMB ANIMAL CAN'T APPRECIATE THE BEAUTIFUL BREAK-THROUGH YOU REPRESENT, MY FRIEND. A CREATURE--
--AN ECOSYSTEM OF SELF-REGENERATIVE MEAT AND PLANT PROTEINS RICH WITH THE... VIRILITY OF BOTH!
WHAT COULD POSSIBLY--
KAKABOOM!

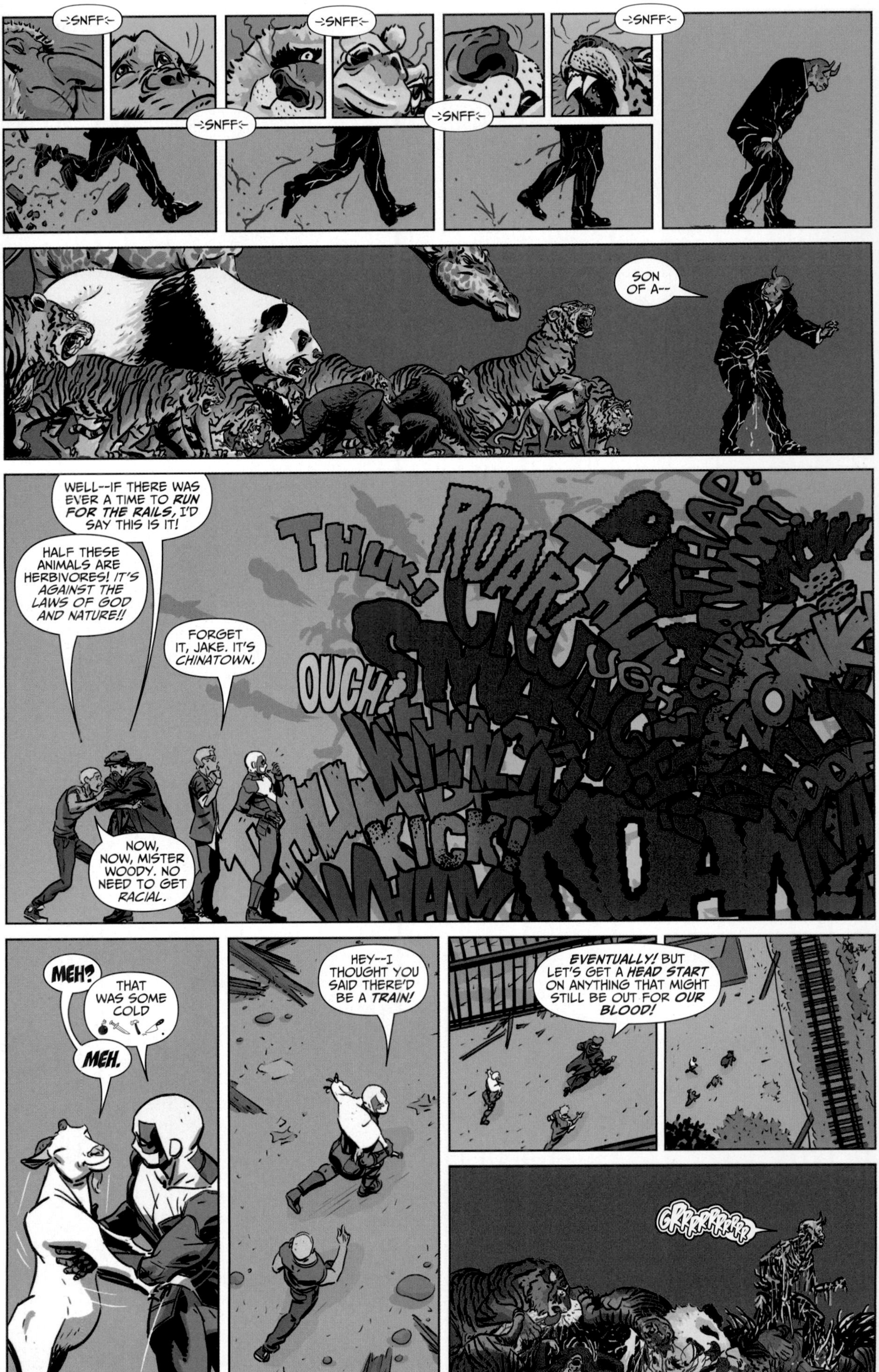
SNFF
SNFF
SNFF
SNFF
SNFF
SON OF A--
WELL--IF THERE WAS EVER A TIME TO *RUN FOR THE RAILS*, I'D SAY THIS IS IT!
HALF THESE ANIMALS ARE HERBIVORES! *IT'S AGAINST THE LAWS OF GOD AND NATURE!!*
FORGET IT, JAKE. IT'S *CHINATOWN.*
NOW, NOW, MISTER WOODY. NO NEED TO GET *RACIAL.*
THUK!
ROAR!
OUCH!
KICK!
WHAM!
MEH?
THAT WAS SOME COLD
MEH.
HEY--I THOUGHT YOU SAID THERE'D BE A *TRAIN!*
EVENTUALLY! BUT LET'S GET A *HEAD START* ON ANYTHING THAT MIGHT STILL BE OUT FOR *OUR BLOOD!*
GRRRRRRRRRR

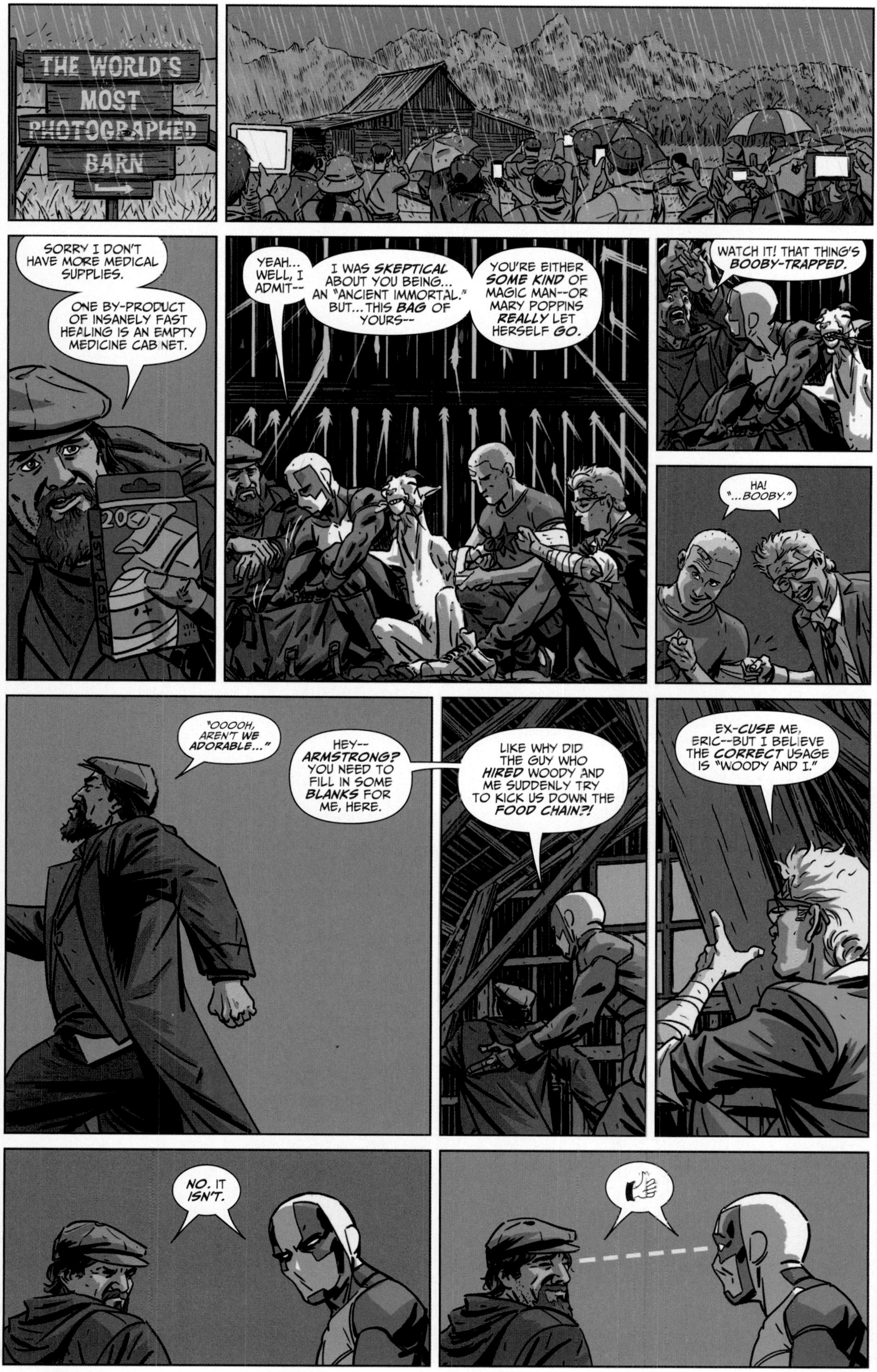

THE WORLD'S MOST PHOTOGRAPHED BARN
SORRY I DON'T HAVE MORE MEDICAL SUPPLIES.
ONE BY-PRODUCT OF INSANELY FAST HEALING IS AN EMPTY MEDICINE CABINET.
YEAH... WELL, I ADMIT--
I WAS SKEPTICAL ABOUT YOU BEING... AN "ANCIENT IMMORTAL." BUT... THIS BAG OF YOURS--
YOU'RE EITHER SOME KIND OF MAGIC MAN--OR MARY POPPINS REALLY LET HERSELF GO.
WATCH IT! THAT THING'S BOOBY-TRAPPED.
HA! "...BOOBY."
"OOOOH, AREN'T WE ADORABLE..."
HEY-- ARMSTRONG? YOU NEED TO FILL IN SOME BLANKS FOR ME, HERE.
LIKE WHY DID THE GUY WHO HIRED WOODY AND ME SUDDENLY TRY TO KICK US DOWN THE FOOD CHAIN?!
EX-CUSE ME, ERIC--BUT I BELIEVE THE CORRECT USAGE IS "WOODY AND I."
NO. IT ISN'T.

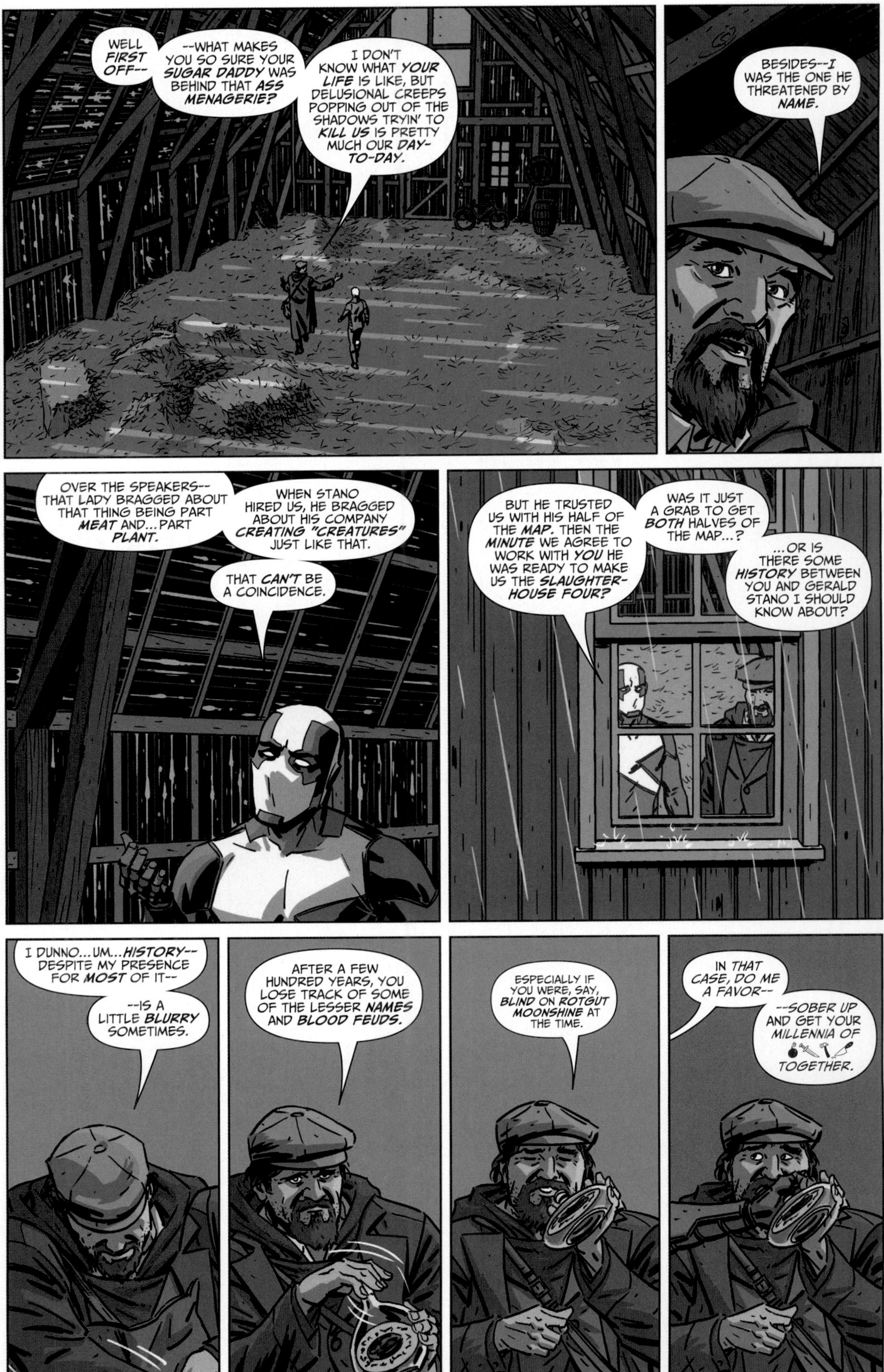
WELL FIRST OFF--
--WHAT MAKES YOU SO SURE YOUR SUGAR DADDY WAS BEHIND THAT ASS MENAGERIE?
I DON'T KNOW WHAT YOUR LIFE IS LIKE, BUT DELUSIONAL CREEPS POPPING OUT OF THE SHADOWS TRYIN' TO KILL US IS PRETTY MUCH OUR DAY-TO-DAY.
BESIDES--I WAS THE ONE HE THREATENED BY NAME.
OVER THE SPEAKERS--THAT LADY BRAGGED ABOUT THAT THING BEING PART MEAT AND...PART PLANT.
WHEN STANO HIRED US, HE BRAGGED ABOUT HIS COMPANY CREATING "CREATURES" JUST LIKE THAT.
THAT CAN'T BE A COINCIDENCE.
BUT HE TRUSTED US WITH HIS HALF OF THE MAP. THEN THE MINUTE WE AGREE TO WORK WITH YOU HE WAS READY TO MAKE US THE SLAUGHTER-HOUSE FOUR?
WAS IT JUST A GRAB TO GET BOTH HALVES OF THE MAP...?
...OR IS THERE SOME HISTORY BETWEEN YOU AND GERALD STANO I SHOULD KNOW ABOUT?
I DUNNO...UM...HISTORY--DESPITE MY PRESENCE FOR MOST OF IT--
--IS A LITTLE BLURRY SOMETIMES.
AFTER A FEW HUNDRED YEARS, YOU LOSE TRACK OF SOME OF THE LESSER NAMES AND BLOOD FEUDS.
ESPECIALLY IF YOU WERE, SAY, BLIND ON ROTGUT MOONSHINE AT THE TIME.
IN THAT CASE, DO ME A FAVOR--
--SOBER UP AND GET YOUR MILLENNIA OF
TOGETHER.

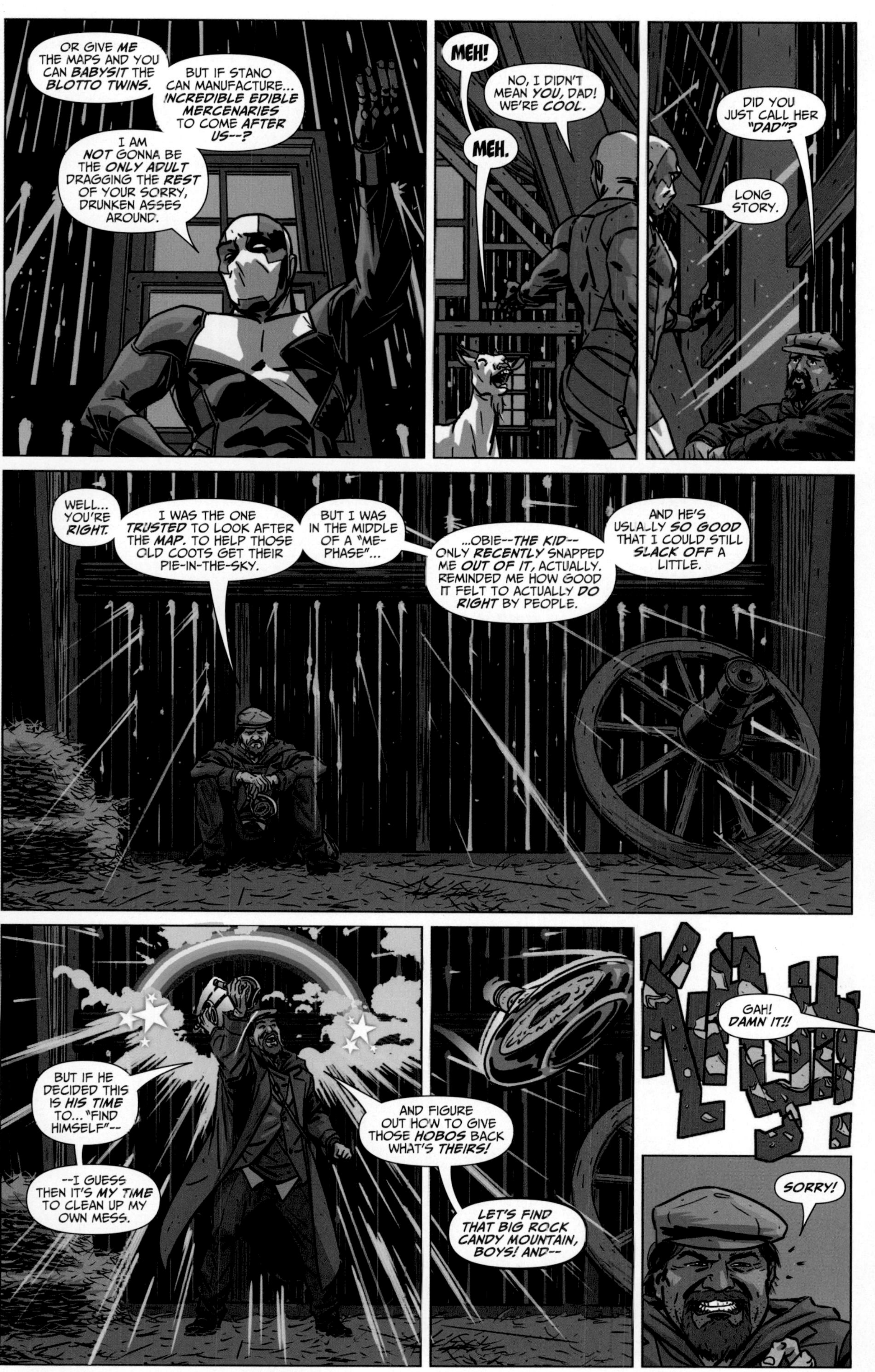
OR GIVE ME THE MAPS AND YOU CAN BABYSIT THE BLOTTO TWINS.
BUT IF STANO CAN MANUFACTURE... INCREDIBLE EDIBLE MERCENARIES TO COME AFTER US--?
I AM NOT GONNA BE THE ONLY ADULT DRAGGING THE REST OF YOUR SORRY, DRUNKEN ASSES AROUND.
MEH!
NO, I DIDN'T MEAN YOU, DAD! WE'RE COOL.
MEH.
DID YOU JUST CALL HER "DAD"?
LONG STORY.
WELL... YOU'RE RIGHT.
I WAS THE ONE TRUSTED TO LOOK AFTER THE MAP. TO HELP THOSE OLD COOTS GET THEIR PIE-IN-THE-SKY.
BUT I WAS IN THE MIDDLE OF A "ME-PHASE"...
...OBIE--THE KID--ONLY RECENTLY SNAPPED ME OUT OF IT, ACTUALLY. REMINDED ME HOW GOOD IT FELT TO ACTUALLY DO RIGHT BY PEOPLE.
AND HE'S USLALLY SO GOOD THAT I COULD STILL SLACK OFF A LITTLE.
BUT IF HE DECIDED THIS IS HIS TIME TO... "FIND HIMSELF"--
--I GUESS THEN IT'S MY TIME TO CLEAN UP MY OWN MESS.
AND FIGURE OUT HOW TO GIVE THOSE HOBOS BACK WHAT'S THEIRS!
LET'S FIND THAT BIG ROCK CANDY MOUNTAIN, BOYS! AND--
GAH! DAMN IT!!
SORRY!

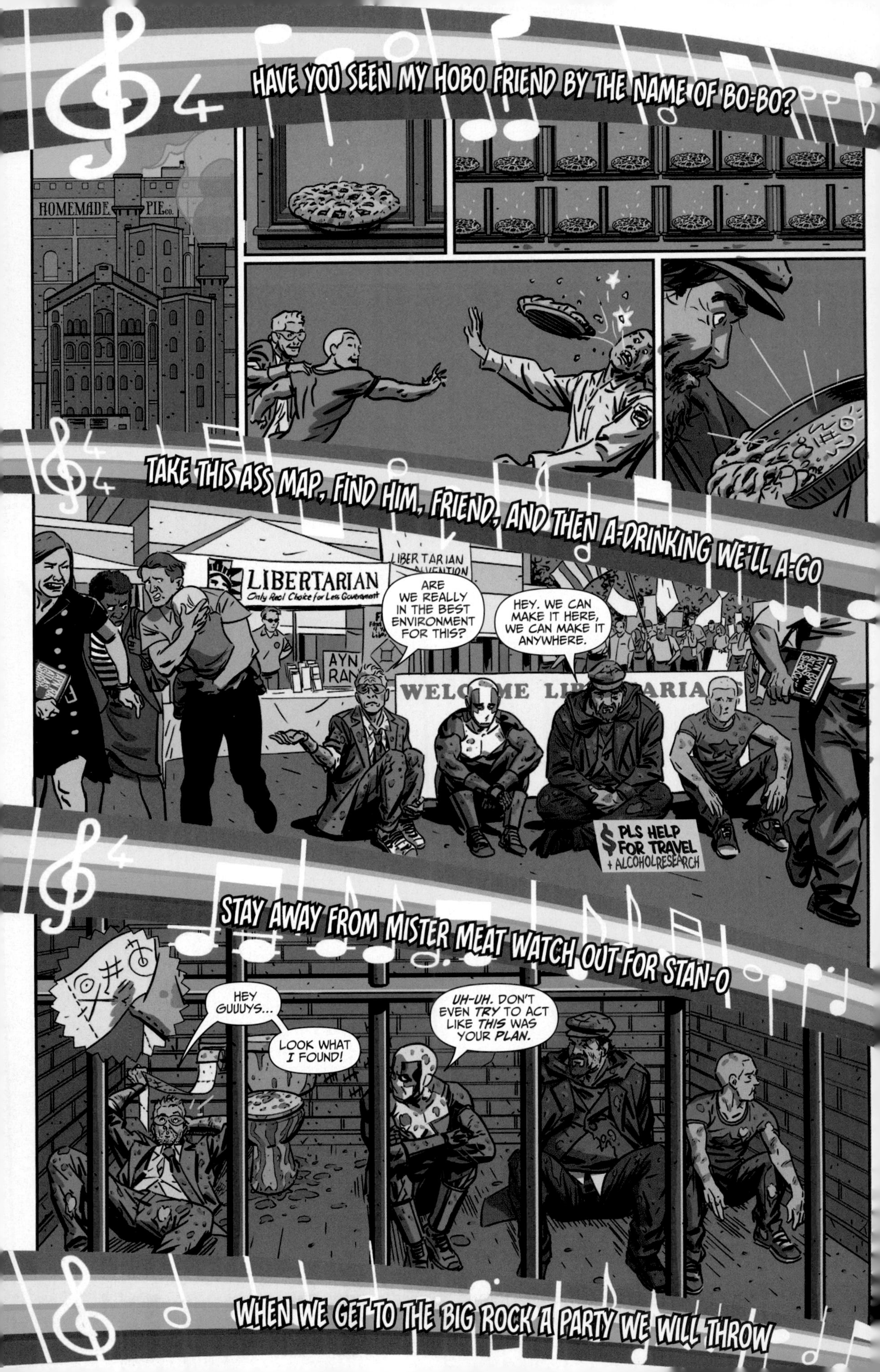
HAVE YOU SEEN MY HOBO FRIEND BY THE NAME OF BO-BO?
HOMEMADE PIE CO.
TAKE THIS ASS MAP, FIND HIM, FRIEND, AND THEN A-DRINKING WE'LL A-GO
LIBERTARIAN
Only Real Choice for Less Government
LIBERTARIAN
ARE WE REALLY IN THE BEST ENVIRONMENT FOR THIS?
HEY. WE CAN MAKE IT HERE, WE CAN MAKE IT ANYWHERE.
$ PLS HELP FOR TRAVEL + ALCOHOLRESEARCH
STAY AWAY FROM MISTER MEAT WATCH OUT FOR STAN-O
HEY GUUUYS...
LOOK WHAT I FOUND!
UH-UH. DON'T EVEN TRY TO ACT LIKE THIS WAS YOUR PLAN.
WHEN WE GET TO THE BIG ROCK A PARTY WE WILL THROW

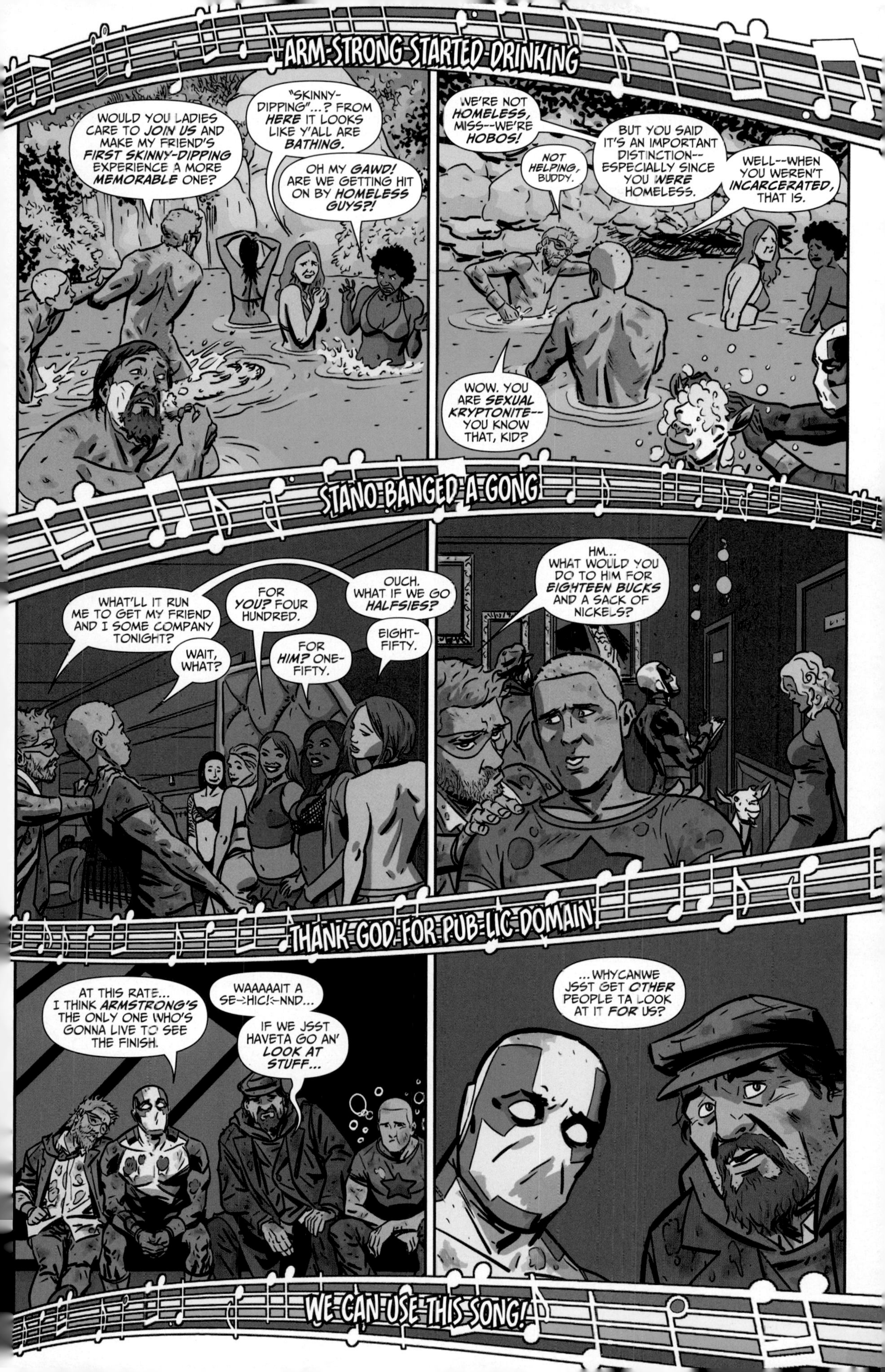
ARM-STRONG STARTED DRINKING
WOULD YOU LADIES CARE TO JOIN US AND MAKE MY FRIEND'S FIRST SKINNY-DIPPING EXPERIENCE A MORE MEMORABLE ONE?
"SKINNY-DIPPING"...? FROM HERE IT LOOKS LIKE Y'ALL ARE BATHING.
OH MY GAWD! ARE WE GETTING HIT ON BY HOMELESS GUYS?!
WE'RE NOT HOMELESS, MISS--WE'RE HOBOS!
NOT HELPING, BUDDY.
BUT YOU SAID IT'S AN IMPORTANT DISTINCTION--ESPECIALLY SINCE YOU WERE HOMELESS.
WELL--WHEN YOU WEREN'T INCARCERATED, THAT IS.
WOW. YOU ARE SEXUAL KRYPTONITE--YOU KNOW THAT, KID?
STANO BANGED A GONG
WHAT'LL IT RUN ME TO GET MY FRIEND AND I SOME COMPANY TONIGHT?
WAIT, WHAT?
FOR YOU? FOUR HUNDRED.
FOR HIM? ONE-FIFTY.
OUCH. WHAT IF WE GO HALFSIES?
EIGHT-FIFTY.
HM... WHAT WOULD YOU DO TO HIM FOR EIGHTEEN BUCKS AND A SACK OF NICKELS?
THANK GOD FOR PUB-LIC DOMAIN
AT THIS RATE... I THINK ARMSTRONG'S THE ONLY ONE WHO'S GONNA LIVE TO SEE THE FINISH.
WAAAAAIT A SE-HIC!-NND...
IF WE JSST HAVETA GO AN' LOOK AT STUFF...
...WHYCANWE JSST GET OTHER PEOPLE TA LOOK AT IT FOR US?
WE CAN USE THIS SONG!

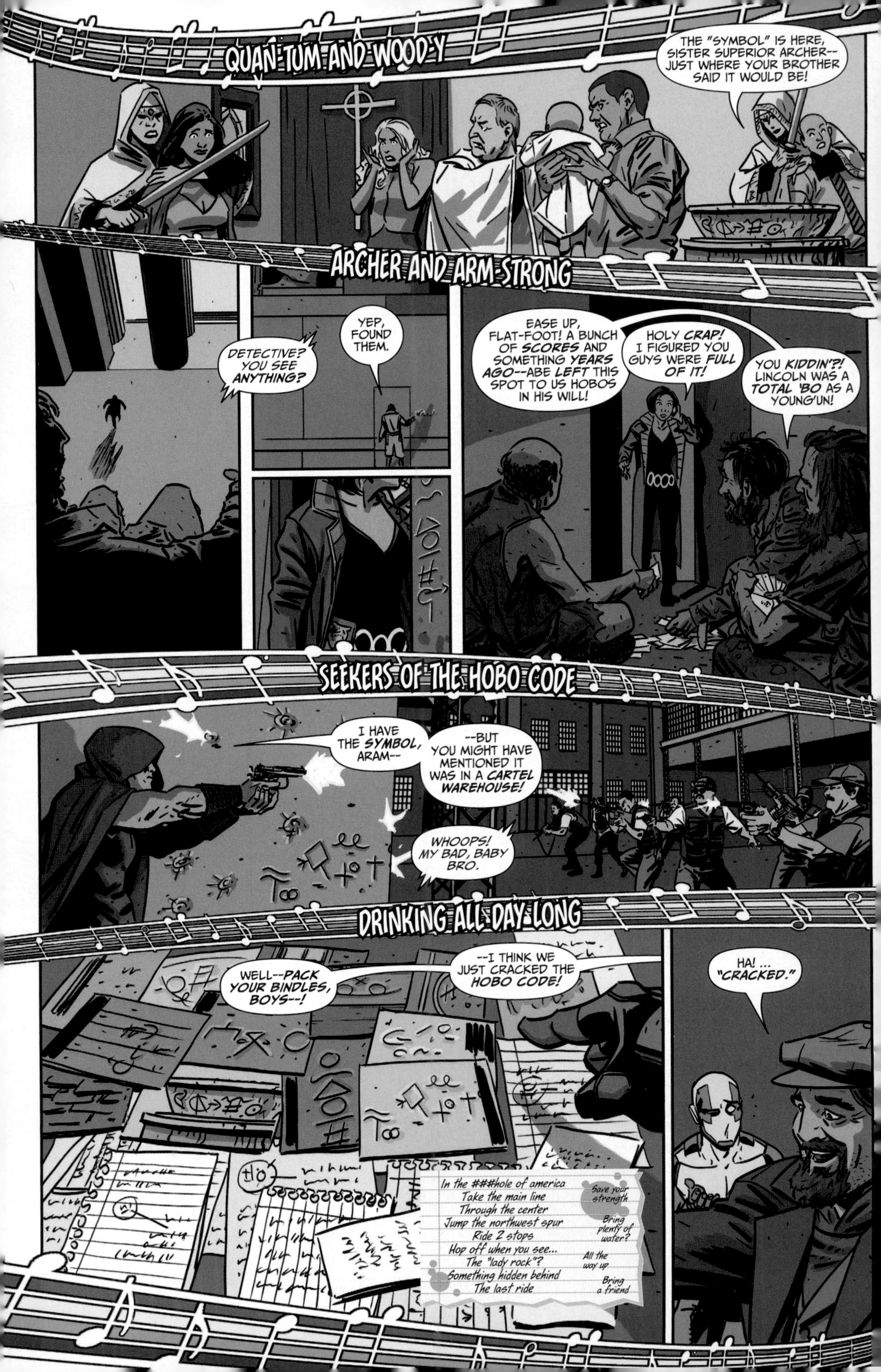
QUAN-TUM AND WOOD-Y
THE "SYMBOL" IS HERE, SISTER SUPERIOR ARCHER-- JUST WHERE YOUR BROTHER SAID IT WOULD BE!
ARCHER AND ARM-STRONG
DETECTIVE? YOU SEE ANYTHING?
YEP, FOUND THEM.
EASE UP, FLAT-FOOT! A BUNCH OF SCORES AND SOMETHING YEARS AGO--ABE LEFT THIS SPOT TO US HOBOS IN HIS WILL!
HOLY CRAP! I FIGURED YOU GUYS WERE FULL OF IT!
YOU KIDDIN'?! LINCOLN WAS A TOTAL 'BO AS A YOUNG'UN!
SEEKERS OF THE HOBO CODE
I HAVE THE SYMBOL, ARAM--
--BUT YOU MIGHT HAVE MENTIONED IT WAS IN A CARTEL WAREHOUSE!
WHOOPS! MY BAD, BABY BRO.
DRINKING ALL DAY LONG
WELL--PACK YOUR BINDLES, BOYS--!
--I THINK WE JUST CRACKED THE HOBO CODE!
HA! ... "CRACKED."
In the ###hole of america
Take the main line
Through the center
Jump the northwest spur
Ride 2 stops
Hop off when you see...
The "lady rock"?
Something hidden behind
The last ride
Save your strength
Bring plenty of water?
All the way up
Bring a friend

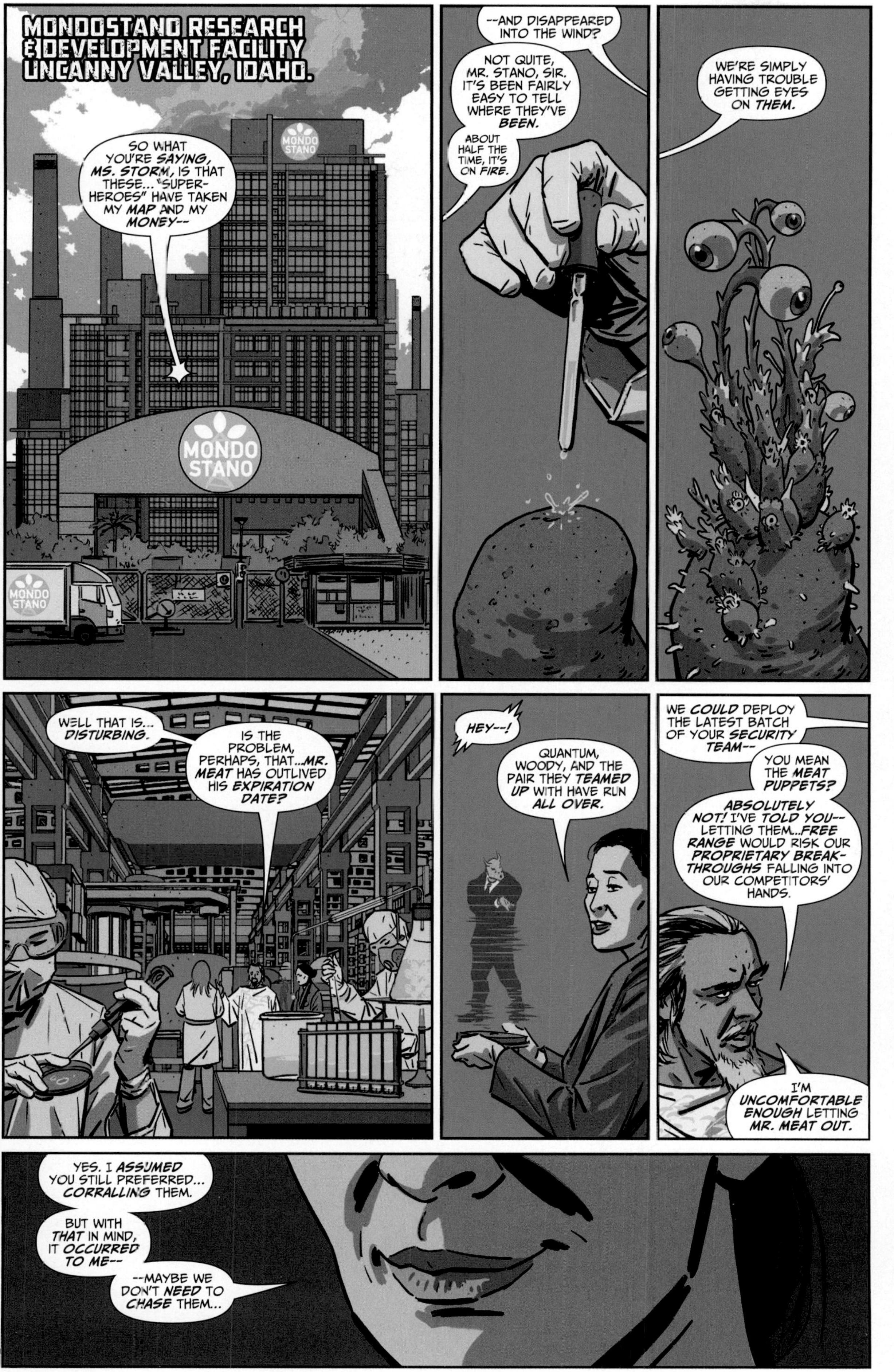
MONDOSTANO RESEARCH & DEVELOPMENT FACILITY UNCANNY VALLEY, IDAHO.
MONDO STANO
SO WHAT YOU'RE SAYING, MS. STORM, IS THAT THESE... "SUPER-HEROES" HAVE TAKEN MY MAP AND MY MONEY--
MONDO STANO
MONDO STANO
--AND DISAPPEARED INTO THE WIND?
NOT QUITE, MR. STANO, SIR. IT'S BEEN FAIRLY EASY TO TELL WHERE THEY'VE BEEN.
ABOUT HALF THE TIME, IT'S ON FIRE.
WE'RE SIMPLY HAVING TROUBLE GETTING EYES ON THEM.
WELL THAT IS... DISTURBING.
IS THE PROBLEM, PERHAPS, THAT... MR. MEAT HAS OUTLIVED HIS EXPIRATION DATE?
HEY--!
QUANTUM, WOODY, AND THE PAIR THEY TEAMED UP WITH HAVE RUN ALL OVER.
WE COULD DEPLOY THE LATEST BATCH OF YOUR SECURITY TEAM--
YOU MEAN THE MEAT PUPPETS?
ABSOLUTELY NOT! I'VE TOLD YOU-- LETTING THEM... FREE RANGE WOULD RISK OUR PROPRIETARY BREAK-THROUGHS FALLING INTO OUR COMPETITORS' HANDS.
I'M UNCOMFORTABLE ENOUGH LETTING MR. MEAT OUT.
YES. I ASSUMED YOU STILL PREFERRED... CORRALLING THEM.
BUT WITH THAT IN MIND, IT OCCURRED TO ME--
--MAYBE WE DON'T NEED TO CHASE THEM...

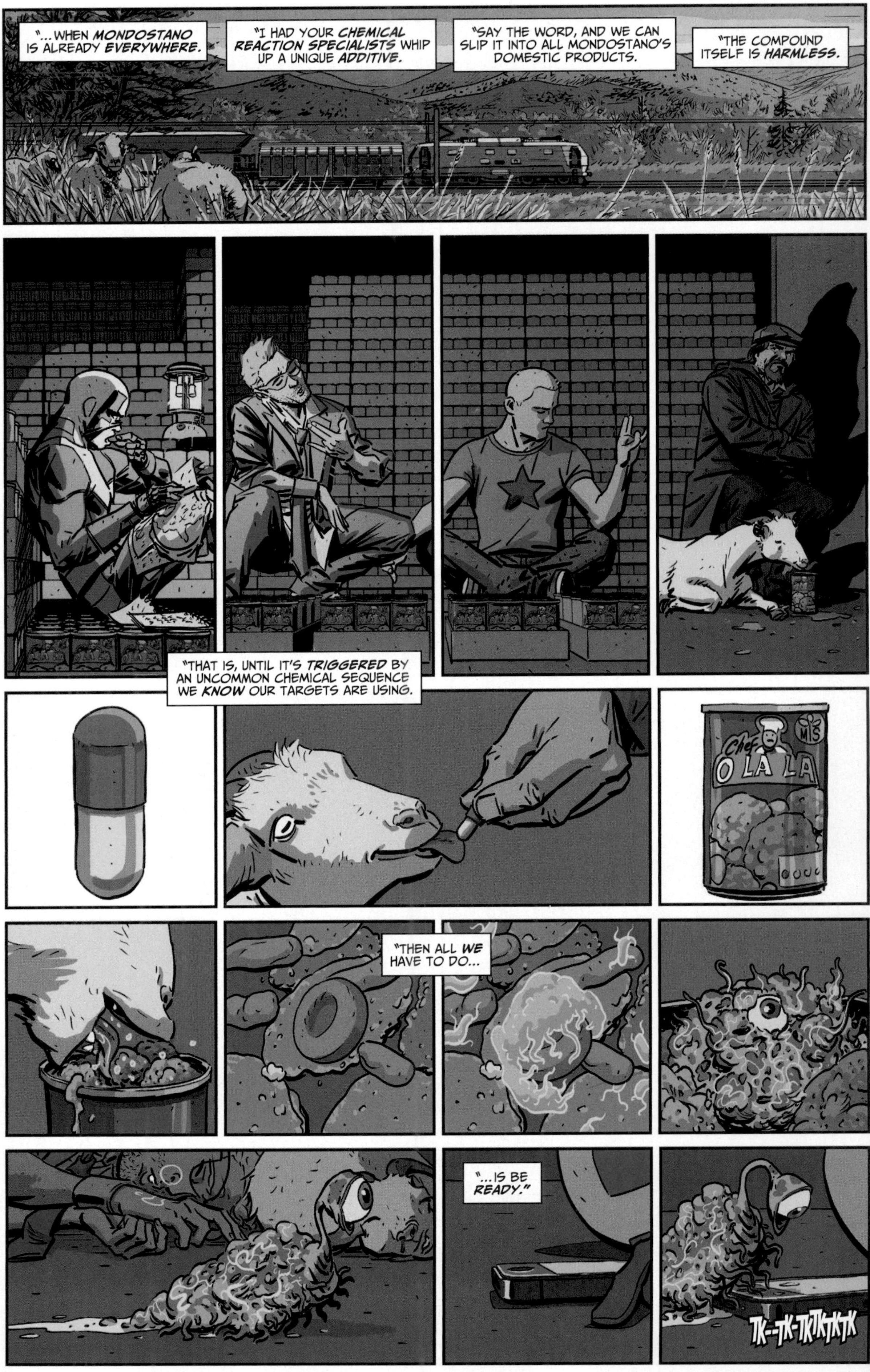
"...WHEN MONDOSTANO IS ALREADY EVERYWHERE.
"I HAD YOUR CHEMICAL REACTION SPECIALISTS WHIP UP A UNIQUE ADDITIVE.
"SAY THE WORD, AND WE CAN SLIP IT INTO ALL MONDOSTANO'S DOMESTIC PRODUCTS.
"THE COMPOUND ITSELF IS HARMLESS.
"THAT IS, UNTIL IT'S TRIGGERED BY AN UNCOMMON CHEMICAL SEQUENCE WE KNOW OUR TARGETS ARE USING.
Chef
M S
O LA LA
"THEN ALL WE HAVE TO DO...
"...IS BE READY."
TK--TK-TKTKTKTK

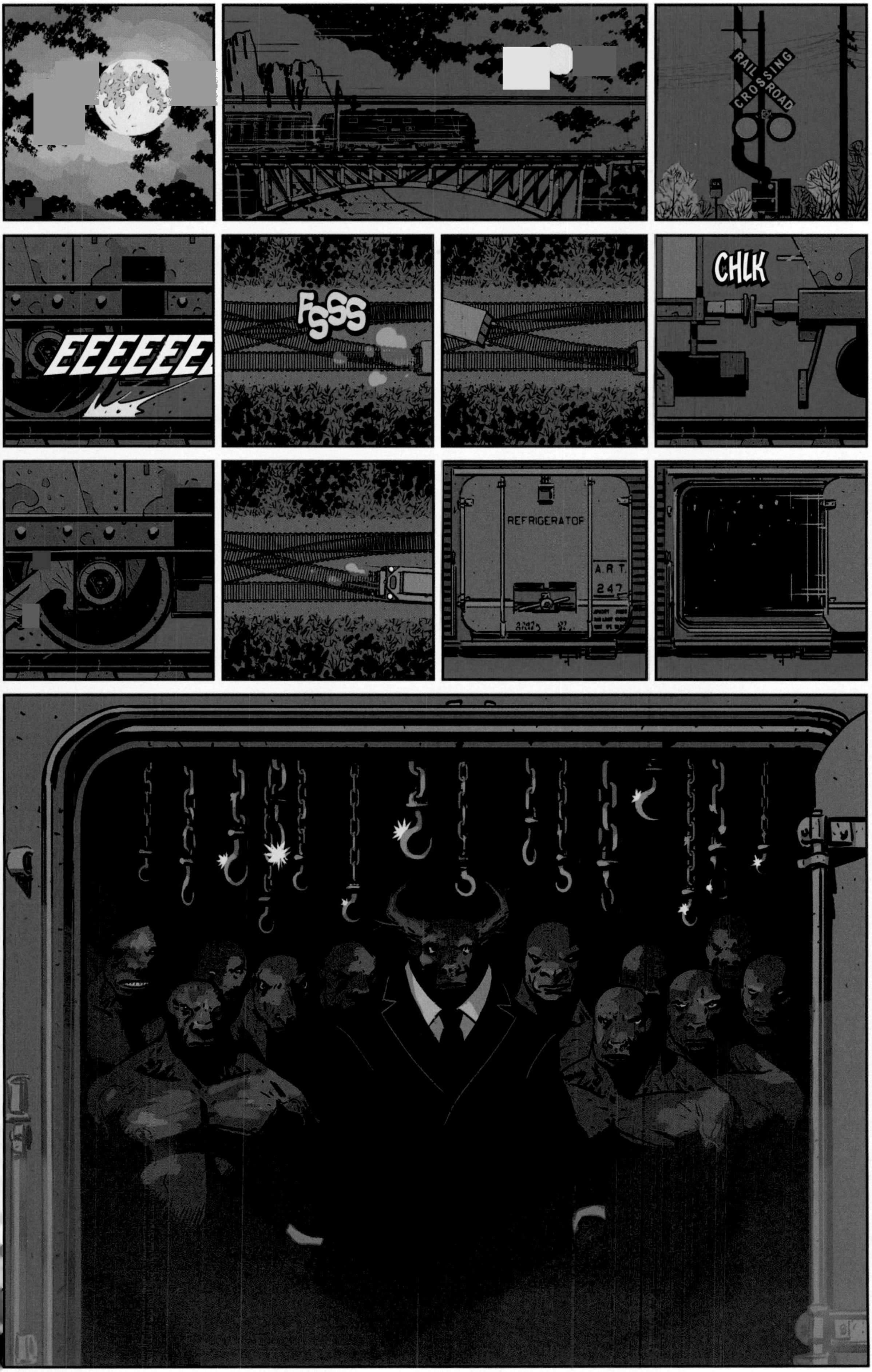

RAIL ROAD
CROSSING
EEEEEEE
FSSS
CHLK
REFRIGERATOR
A.R.T.
247

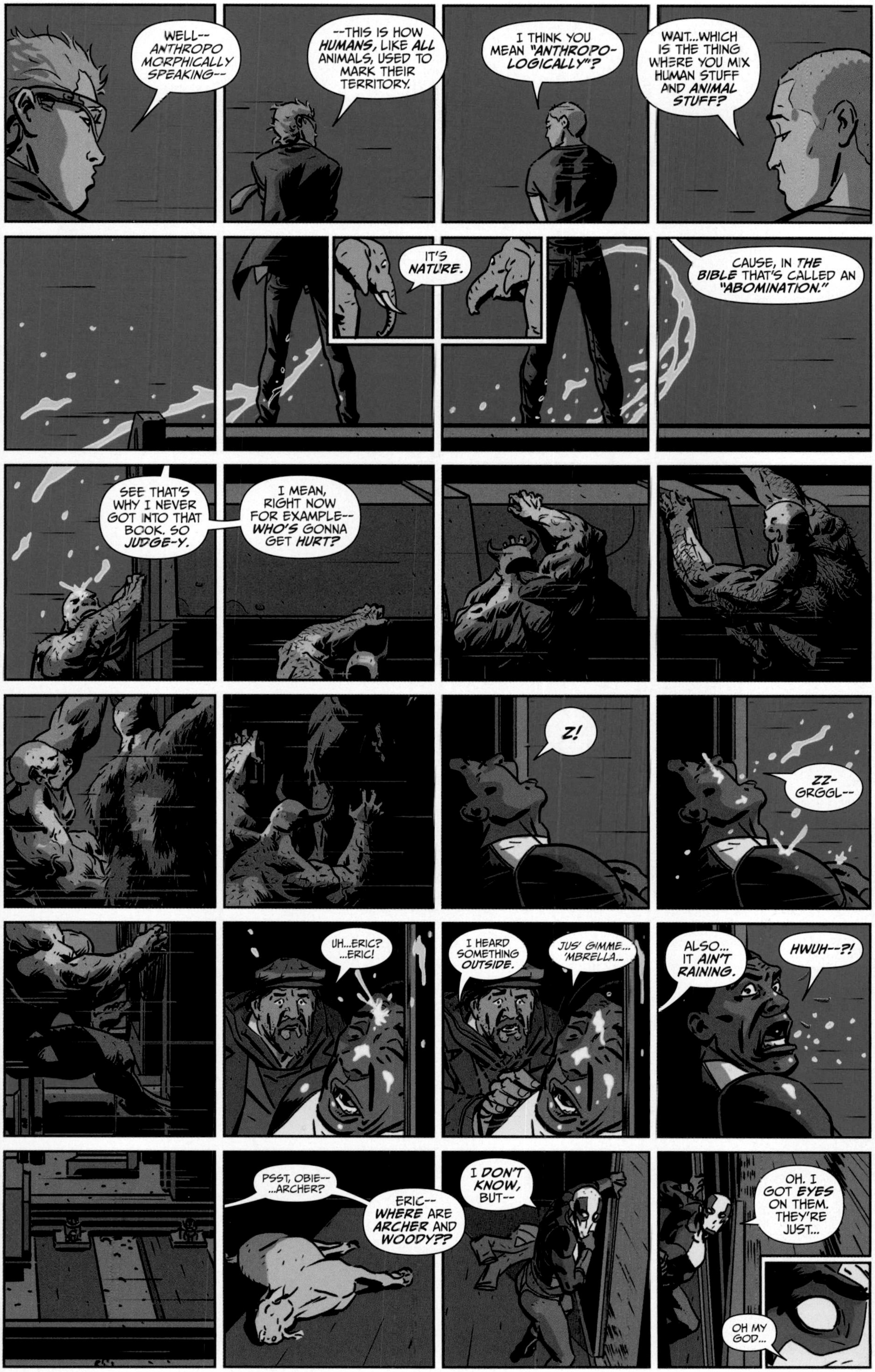
WELL-- ANTHROPO MORPHICALLY SPEAKING--
--THIS IS HOW HUMANS, LIKE ALL ANIMALS, USED TO MARK THEIR TERRITORY.
I THINK YOU MEAN "ANTHROPO-LOGICALLY"?
WAIT...WHICH IS THE THING WHERE YOU MIX HUMAN STUFF AND ANIMAL STUFF?
IT'S NATURE.
CAUSE, IN THE BIBLE THAT'S CALLED AN "ABOMINATION."
SEE THAT'S WHY I NEVER GOT INTO THAT BOOK. SO JUDGE-Y.
I MEAN, RIGHT NOW FOR EXAMPLE-- WHO'S GONNA GET HURT?
Z!
ZZ-GRGGL--
UH...ERIC? ...ERIC!
I HEARD SOMETHING OUTSIDE.
JUS' GIMME... 'MBRELLA..
ALSO... IT AIN'T RAINING.
HWUH--?!
PSST, OBIE-- ...ARCHER?
ERIC-- WHERE ARE ARCHER AND WOODY??
I DON'T KNOW, BUT--
OH. I GOT EYES ON THEM. THEY'RE JUST...
OH MY GOD...

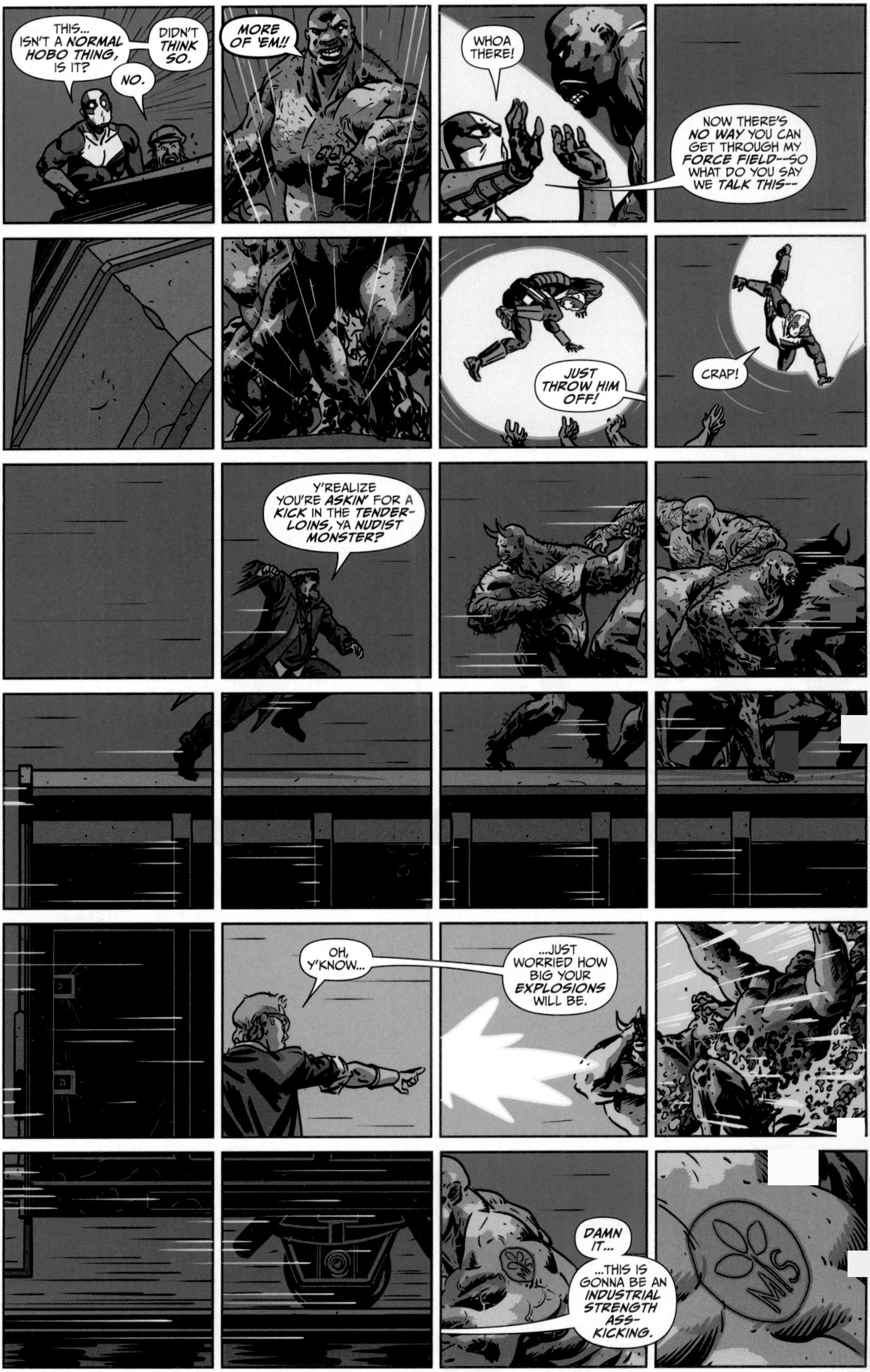
THIS... ISN'T A NORMAL HOBO THING, IS IT?
DIDN'T THINK SO.
NO.
MORE OF 'EM!!
WHOA THERE!
NOW THERE'S NO WAY YOU CAN GET THROUGH MY FORCE FIELD--SO WHAT DO YOU SAY WE TALK THIS--
JUST THROW HIM OFF!
CRAP!
Y'REALIZE YOU'RE ASKIN' FOR A KICK IN THE TENDER-LOINS, YA NUDIST MONSTER?
OH, Y'KNOW...
...JUST WORRIED HOW BIG YOUR EXPLOSIONS WILL BE.
DAMN IT...
...THIS IS GONNA BE AN INDUSTRIAL STRENGTH ASS-KICKING.
MS

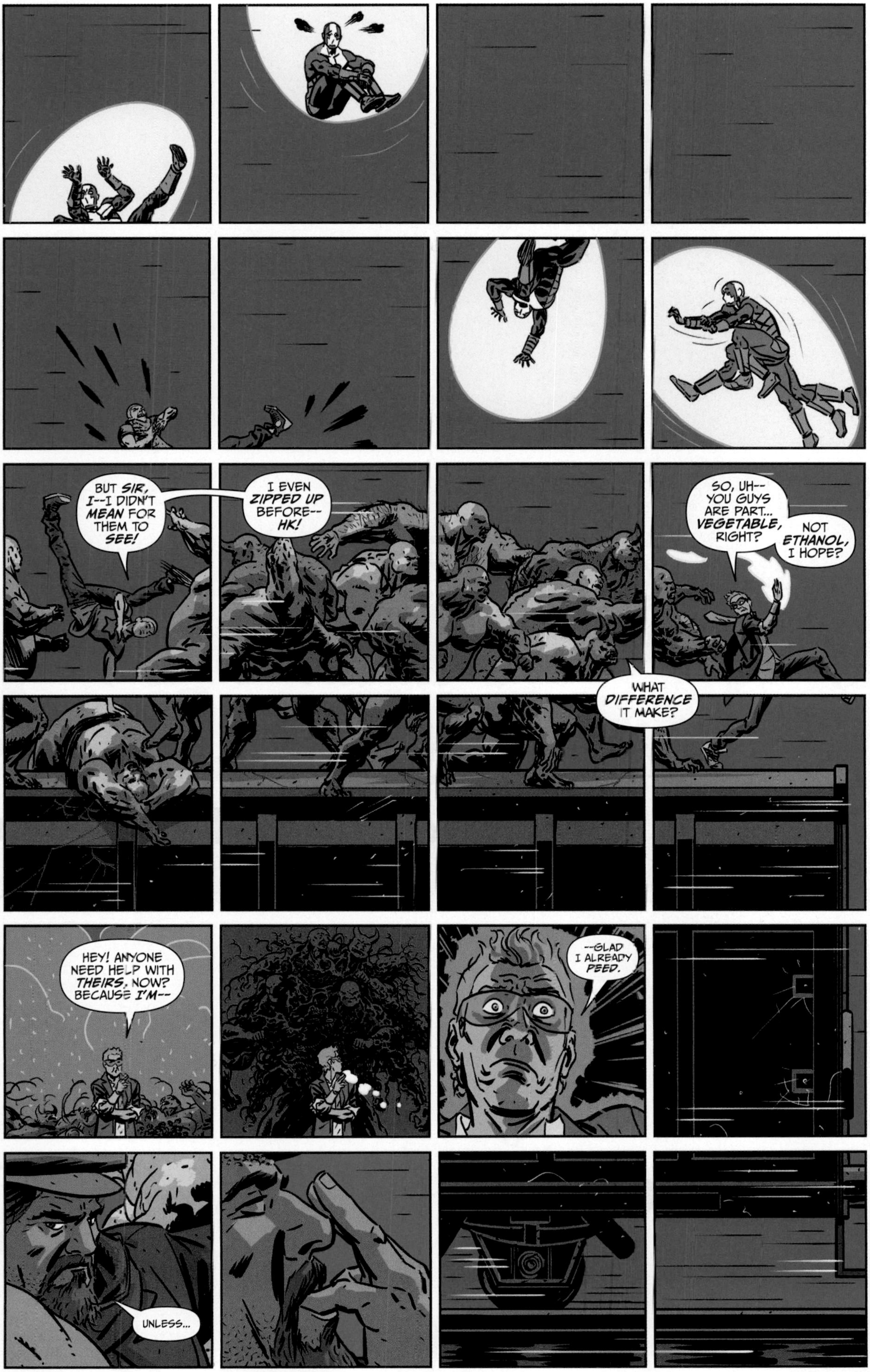
BUT SIR, I--I DIDN'T MEAN FOR THEM TO SEE!
I EVEN ZIPPED UP BEFORE-- HK!
SO, UH-- YOU GUYS ARE PART... VEGETABLE, RIGHT?
NOT ETHANOL, I HOPE?
WHAT DIFFERENCE IT MAKE?
HEY! ANYONE NEED HELP WITH THEIRS, NOW? BECAUSE I'M--
--GLAD I ALREADY PEED.
UNLESS...

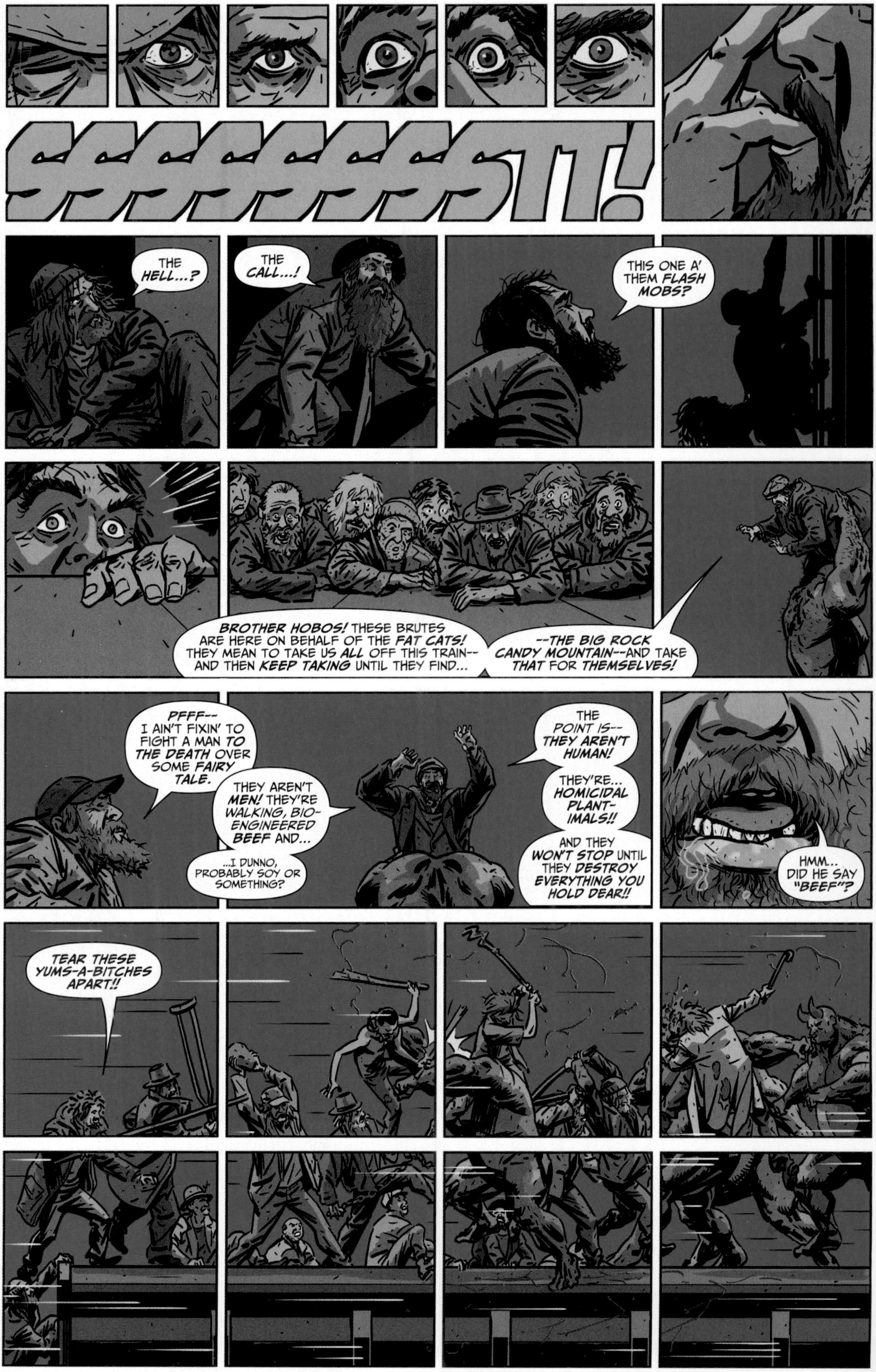

SSSSSSSSTT!
THE HELL...?
THE CALL...!
THIS ONE A' THEM FLASH MOBS?
BROTHER HOBOS! THESE BRUTES ARE HERE ON BEHALF OF THE FAT CATS! THEY MEAN TO TAKE US ALL OFF THIS TRAIN-- AND THEN KEEP TAKING UNTIL THEY FIND...
--THE BIG ROCK CANDY MOUNTAIN--AND TAKE THAT FOR THEMSELVES!
PFFF-- I AIN'T FIXIN' TO FIGHT A MAN TO THE DEATH OVER SOME FAIRY TALE.
THEY AREN'T MEN! THEY'RE WALKING, BIO-ENGINEERED BEEF AND...
...I DUNNO, PROBABLY SOY OR SOMETHING?
THE POINT IS-- THEY AREN'T HUMAN!
THEY'RE... HOMICIDAL PLANT-IMALS!!
AND THEY WON'T STOP UNTIL THEY DESTROY EVERYTHING YOU HOLD DEAR!!
HMM... DID HE SAY "BEEF"?
TEAR THESE YUMS-A-BITCHES APART!!

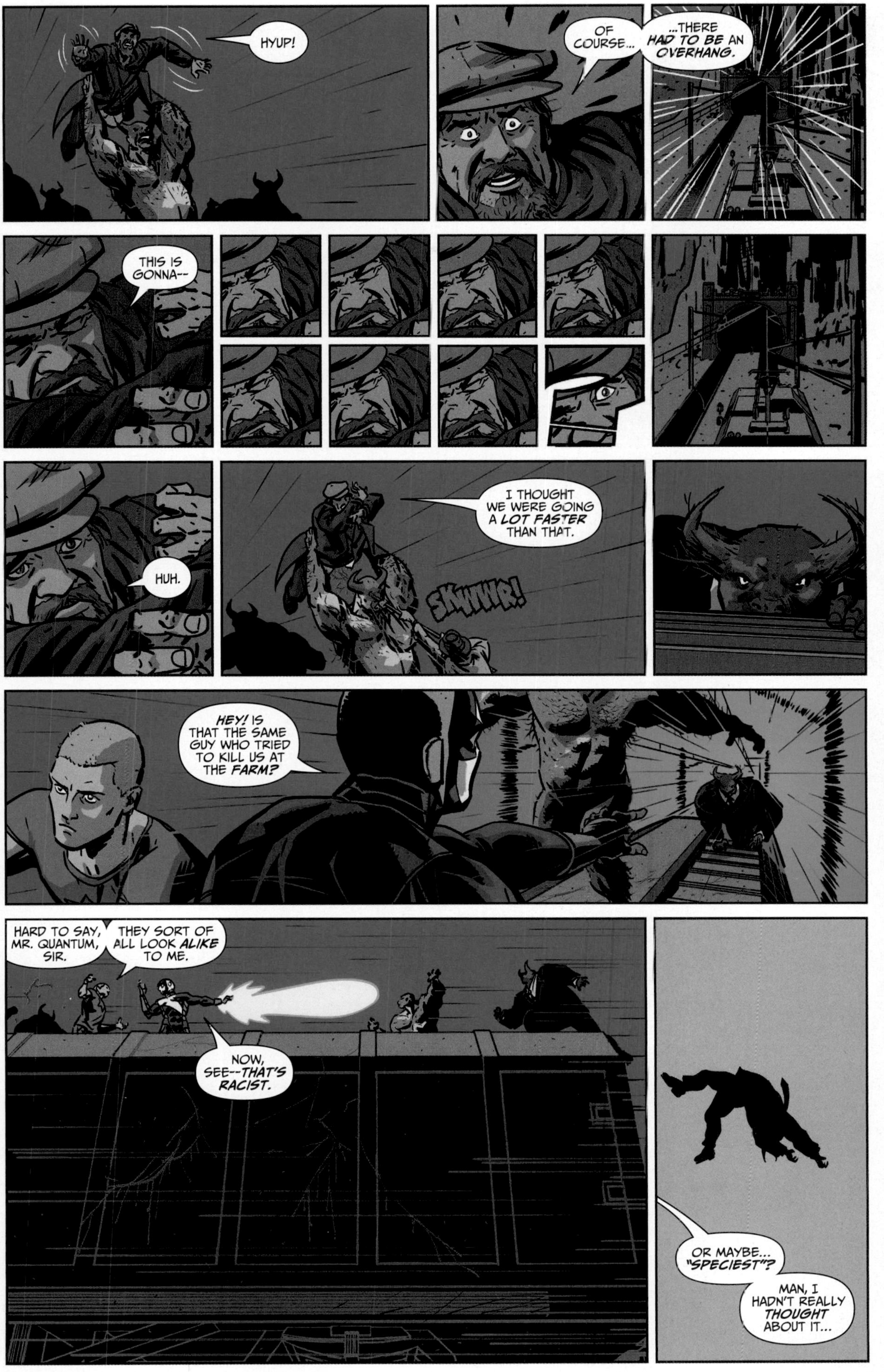
HYUP!
OF COURSE...
...THERE HAD TO BE AN OVERHANG.
THIS IS GONNA--
HUH.
I THOUGHT WE WERE GOING A LOT FASTER THAN THAT.
SKWWR!
HEY! IS THAT THE SAME GUY WHO TRIED TO KILL US AT THE FARM?
HARD TO SAY, MR. QUANTUM, SIR.
THEY SORT OF ALL LOOK ALIKE TO ME.
NOW, SEE--THAT'S RACIST.
OR MAYBE... "SPECIEST"?
MAN, I HADN'T REALLY THOUGHT ABOUT IT...

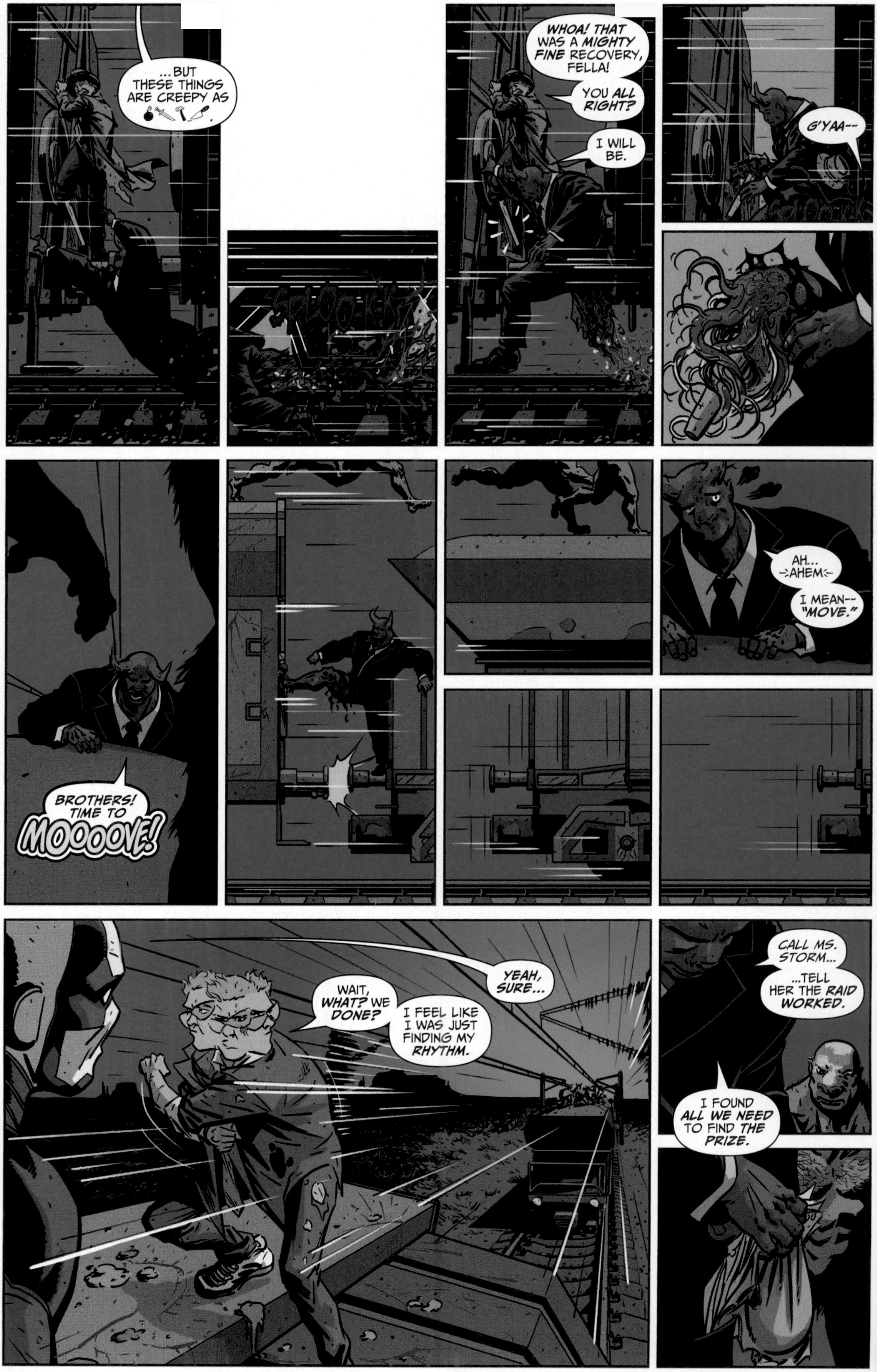
...BUT THESE THINGS ARE CREEPY AS
WHOA! THAT WAS A MIGHTY FINE RECOVERY, FELLA!
YOU ALL RIGHT?
I WILL BE.
G'YAA--
BROTHERS! TIME TO MOOOOVE!
AH... AHEM
I MEAN-- "MOVE."
WAIT, WHAT? WE DONE?
I FEEL LIKE I WAS JUST FINDING MY RHYTHM.
YEAH, SURE...
CALL MS. STORM...
...TELL HER THE RAID WORKED.
I FOUND ALL WE NEED TO FIND THE PRIZE.

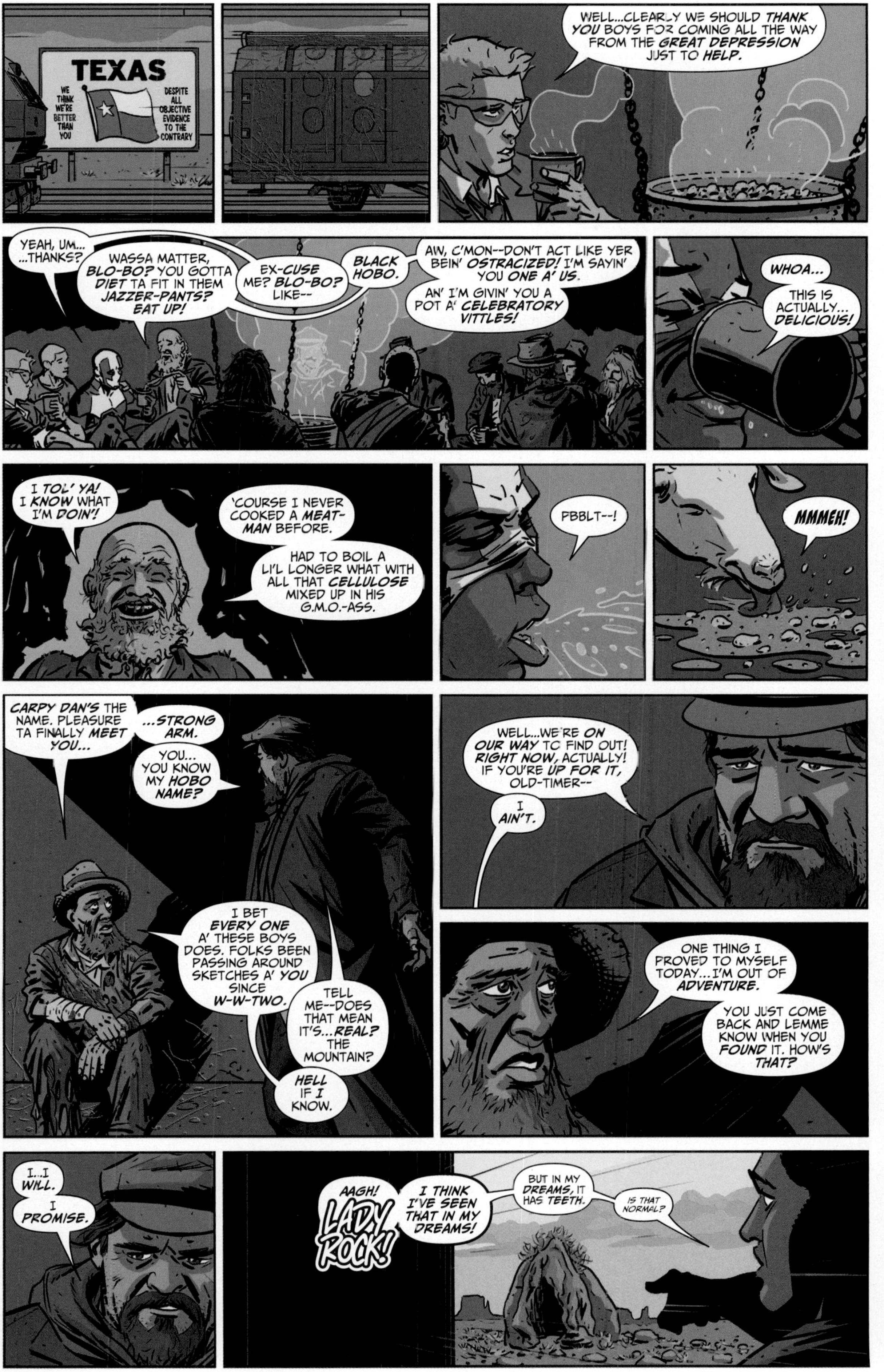
TEXAS
WE THINK WE'RE BETTER THAN YOU
DESPITE ALL OBJECTIVE EVIDENCE TO THE CONTRARY
WELL...CLEARLY WE SHOULD THANK YOU BOYS FOR COMING ALL THE WAY FROM THE GREAT DEPRESSION JUST TO HELP.
YEAH, UM... ...THANKS?
WASSA MATTER, BLO-BO? YOU GOTTA DIET TA FIT IN THEM JAZZER-PANTS? EAT UP!
EX-CUSE ME? BLO-BO? LIKE--
BLACK HOBO.
AW, C'MON--DON'T ACT LIKE YER BEIN' OSTRACIZED! I'M SAYIN' YOU ONE A' US.
AN' I'M GIVIN' YOU A POT A' CELEBRATORY VITTLES!
WHOA...
THIS IS ACTUALLY... DELICIOUS!
I TOL' YA! I KNOW WHAT I'M DOIN'!
'COURSE I NEVER COOKED A MEAT-MAN BEFORE.
HAD TO BOIL A LI'L LONGER WHAT WITH ALL THAT CELLULOSE MIXED UP IN HIS G.M.O.-ASS.
PBBLT--!
MMMEH!
CARPY DAN'S THE NAME. PLEASURE TA FINALLY MEET YOU...
...STRONG ARM.
YOU... YOU KNOW MY HOBO NAME?
I BET EVERY ONE A' THESE BOYS DOES. FOLKS BEEN PASSING AROUND SKETCHES A' YOU SINCE W-W-TWO.
TELL ME--DOES THAT MEAN IT'S...REAL? THE MOUNTAIN?
HELL IF I KNOW.
WELL...WE'RE ON OUR WAY TO FIND OUT! RIGHT NOW, ACTUALLY! IF YOU'RE UP FOR IT, OLD-TIMER--
I AIN'T.
ONE THING I PROVED TO MYSELF TODAY...I'M OUT OF ADVENTURE.
YOU JUST COME BACK AND LEMME KNOW WHEN YOU FOUND IT. HOW'S THAT?
I...I WILL. I PROMISE.
AAGH! LADY ROCK!
I THINK I'VE SEEN THAT IN MY DREAMS!
BUT IN MY DREAMS, IT HAS TEETH.
IS THAT NORMAL?

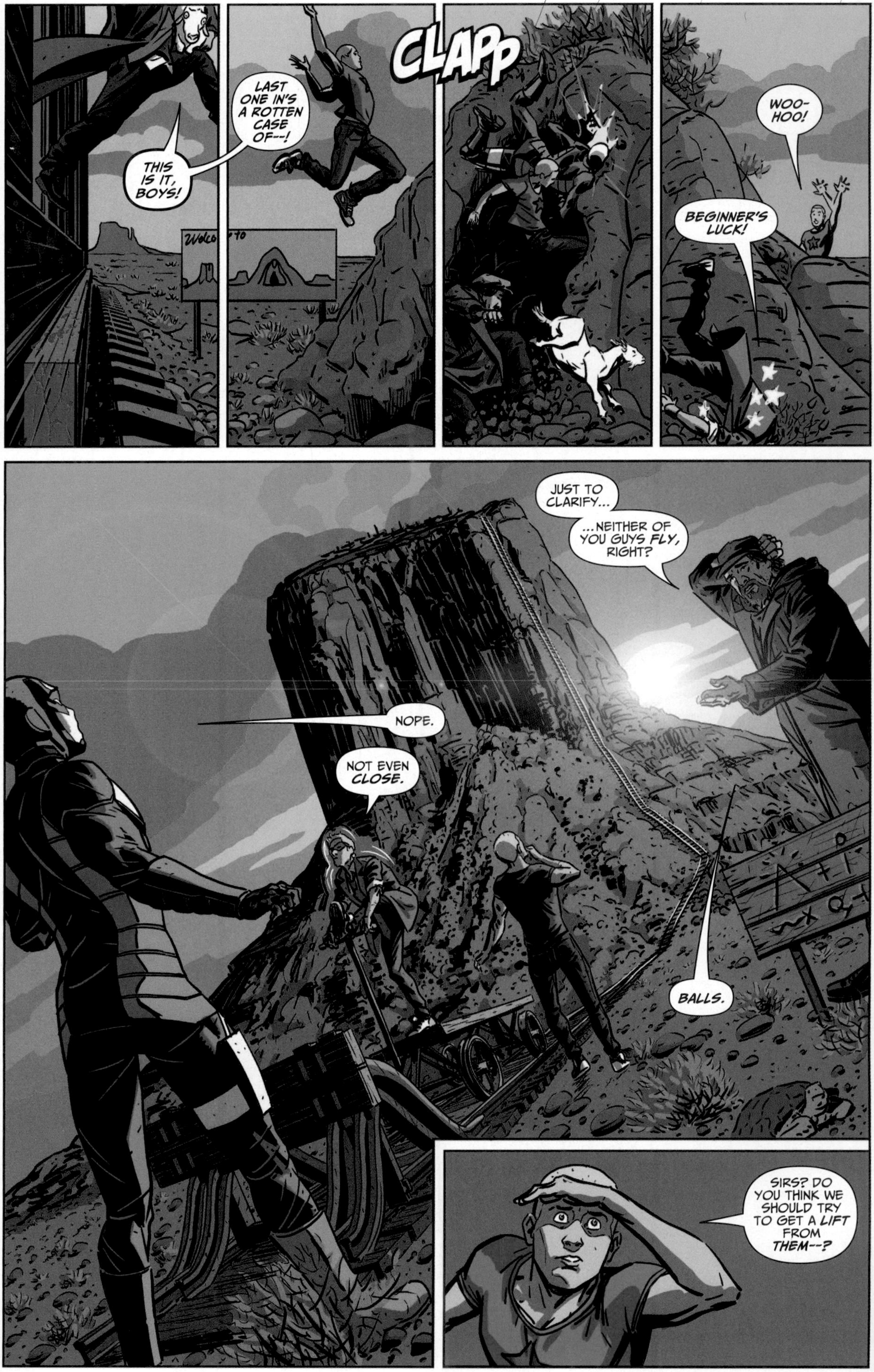
THIS IS IT, BOYS!
LAST ONE IN'S A ROTTEN CASE OF--!
CLAPP
WOO-HOO!
BEGINNER'S LUCK!
JUST TO CLARIFY...
...NEITHER OF YOU GUYS FLY, RIGHT?
NOPE.
NOT EVEN CLOSE.
BALLS.
SIRS? DO YOU THINK WE SHOULD TRY TO GET A LIFT FROM THEM--?

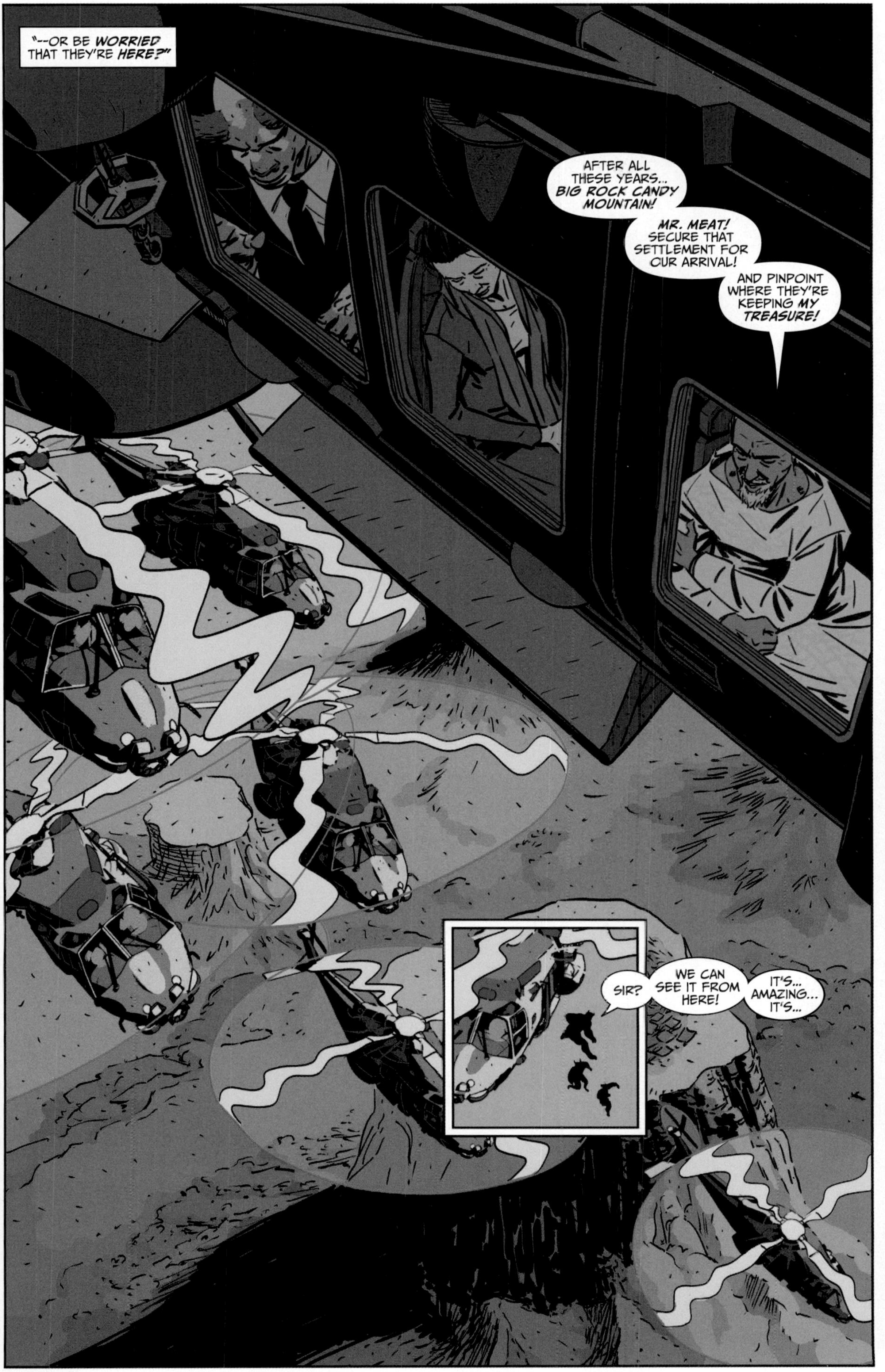
"--OR BE WORRIED THAT THEY'RE HERE?"
AFTER ALL THESE YEARS... BIG ROCK CANDY MOUNTAIN!
MR. MEAT! SECURE THAT SETTLEMENT FOR OUR ARRIVAL!
AND PINPOINT WHERE THEY'RE KEEPING MY TREASURE!
SIR?
WE CAN SEE IT FROM HERE!
IT'S... AMAZING... IT'S...

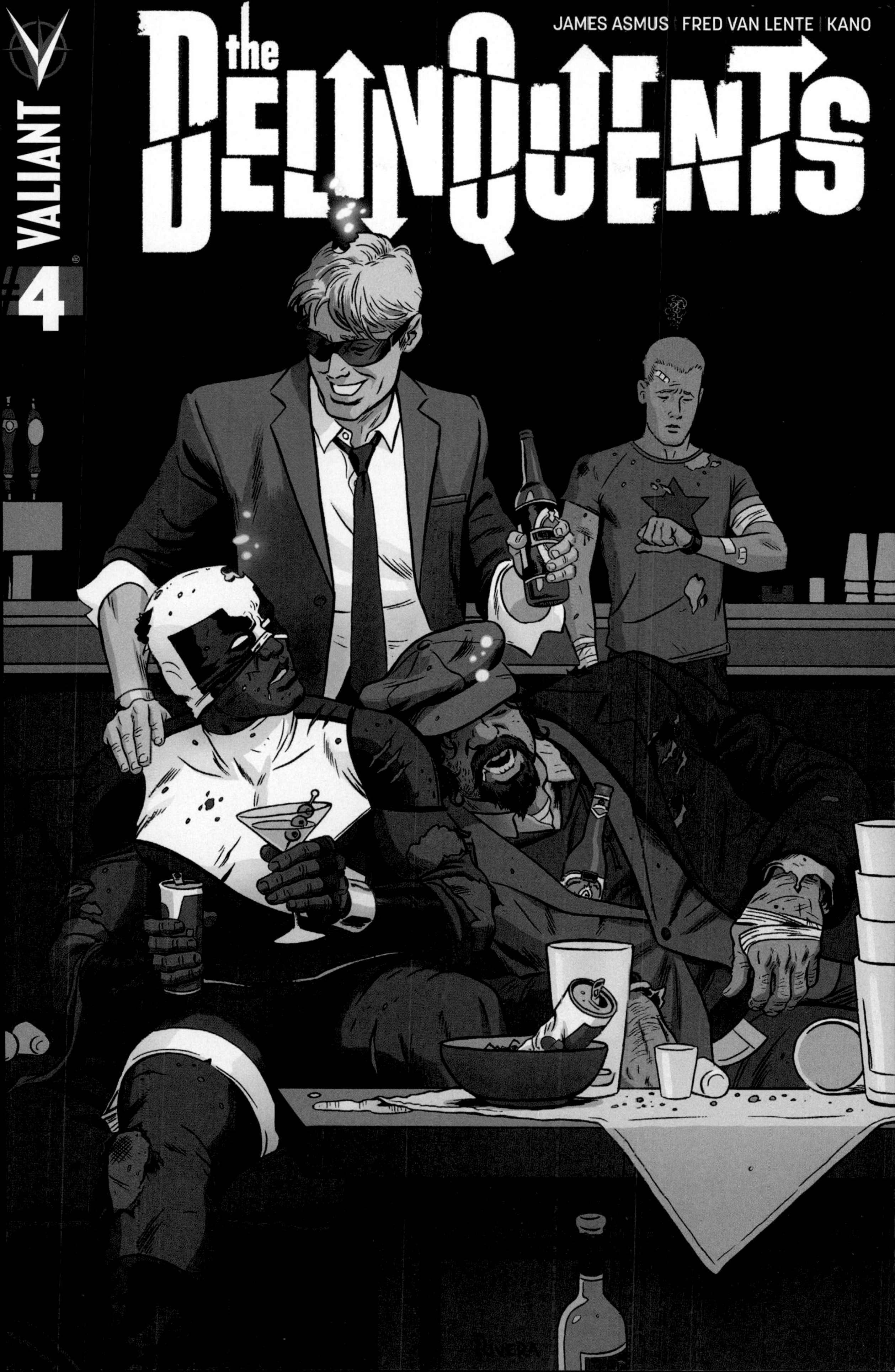
VALIANT
#4
the DELINQUENTS
JAMES ASMUS | FRED VAN LENTE | KANO

the DELINQUENTS

Hgt: 6-2   Wgt: 200
Sex: M   Eyes: Brown

Washington, D.C.
DRIVERS LICENSE

Eric "Quantum" Henderson
Eric and his foster brother, Woody, were transformed by an explosion in their father's lab. Eric became Quantum, and acquired the ability to create force fields. As a hero for gainful employment, he is currently selling his services to the Mondostano Corporation, using a mysterious ass map to find the lost treasure of the hobos. Unfortunately... he only has half the map.

NEW YORK STATE

DRIVERS LICENSE

Aram "Armstrong" Anni-Padda
Hgt: 6-7   Wgt: 325   Sex: M   Eyes: Brown

Effectively immortal, Armstrong is Archer's usually drunk and carousing partner, and a former hobo tasked with guarding the map to the lost treasure of the hobos.

DL   Class D   **Ohio**
DRIVER LICENSE

Obadiah Archer
Sheltered from the world, Obadiah Archer's parents raised him as a weapon to destroy Armstrong–who is now his best friend. Archer and Armstrong now possess the other half of a continent-spanning ass map leading to the lost treasure of the hobos.

Hgt: 5-09   Wgt: 155
Sex: M   Eyes: Blue

DL   Class C   Drivers License   *Maryland*

Hgt: 5-11   Wgt: 180
Sex: M   Eyes: Blue

Woodroe "Woody" Henderson
Trapped in the same lab accident that turned his brother into Quantum, this guy developed the ability to shoot glowy energy blasts from his hands. Former con artist. Banned for life from Belgium.

KANSAS
DRIVER'S LICENSE
USA KS

The Goat
This old girl is the traveling companion of Quantum and Woody, mysteriously imbued with various unnatural superpowers, as well as the mind of their late father. She's also in a delicate condition (pregnant). Approach with extreme caution.

Hgt: 2-06   Wgt: 114
Sex: F   Eyes: Glowing Red?

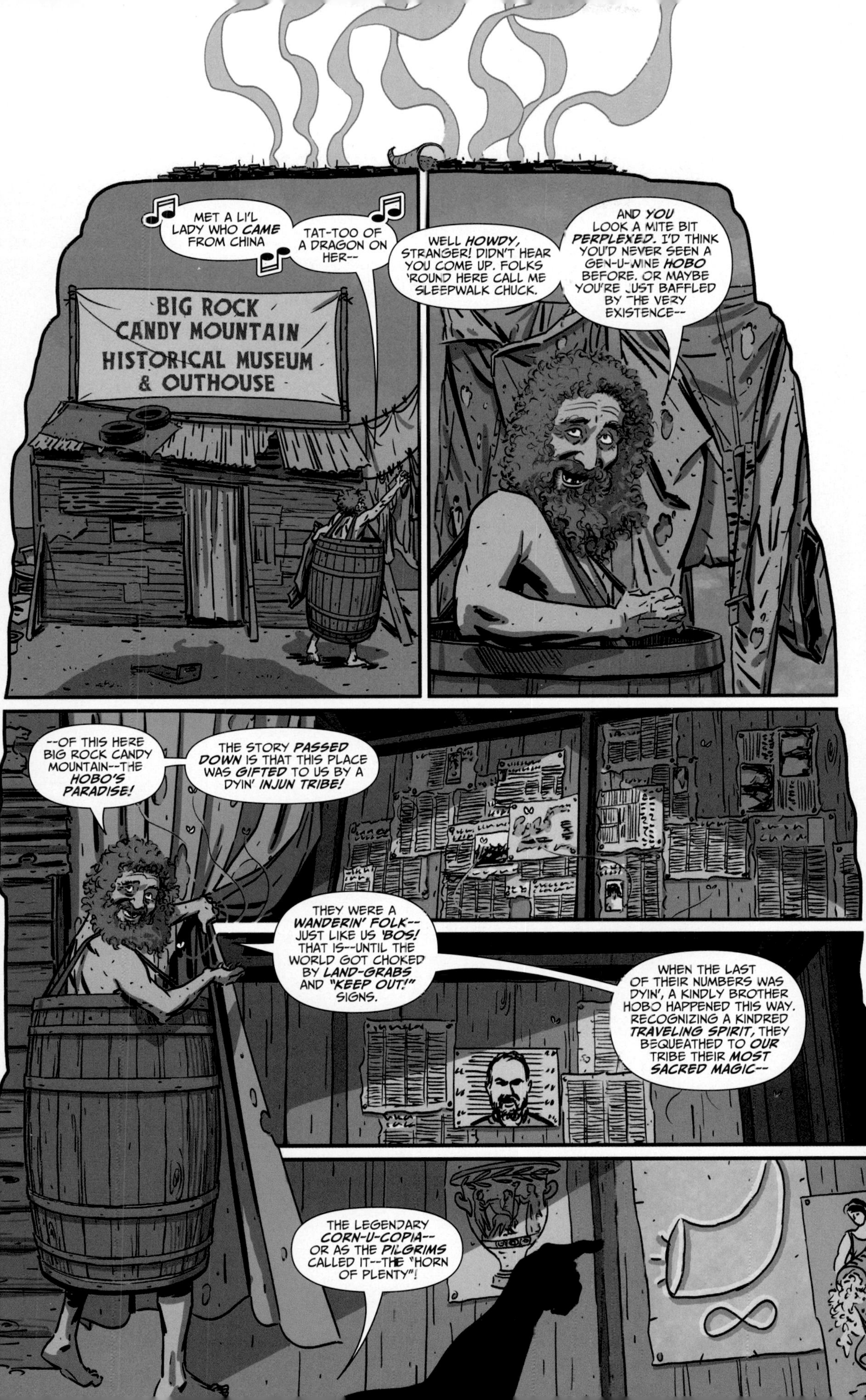
MET A LI'L LADY WHO CAME FROM CHINA
TAT-TOO OF A DRAGON ON HER--
BIG ROCK CANDY MOUNTAIN HISTORICAL MUSEUM & OUTHOUSE
WELL HOWDY, STRANGER! DIDN'T HEAR YOU COME UP. FOLKS 'ROUND HERE CALL ME SLEEPWALK CHUCK.
AND YOU LOOK A MITE BIT PERPLEXED. I'D THINK YOU'D NEVER SEEN A GEN-U-WINE HOBO BEFORE. OR MAYBE YOU'RE JUST BAFFLED BY THE VERY EXISTENCE--
--OF THIS HERE BIG ROCK CANDY MOUNTAIN--THE HOBO'S PARADISE!
THE STORY PASSED DOWN IS THAT THIS PLACE WAS GIFTED TO US BY A DYIN' INJUN TRIBE!
THEY WERE A WANDERIN' FOLK--JUST LIKE US 'BOS! THAT IS--UNTIL THE WORLD GOT CHOKED BY LAND-GRABS AND "KEEP OUT!" SIGNS.
WHEN THE LAST OF THEIR NUMBERS WAS DYIN', A KINDLY BROTHER HOBO HAPPENED THIS WAY. RECOGNIZING A KINDRED TRAVELING SPIRIT, THEY BEQUEATHED TO OUR TRIBE THEIR MOST SACRED MAGIC--
THE LEGENDARY CORN-U-COPIA--OR AS THE PILGRIMS CALLED IT--THE "HORN OF PLENTY"!

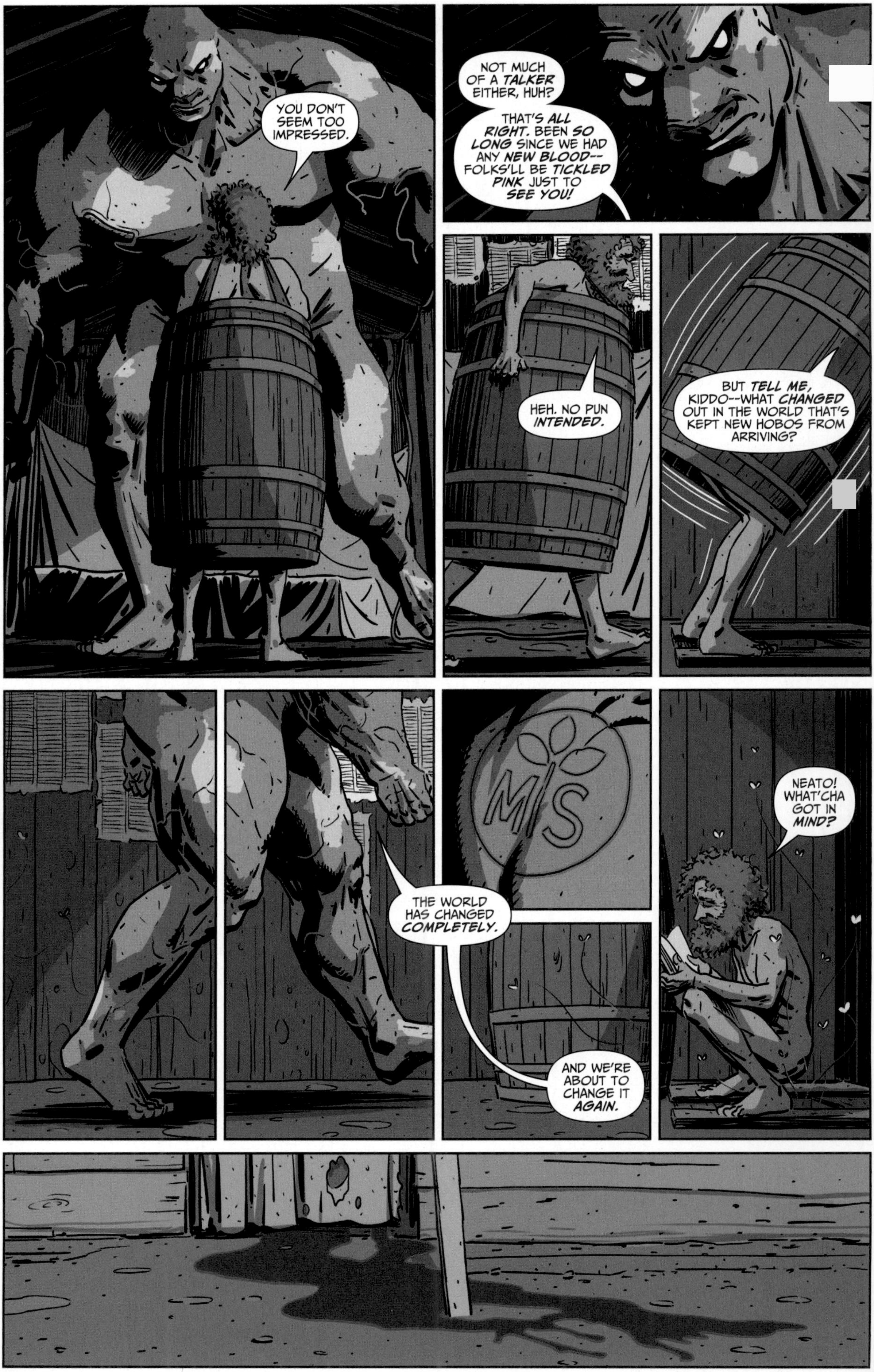

YOU DON'T SEEM TOO IMPRESSED.
NOT MUCH OF A TALKER EITHER, HUH?
THAT'S ALL RIGHT. BEEN SO LONG SINCE WE HAD ANY NEW BLOOD-- FOLKS'LL BE TICKLED PINK JUST TO SEE YOU!
HEH. NO PUN INTENDED.
BUT TELL ME, KIDDO--WHAT CHANGED OUT IN THE WORLD THAT'S KEPT NEW HOBOS FROM ARRIVING?
THE WORLD HAS CHANGED COMPLETELY.
M S
AND WE'RE ABOUT TO CHANGE IT AGAIN.
NEATO! WHAT'CHA GOT IN MIND?

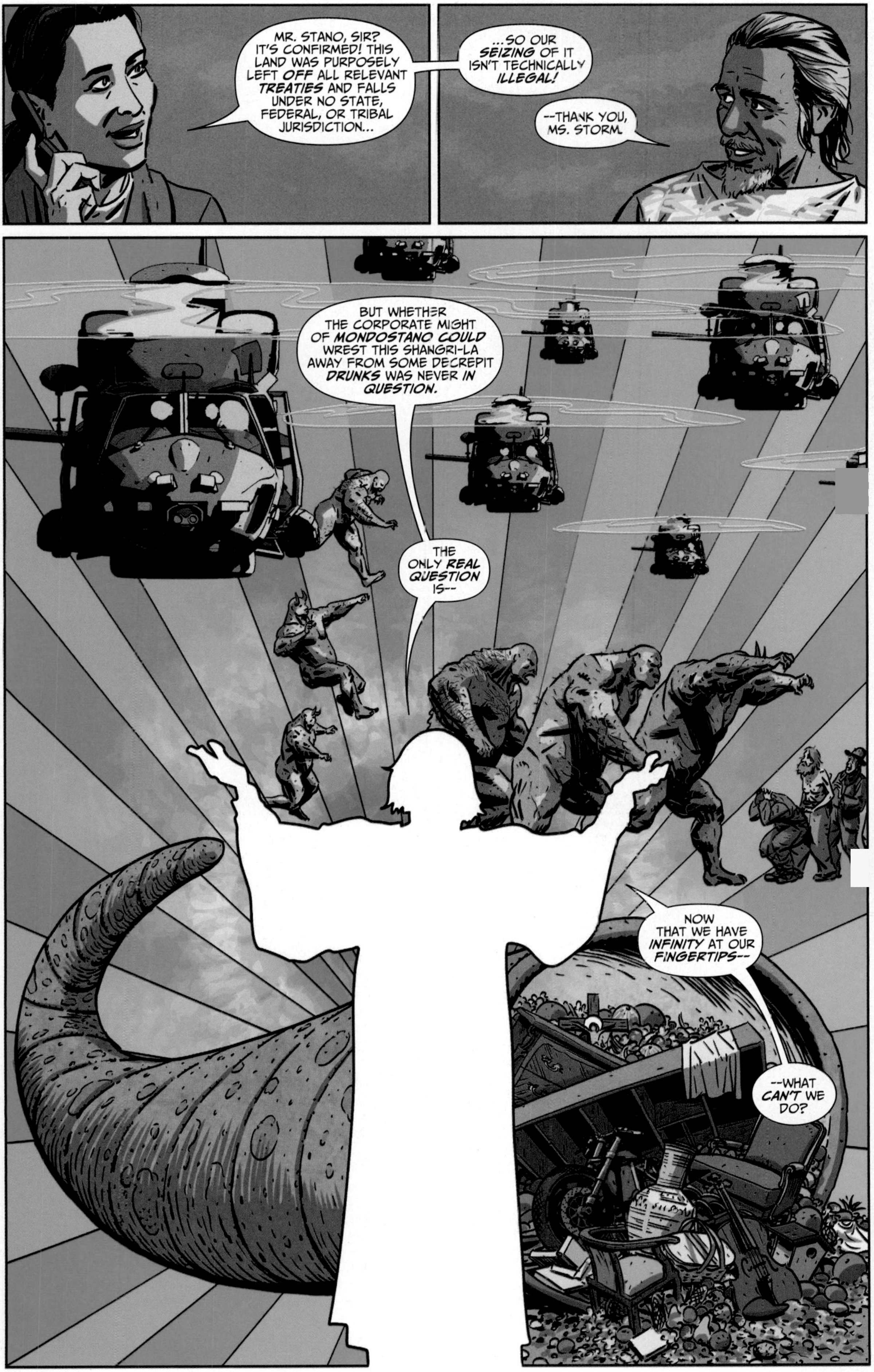
MR. STANO, SIR? IT'S CONFIRMED! THIS LAND WAS PURPOSELY LEFT *OFF* ALL RELEVANT *TREATIES* AND FALLS UNDER NO STATE, FEDERAL, OR TRIBAL JURISDICTION...
...SO OUR *SEIZING* OF IT ISN'T TECHNICALLY *ILLEGAL!*
--THANK YOU, MS. STORM.
BUT WHETHER THE CORPORATE MIGHT OF *MONDOSTANO COULD* WREST THIS SHANGRI-LA AWAY FROM SOME DECREPIT *DRUNKS* WAS NEVER *IN QUESTION.*
THE ONLY *REAL QUESTION* IS--
NOW THAT WE HAVE *INFINITY* AT OUR *FINGERTIPS*--
--WHAT *CAN'T* WE DO?

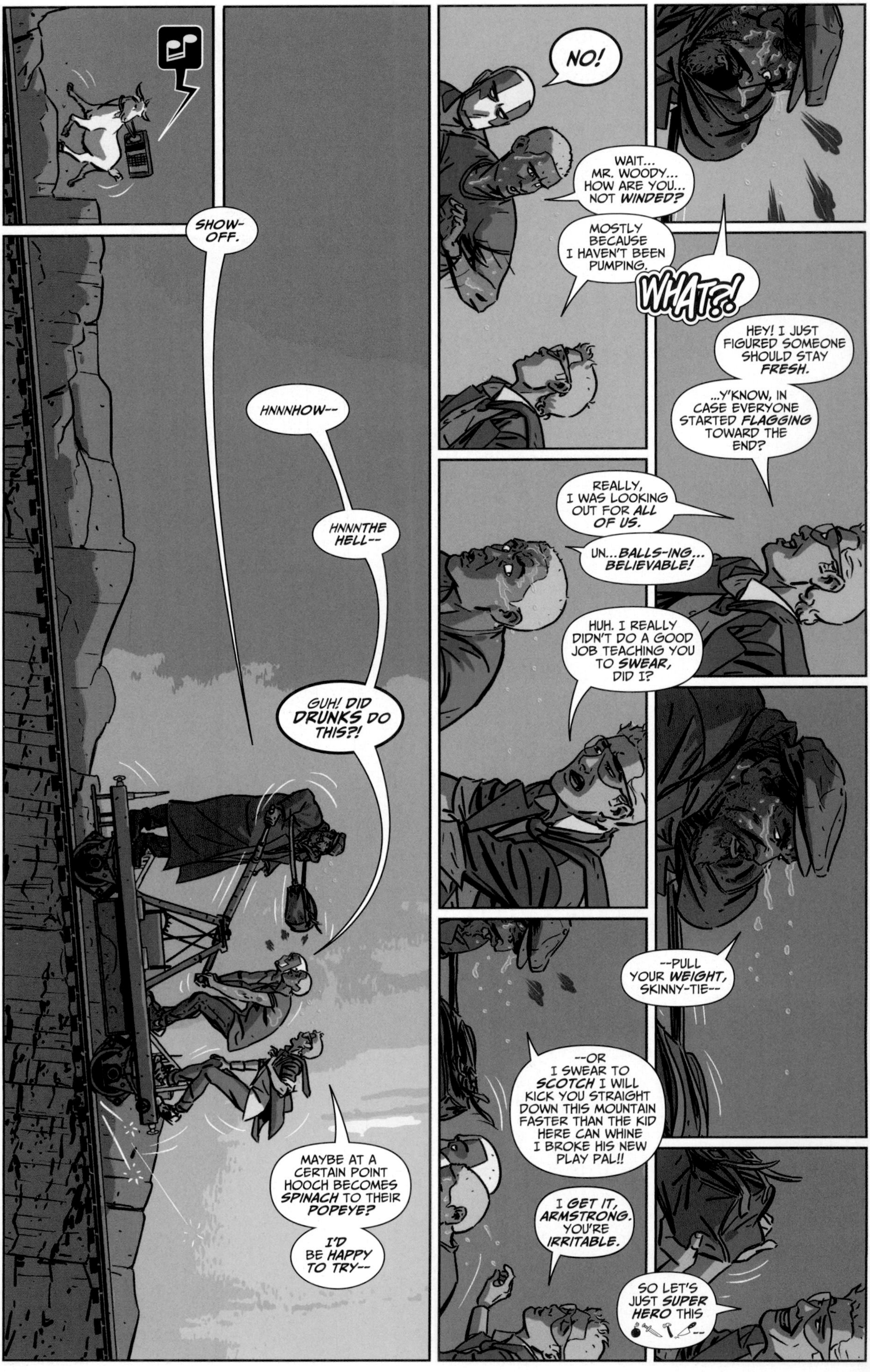
SHOW-OFF.
HNNNHOW--
HNNNTHE HELL--
GUH! DID DRUNKS DO THIS?!
MAYBE AT A CERTAIN POINT HOOCH BECOMES SPINACH TO THEIR POPEYE?
I'D BE HAPPY TO TRY--
NO!
WAIT... MR. WOODY... HOW ARE YOU... NOT WINDED?
MOSTLY BECAUSE I HAVEN'T BEEN PUMPING.
WHAT?!
HEY! I JUST FIGURED SOMEONE SHOULD STAY FRESH.
...Y'KNOW, IN CASE EVERYONE STARTED FLAGGING TOWARD THE END?
REALLY, I WAS LOOKING OUT FOR ALL OF US.
UN...BALLS-ING... BELIEVABLE!
HUH. I REALLY DIDN'T DO A GOOD JOB TEACHING YOU TO SWEAR, DID I?
--PULL YOUR WEIGHT, SKINNY-TIE--
--OR I SWEAR TO SCOTCH I WILL KICK YOU STRAIGHT DOWN THIS MOUNTAIN FASTER THAN THE KID HERE CAN WHINE I BROKE HIS NEW PLAY PAL!!
I GET IT, ARMSTRONG. YOU'RE IRRITABLE.
SO LET'S JUST SUPER HERO THIS --

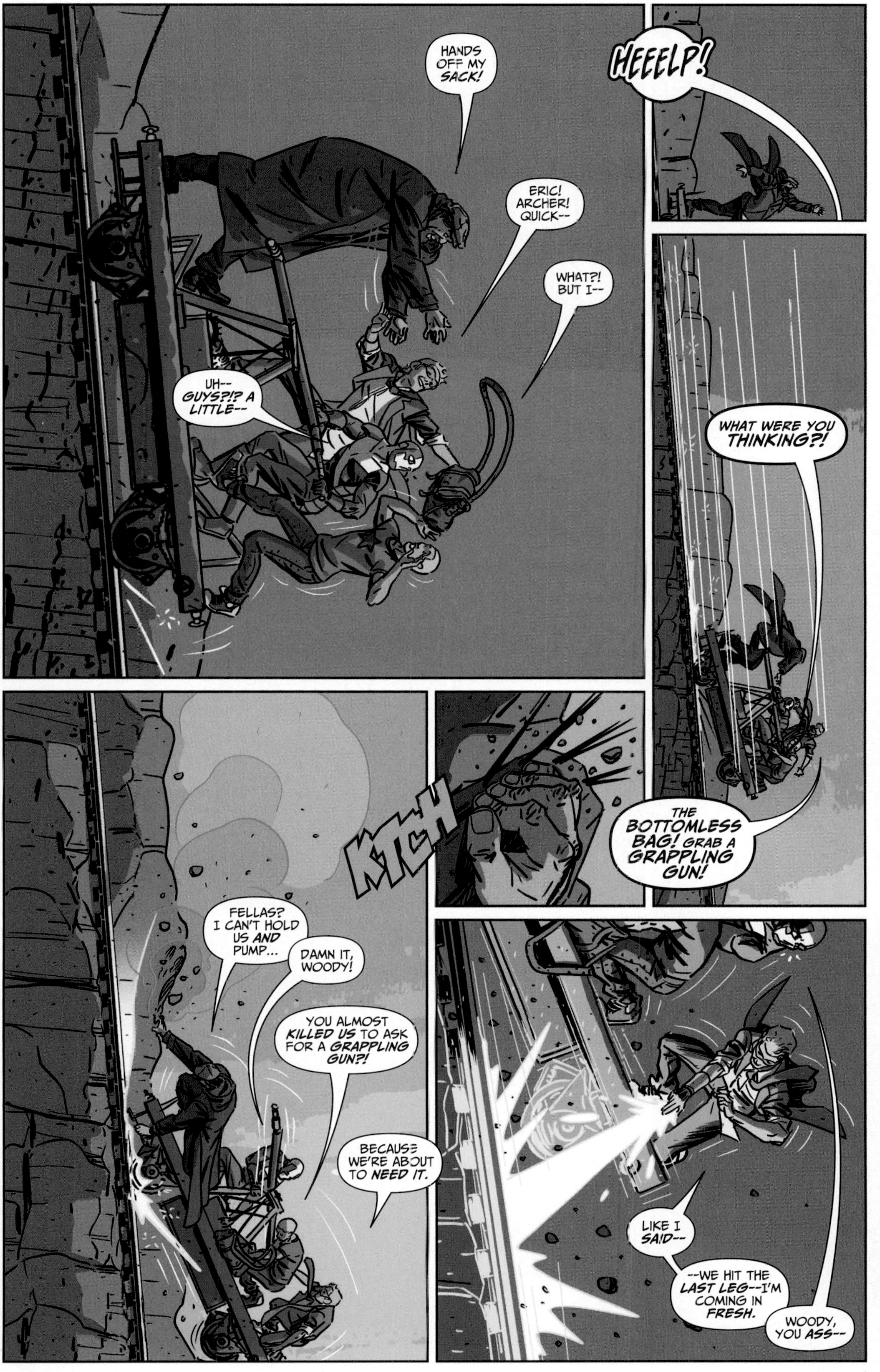
HANDS OFF MY SACK!
ERIC! ARCHER! QUICK--
WHAT?! BUT I--
UH-- GUYS?!? A LITTLE--
HEEEELP!
WHAT WERE YOU THINKING?!
THE BOTTOMLESS BAG! GRAB A GRAPPLING GUN!
KTCH
FELLAS? I CAN'T HOLD US AND PUMP...
DAMN IT, WOODY!
YOU ALMOST KILLED US TO ASK FOR A GRAPPLING GUN?!
BECAUSE WE'RE ABOUT TO NEED IT.
LIKE I SAID--
--WE HIT THE LAST LEG--I'M COMING IN FRESH.
WOODY, YOU ASS--

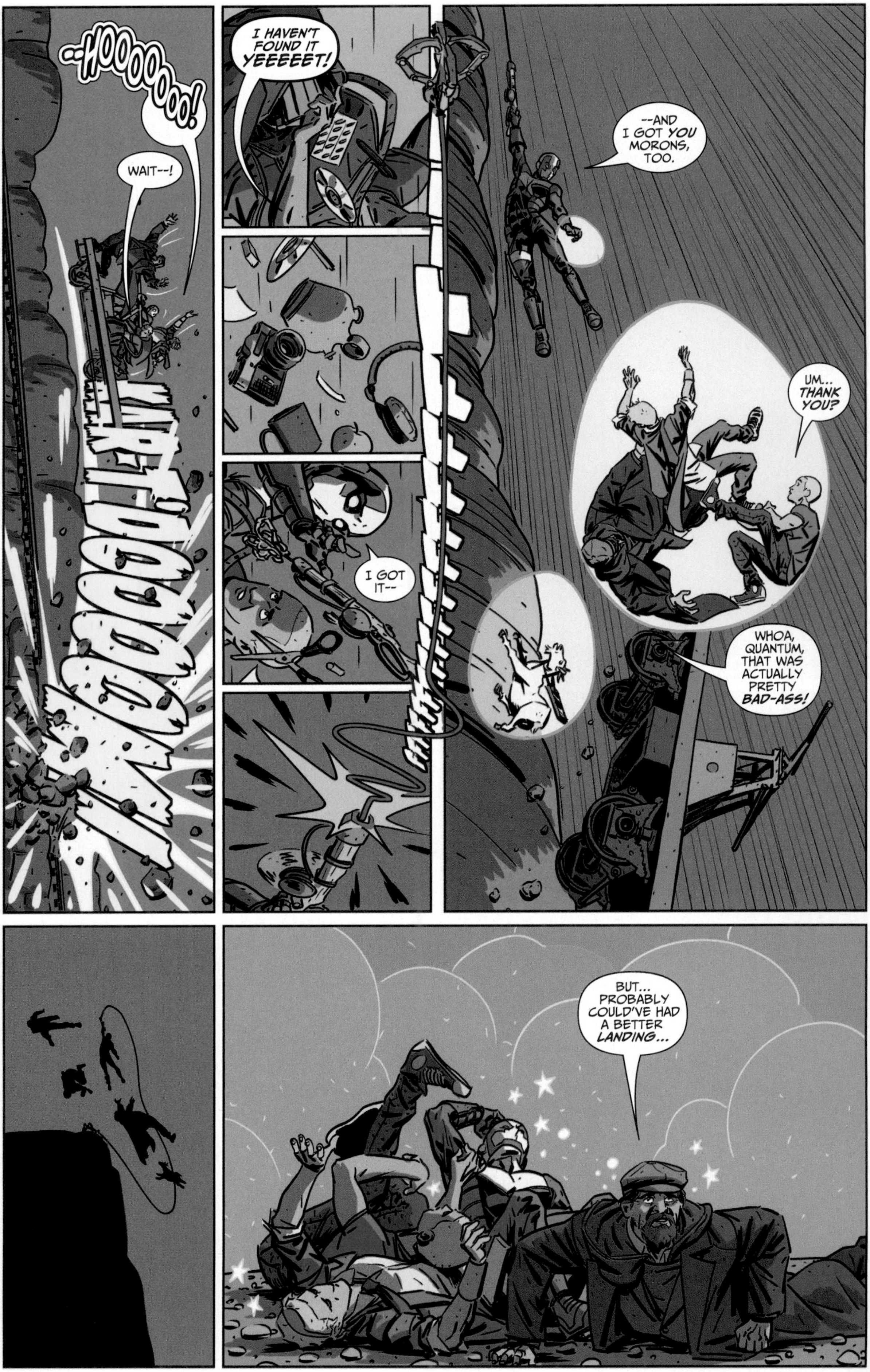

--HOOOOOOOO!
WAIT--!
WHOOOOOOM
I HAVEN'T FOUND IT YEEEEEET!
I GOT IT--
--AND I GOT YOU MORONS, TOO.
UM... THANK YOU?
WHOA, QUANTUM, THAT WAS ACTUALLY PRETTY BAD-ASS!
BUT... PROBABLY COULD'VE HAD A BETTER LANDING...

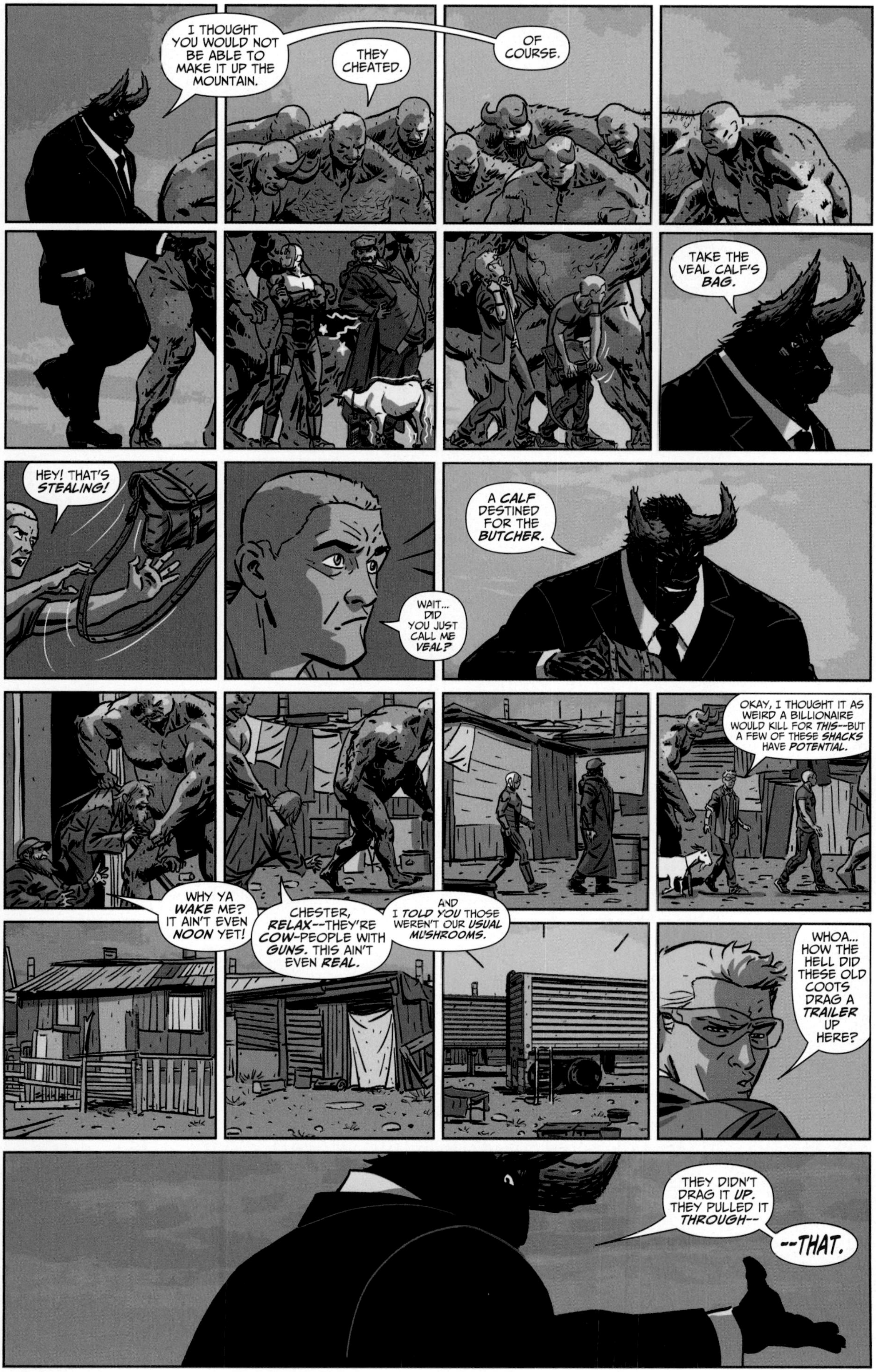
I THOUGHT YOU WOULD NOT BE ABLE TO MAKE IT UP THE MOUNTAIN.
THEY CHEATED.
OF COURSE.
TAKE THE VEAL CALF'S BAG.
HEY! THAT'S STEALING!
WAIT... DID YOU JUST CALL ME VEAL?
A CALF DESTINED FOR THE BUTCHER.
OKAY, I THOUGHT IT AS WEIRD A BILLIONAIRE WOULD KILL FOR THIS--BUT A FEW OF THESE SHACKS HAVE POTENTIAL.
WHY YA WAKE ME? IT AIN'T EVEN NOON YET!
CHESTER, RELAX--THEY'RE COW-PEOPLE WITH GUNS. THIS AIN'T EVEN REAL.
AND I TOLD YOU THOSE WEREN'T OUR USUAL MUSHROOMS.
WHOA... HOW THE HELL DID THESE OLD COOTS DRAG A TRAILER UP HERE?
THEY DIDN'T DRAG IT UP. THEY PULLED IT THROUGH--
--THAT.

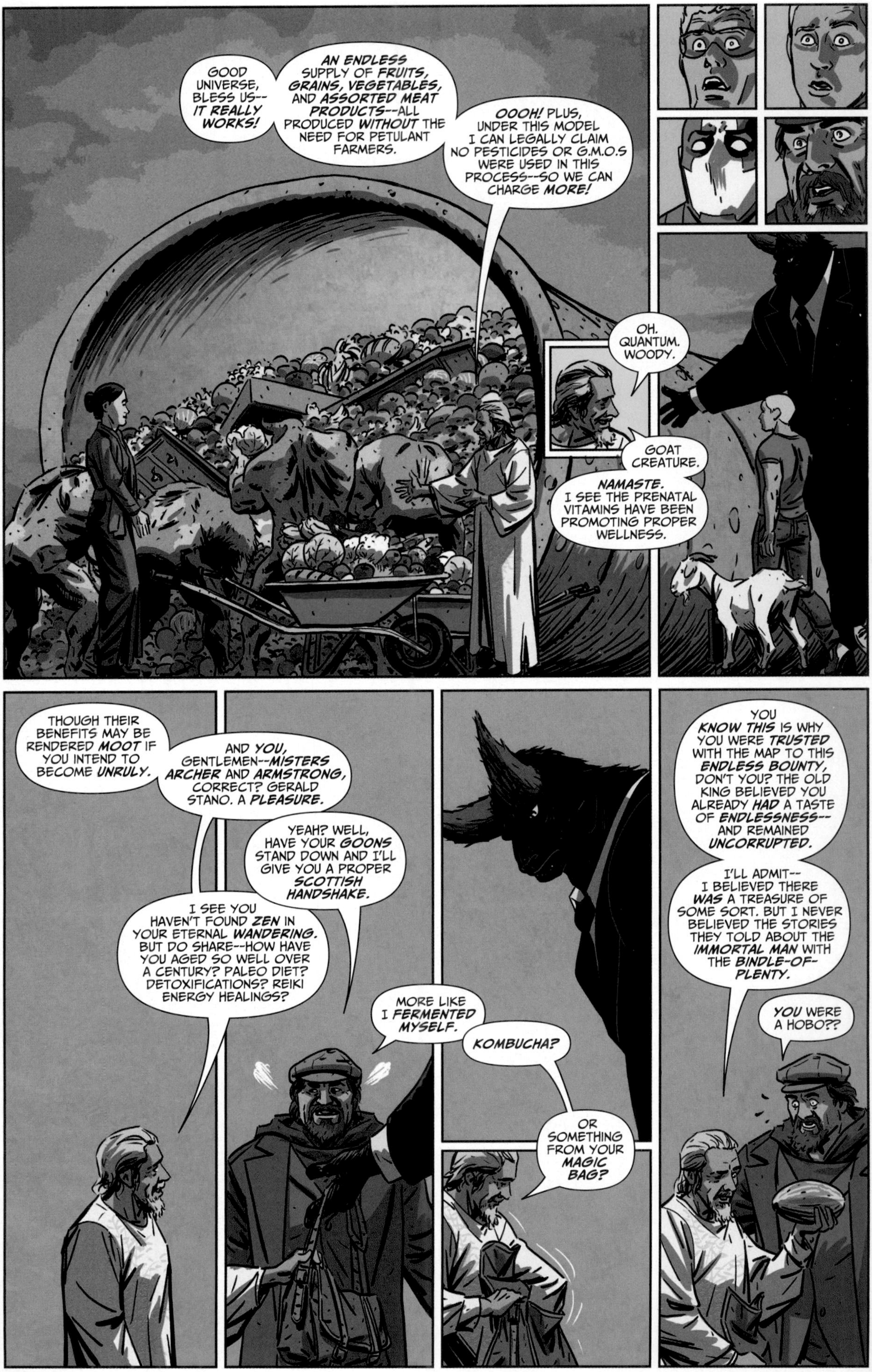
GOOD UNIVERSE, BLESS US-- IT REALLY WORKS!
AN ENDLESS SUPPLY OF FRUITS, GRAINS, VEGETABLES, AND ASSORTED MEAT PRODUCTS--ALL PRODUCED WITHOUT THE NEED FOR PETULANT FARMERS.
OOOH! PLUS, UNDER THIS MODEL I CAN LEGALLY CLAIM NO PESTICIDES OR G.M.O.S WERE USED IN THIS PROCESS--SO WE CAN CHARGE MORE!
OH. QUANTUM. WOODY.
GOAT CREATURE.
NAMASTE. I SEE THE PRENATAL VITAMINS HAVE BEEN PROMOTING PROPER WELLNESS.
THOUGH THEIR BENEFITS MAY BE RENDERED MOOT IF YOU INTEND TO BECOME UNRULY.
AND YOU, GENTLEMEN--MISTERS ARCHER AND ARMSTRONG, CORRECT? GERALD STANO. A PLEASURE.
YEAH? WELL, HAVE YOUR GOONS STAND DOWN AND I'LL GIVE YOU A PROPER SCOTTISH HANDSHAKE.
I SEE YOU HAVEN'T FOUND ZEN IN YOUR ETERNAL WANDERING. BUT DO SHARE--HOW HAVE YOU AGED SO WELL OVER A CENTURY? PALEO DIET? DETOXIFICATIONS? REIKI ENERGY HEALINGS?
MORE LIKE I FERMENTED MYSELF.
KOMBUCHA?
OR SOMETHING FROM YOUR MAGIC BAG?
YOU KNOW THIS IS WHY YOU WERE TRUSTED WITH THE MAP TO THIS ENDLESS BOUNTY, DON'T YOU? THE OLD KING BELIEVED YOU ALREADY HAD A TASTE OF ENDLESSNESS-- AND REMAINED UNCORRUPTED.
I'LL ADMIT-- I BELIEVED THERE WAS A TREASURE OF SOME SORT. BUT I NEVER BELIEVED THE STORIES THEY TOLD ABOUT THE IMMORTAL MAN WITH THE BINDLE-OF-PLENTY.
YOU WERE A HOBO??

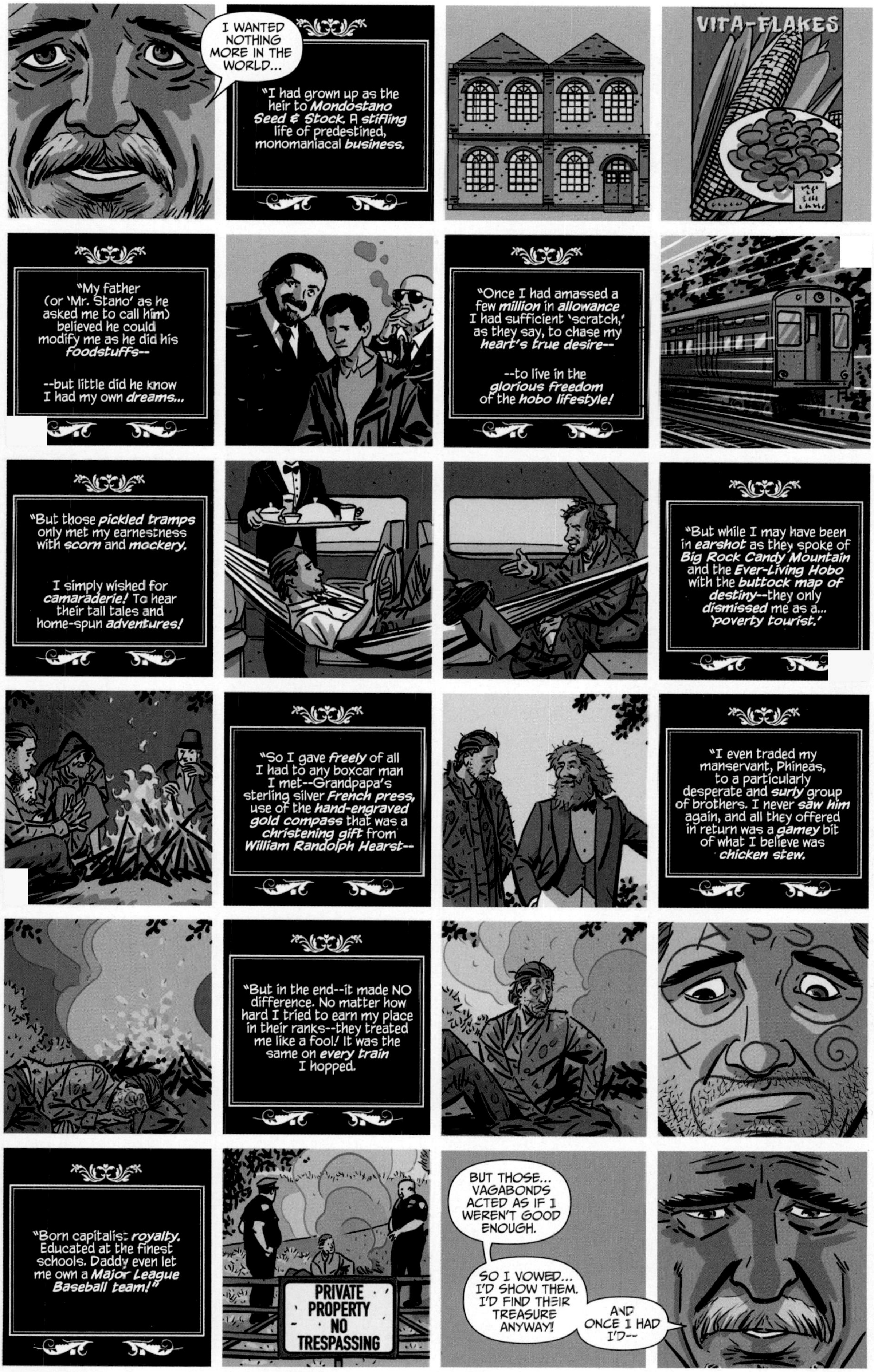
I WANTED NOTHING MORE IN THE WORLD...
"I had grown up as the heir to Mondostano Seed & Stock. A stifling life of predestined, monomaniacal business.
VITA-FLAKES
"My father (or 'Mr. Stano' as he asked me to call him) believed he could modify me as he did his foodstuffs--
--but little did he know I had my own dreams...
"Once I had amassed a few million in allowance I had sufficient 'scratch,' as they say, to chase my heart's true desire--
--to live in the glorious freedom of the hobo lifestyle!
"But those pickled tramps only met my earnestness with scorn and mockery.
I simply wished for camaraderie! To hear their tall tales and home-spun adventures!
"But while I may have been in earshot as they spoke of Big Rock Candy Mountain and the Ever-Living Hobo with the buttock map of destiny--they only dismissed me as a... 'poverty tourist.'
"So I gave freely of all I had to any boxcar man I met--Grandpapa's sterling silver French press, use of the hand-engraved gold compass that was a christening gift from William Randolph Hearst--
"I even traded my manservant, Phineas, to a particularly desperate and surly group of brothers. I never saw him again, and all they offered in return was a gamey bit of what I believe was chicken stew.
"But in the end--it made NO difference. No matter how hard I tried to earn my place in their ranks--they treated me like a fool! It was the same on every train I hopped.
"Born capitalist royalty. Educated at the finest schools. Daddy even let me own a Major League Baseball team!"
PRIVATE PROPERTY NO TRESPASSING
BUT THOSE... VAGABONDS ACTED AS IF I WEREN'T GOOD ENOUGH.
SO I VOWED... I'D SHOW THEM. I'D FIND THEIR TREASURE ANYWAY!
AND ONCE I HAD I'D--

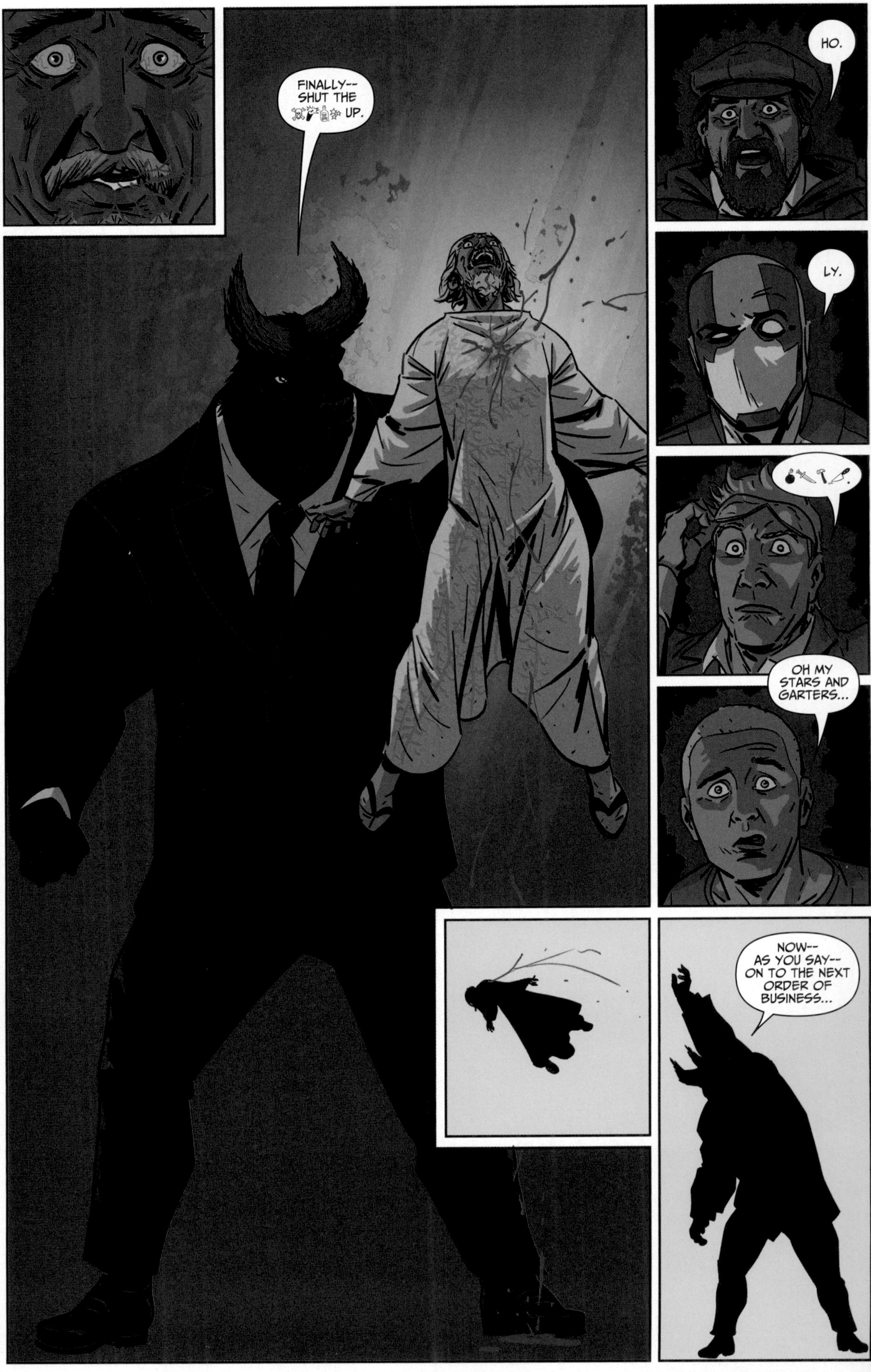
FINALLY--
SHUT THE [grawlix] UP.
HO.
LY.
[grawlix]
OH MY STARS AND GARTERS...
NOW--
AS YOU SAY--
ON TO THE NEXT ORDER OF BUSINESS...

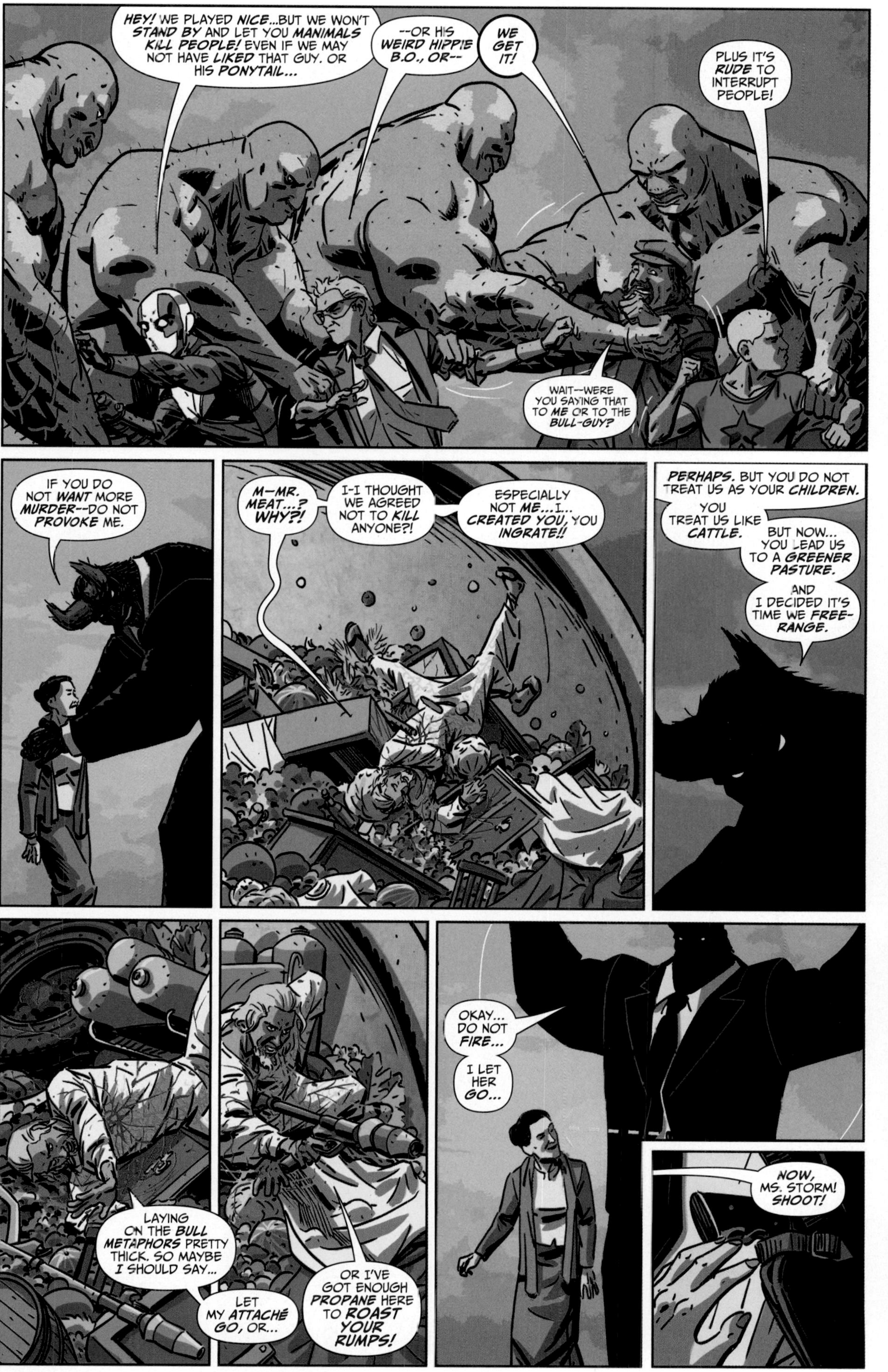
HEY! WE PLAYED NICE...BUT WE WON'T STAND BY AND LET YOU MANIMALS KILL PEOPLE! EVEN IF WE MAY NOT HAVE LIKED THAT GUY. OR HIS PONYTAIL...
--OR HIS WEIRD HIPPIE B.O., OR--
WE GET IT!
PLUS IT'S RUDE TO INTERRUPT PEOPLE!
WAIT--WERE YOU SAYING THAT TO ME OR TO THE BULL-GUY?
IF YOU DO NOT WANT MORE MURDER--DO NOT PROVOKE ME.
M--MR. MEAT...? WHY?!
I-I THOUGHT WE AGREED NOT TO KILL ANYONE?!
ESPECIALLY NOT ME...I... CREATED YOU, YOU INGRATE!!
PERHAPS. BUT YOU DO NOT TREAT US AS YOUR CHILDREN.
YOU TREAT US LIKE CATTLE.
BUT NOW... YOU LEAD US TO A GREENER PASTURE.
AND I DECIDED IT'S TIME WE FREE-RANGE.
LAYING ON THE BULL METAPHORS PRETTY THICK. SO MAYBE I SHOULD SAY...
LET MY ATTACHÉ GO, OR...
OR I'VE GOT ENOUGH PROPANE HERE TO ROAST YOUR RUMPS!
OKAY... DO NOT FIRE...
I LET HER GO...
NOW, MS. STORM! SHOOT!

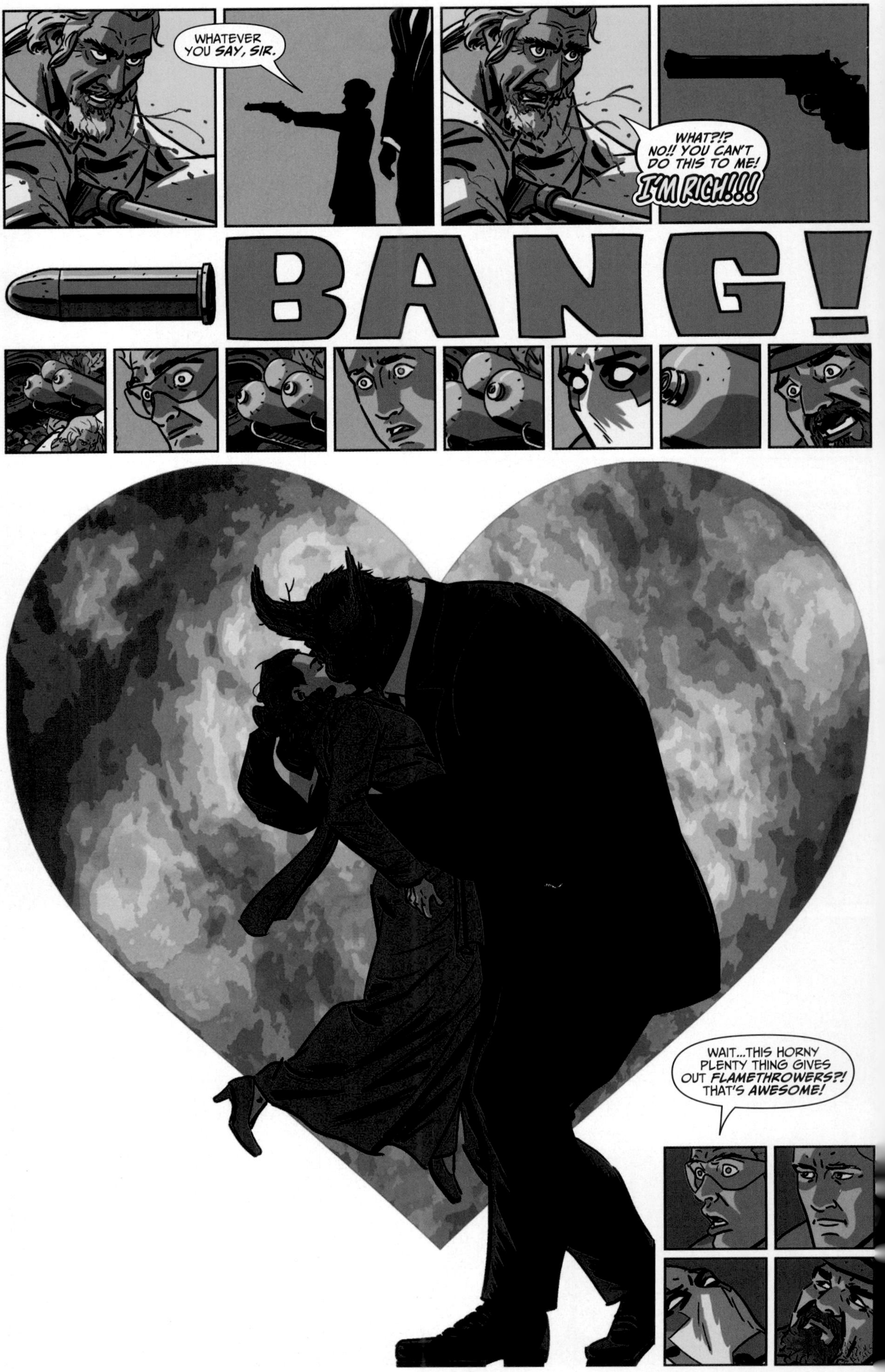
WHATEVER YOU SAY, SIR.
WHAT?!? NO!! YOU CAN'T DO THIS TO ME!
I'M RICH!!!
BANG!
WAIT...THIS HORNY PLENTY THING GIVES OUT FLAMETHROWERS?! THAT'S AWESOME!

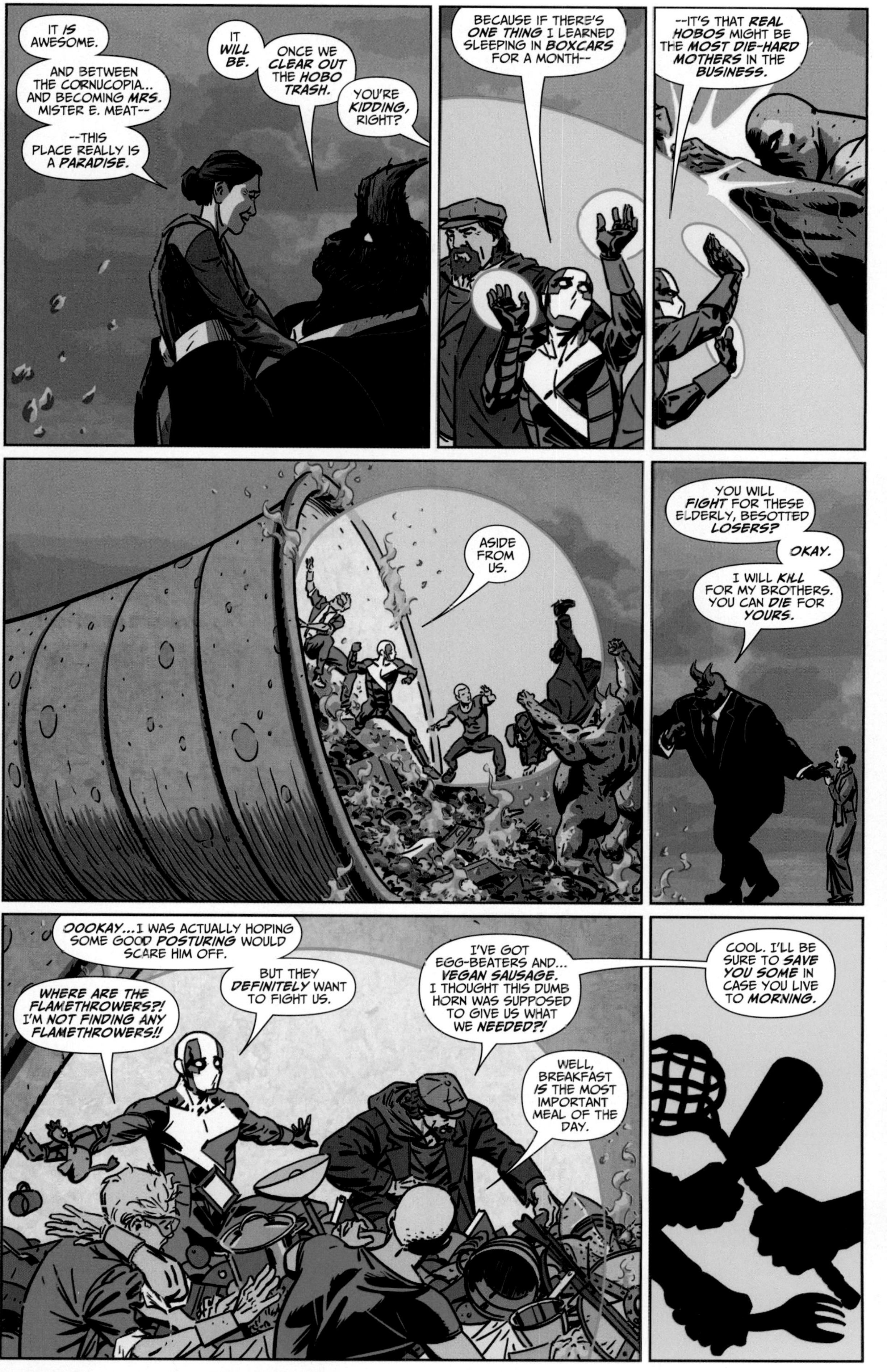
IT IS AWESOME.
AND BETWEEN THE CORNUCOPIA... AND BECOMING MRS. MISTER E. MEAT--
--THIS PLACE REALLY IS A PARADISE.
IT WILL BE.
ONCE WE CLEAR OUT THE HOBO TRASH.
YOU'RE KIDDING, RIGHT?
BECAUSE IF THERE'S ONE THING I LEARNED SLEEPING IN BOXCARS FOR A MONTH--
--IT'S THAT REAL HOBOS MIGHT BE THE MOST DIE-HARD MOTHERS IN THE BUSINESS.
ASIDE FROM US.
YOU WILL FIGHT FOR THESE ELDERLY, BESOTTED LOSERS?
OKAY.
I WILL KILL FOR MY BROTHERS. YOU CAN DIE FOR YOURS.
OOOKAY...I WAS ACTUALLY HOPING SOME GOOD POSTURING WOULD SCARE HIM OFF.
BUT THEY DEFINITELY WANT TO FIGHT US.
WHERE ARE THE FLAMETHROWERS?! I'M NOT FINDING ANY FLAMETHROWERS!!
I'VE GOT EGG-BEATERS AND... VEGAN SAUSAGE. I THOUGHT THIS DUMB HORN WAS SUPPOSED TO GIVE US WHAT WE NEEDED?!
WELL, BREAKFAST IS THE MOST IMPORTANT MEAL OF THE DAY.
COOL. I'LL BE SURE TO SAVE YOU SOME IN CASE YOU LIVE TO MORNING.

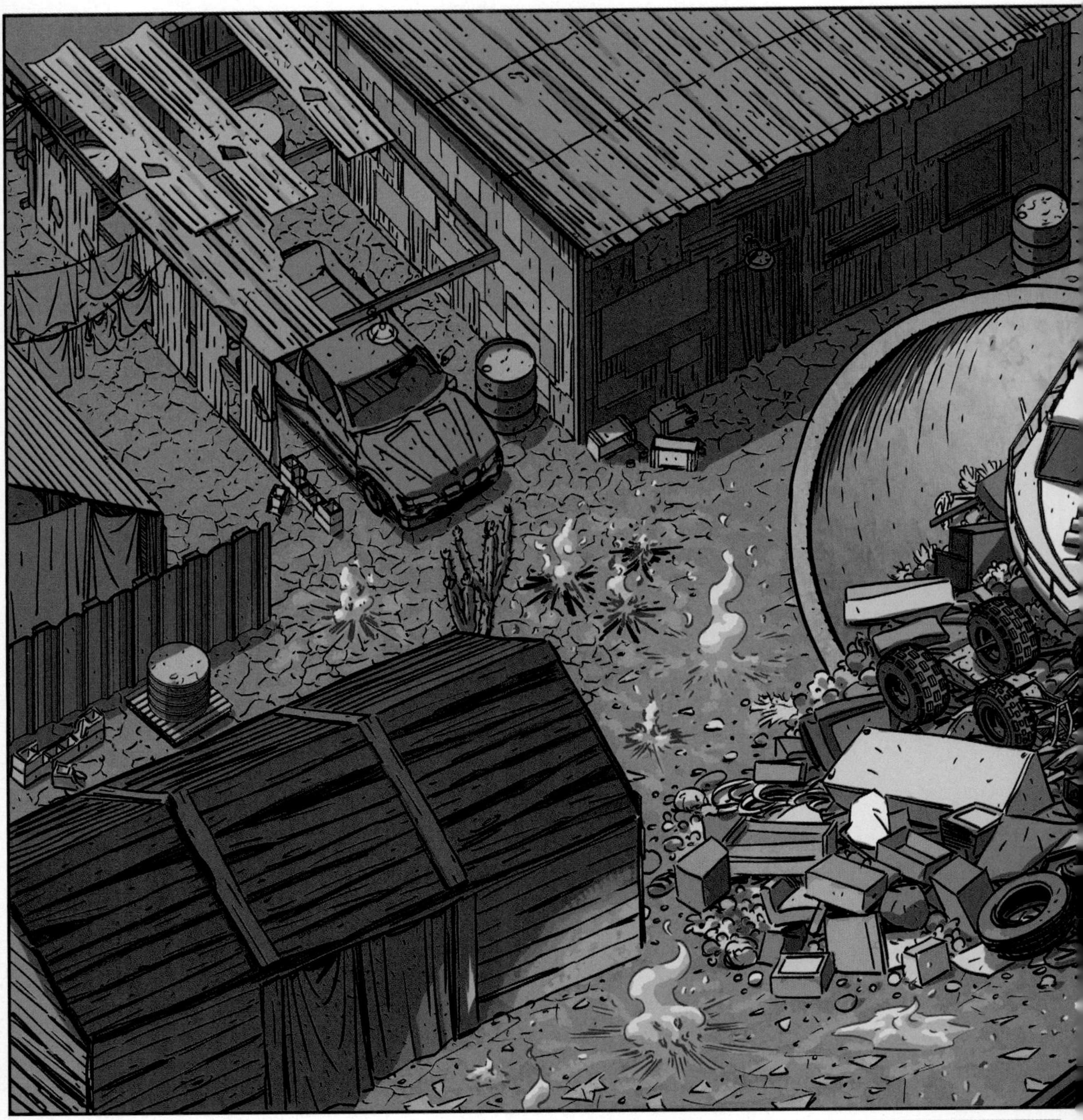

HEY KIDS! WE KNOW THAT COMIC BOOK STORIES USUALLY END IN GIANT FIGHT SEQUENCES--SOMETIMES LASTING THE ENTIRE ISSUE. BUT AS OUR GOAL HAS BEEN TO TELL A JAM-PACKED STORY--WE DECIDED TO ALLOW YOU, THE READER, TO SPEND AS MUCH TIME CRASHING THE CHARACTERS TOGETHER IN AS MANY MINDLESS FEATS OF VIOLENCE AS YOU NEED IN ORDER TO FEEL FULFILLED--WITHOUT SACRIFICING ANY PAGES OF OUR NARRATIVE! IT'S A WIN-WIN! JUST CUT OUT THE FIGURES AND ***HAVE FUN!****

****NOTE:*** IF YOU DO ***NOT*** HAVE FUN, THAT IS ENTIRELY THE FAULT OF YOUR OWN IMAGINATION AND THEREFORE CANNOT REASONABLY BE HELD AGAINST THE CREATORS OF THIS COMIC IN ANY CRITICAL REVIEW / DISCUSSION OF THIS ISSUE.

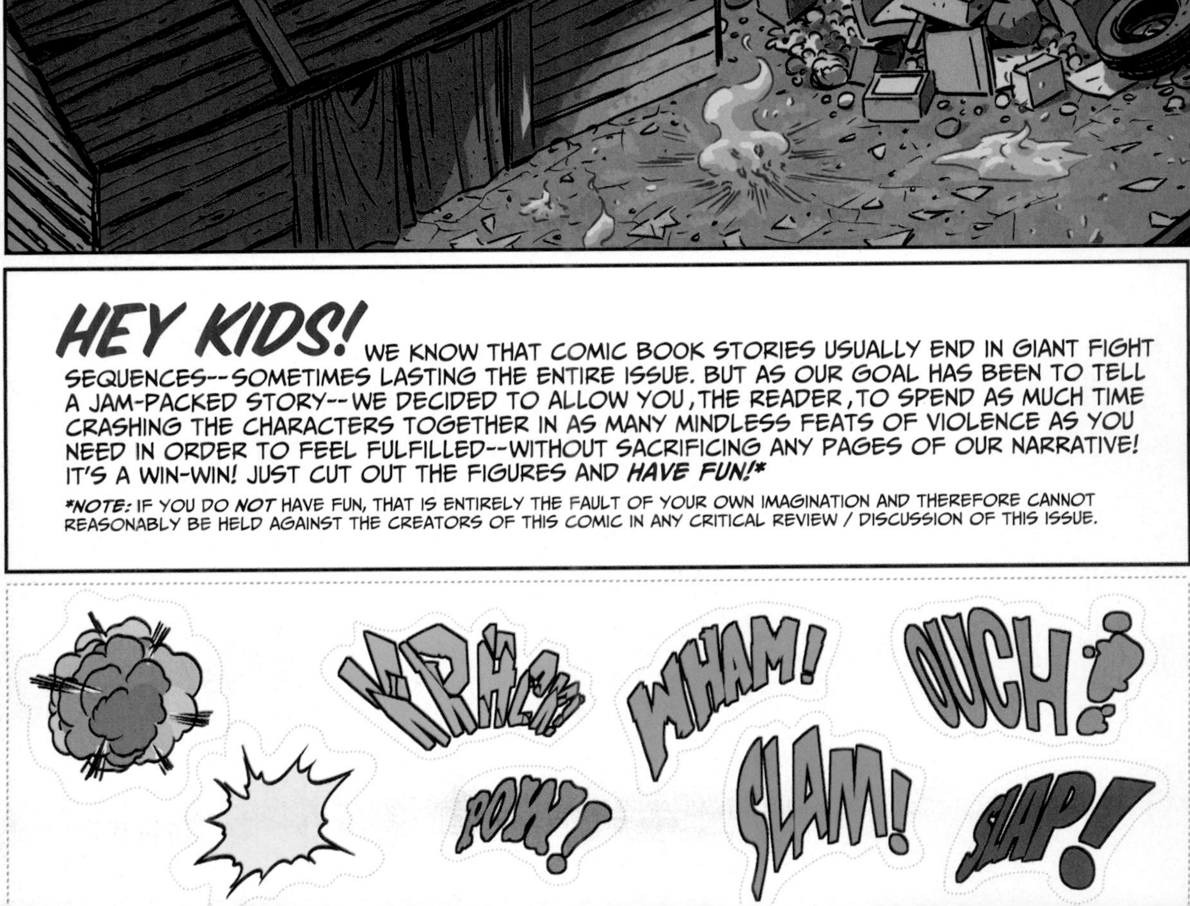
WHAM!
OUCH!
POW!
SLAM!
SLAP!

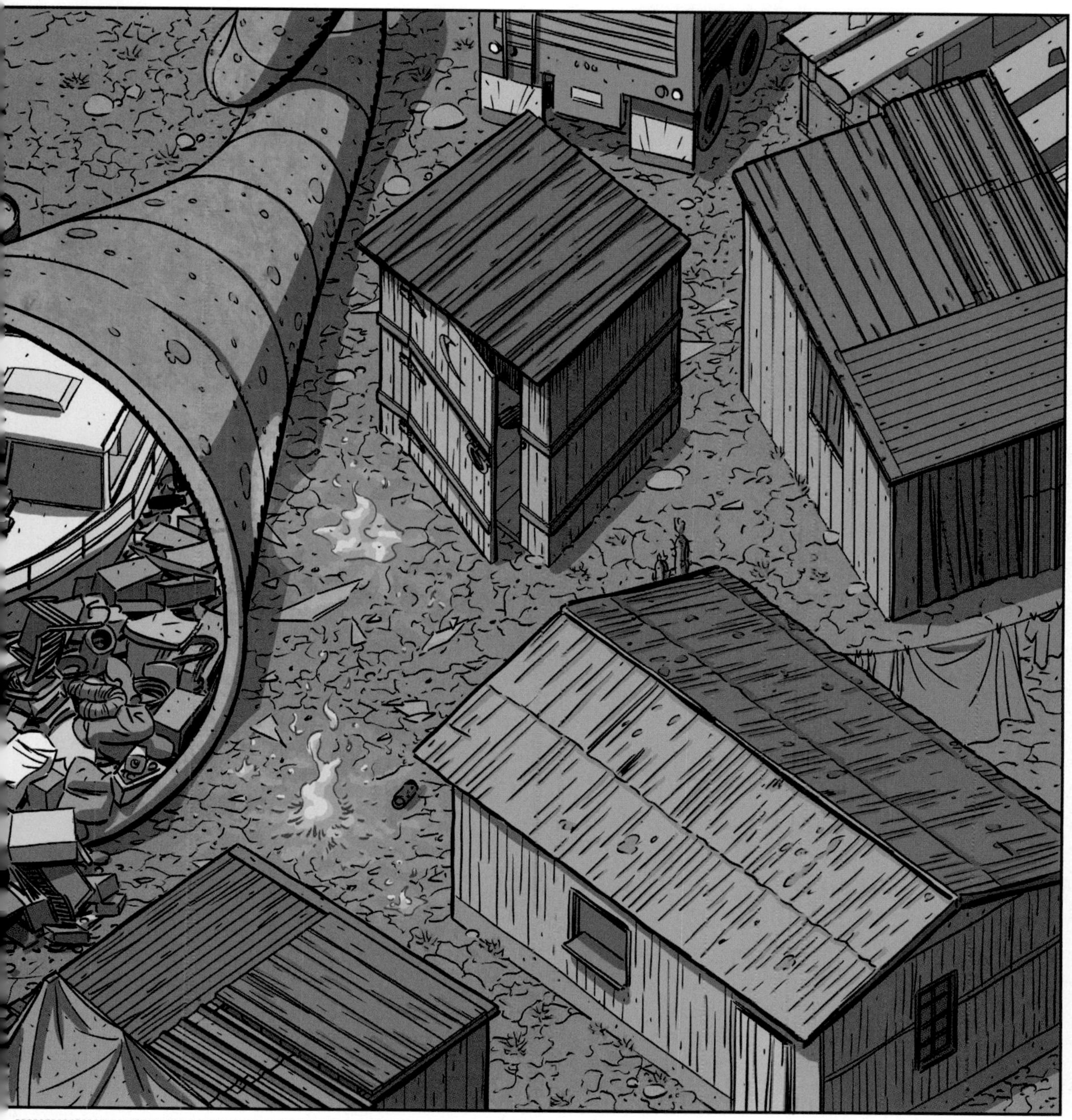

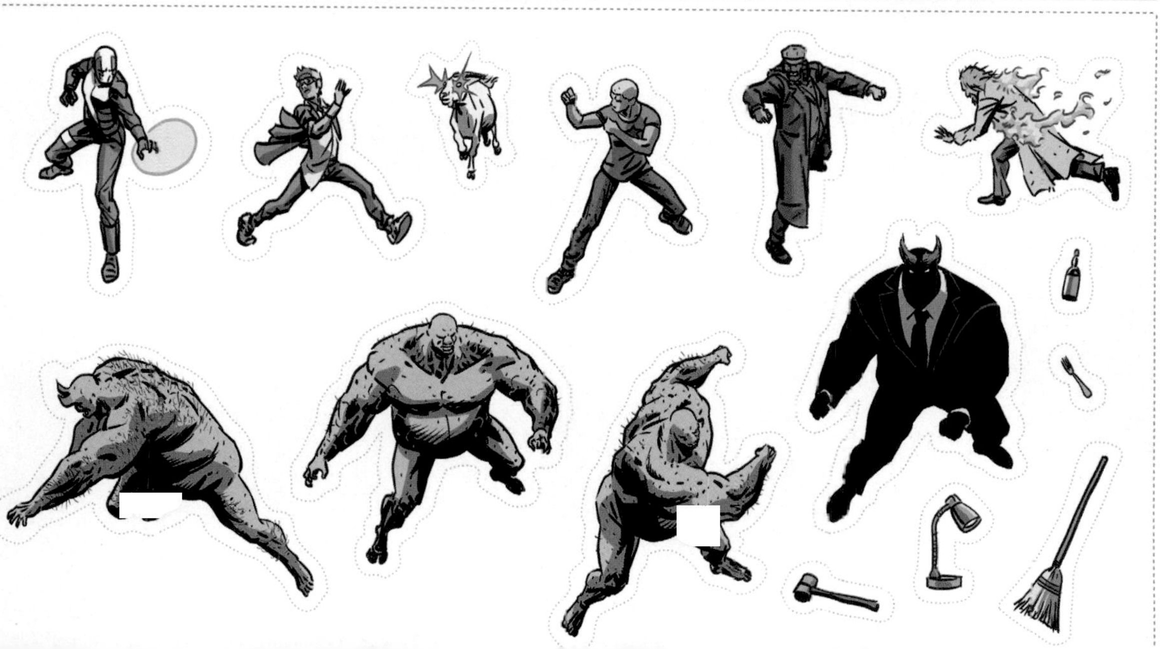

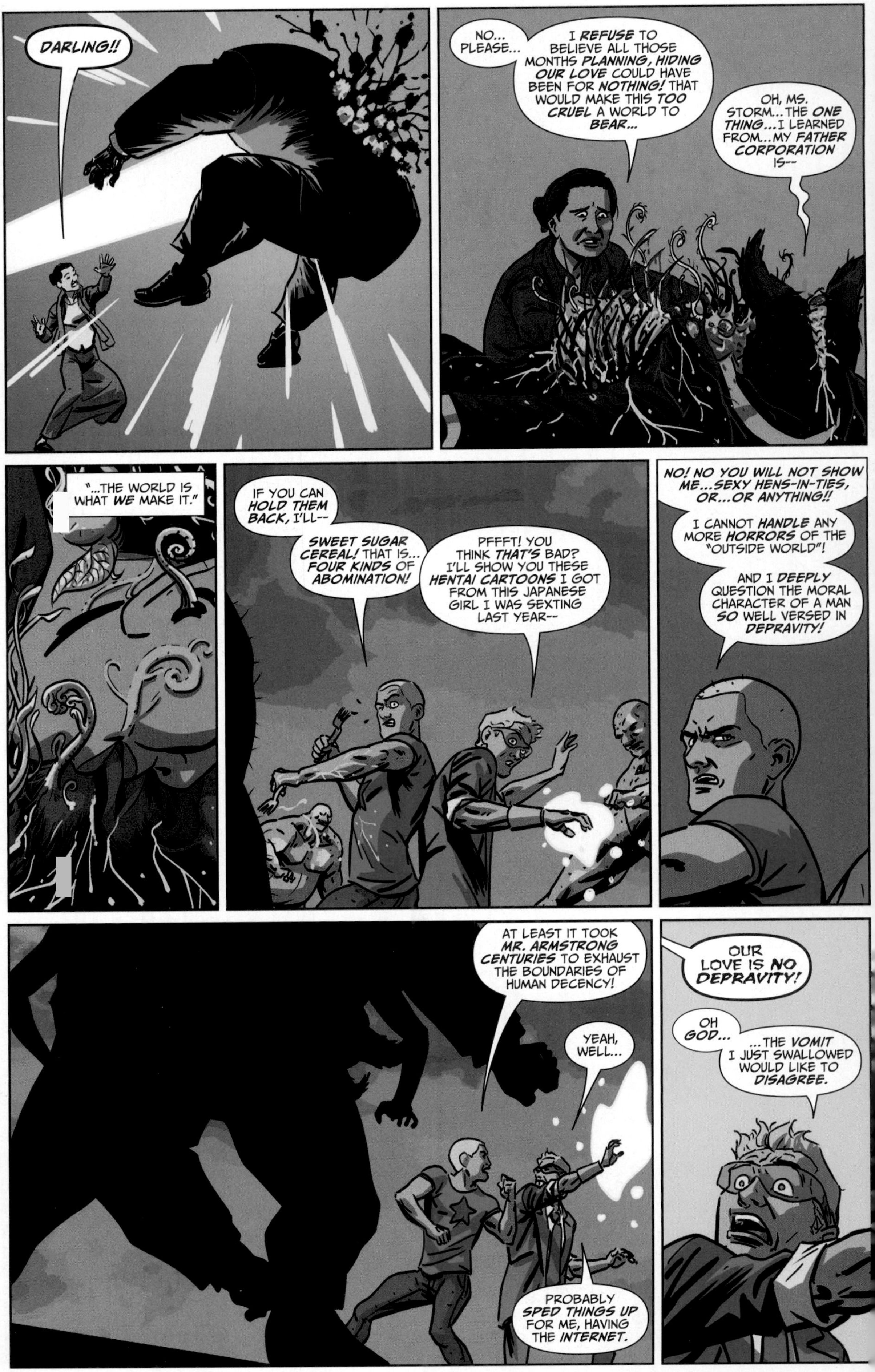
DARLING!!
NO... PLEASE...
I REFUSE TO BELIEVE ALL THOSE MONTHS PLANNING, HIDING OUR LOVE COULD HAVE BEEN FOR NOTHING! THAT WOULD MAKE THIS TOO CRUEL A WORLD TO BEAR...
OH, MS. STORM...THE ONE THING...I LEARNED FROM...MY FATHER CORPORATION IS--
"...THE WORLD IS WHAT WE MAKE IT."
IF YOU CAN HOLD THEM BACK, I'LL--
SWEET SUGAR CEREAL! THAT IS... FOUR KINDS OF ABOMINATION!
PFFFT! YOU THINK THAT'S BAD? I'LL SHOW YOU THESE HENTAI CARTOONS I GOT FROM THIS JAPANESE GIRL I WAS SEXTING LAST YEAR--
NO! NO YOU WILL NOT SHOW ME...SEXY HENS-IN-TIES, OR...OR ANYTHING!!
I CANNOT HANDLE ANY MORE HORRORS OF THE "OUTSIDE WORLD"!
AND I DEEPLY QUESTION THE MORAL CHARACTER OF A MAN SO WELL VERSED IN DEPRAVITY!
AT LEAST IT TOOK MR. ARMSTRONG CENTURIES TO EXHAUST THE BOUNDARIES OF HUMAN DECENCY!
YEAH, WELL...
PROBABLY SPED THINGS UP FOR ME, HAVING THE INTERNET.
OUR LOVE IS NO DEPRAVITY!
OH GOD...
...THE VOMIT I JUST SWALLOWED WOULD LIKE TO DISAGREE.

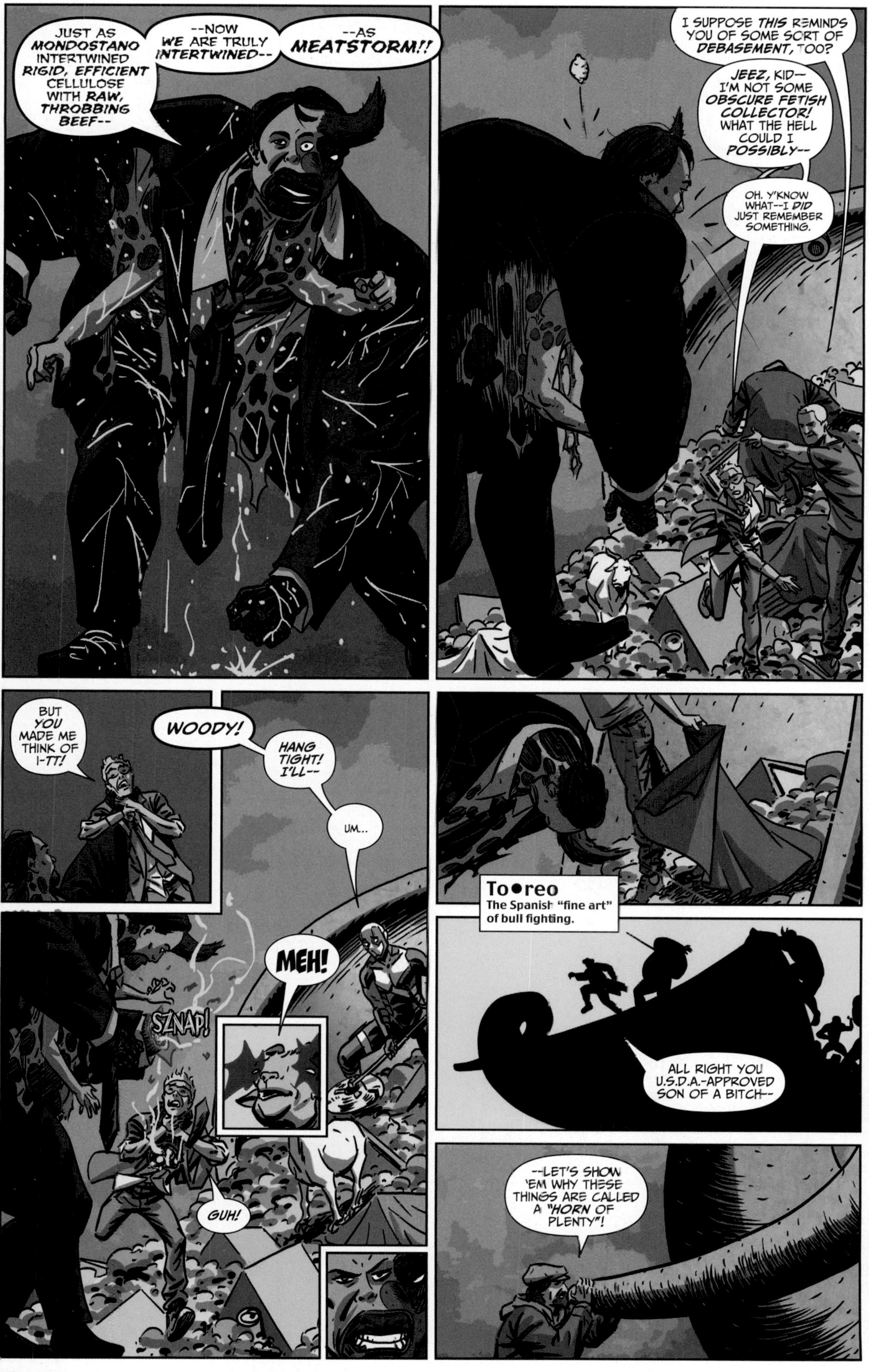
JUST AS MONDOSTANO INTERTWINED RIGID, EFFICIENT CELLULOSE WITH RAW, THROBBING BEEF--
--NOW WE ARE TRULY INTERTWINED--
--AS MEATSTORM!!
I SUPPOSE THIS REMINDS YOU OF SOME SORT OF DEBASEMENT, TOO?
JEEZ, KID— I'M NOT SOME OBSCURE FETISH COLLECTOR! WHAT THE HELL COULD I POSSIBLY--
OH. Y'KNOW WHAT--I DID JUST REMEMBER SOMETHING.
BUT YOU MADE ME THINK OF I-TT!
WOODY!
HANG TIGHT! I'LL--
UM...
MEH!
SZNAP!
GUH!
To●reo
The Spanish "fine art" of bull fighting.
ALL RIGHT YOU U.S.D.A.-APPROVED SON OF A BITCH--
--LET'S SHOW 'EM WHY THESE THINGS ARE CALLED A "HORN OF PLENTY"!

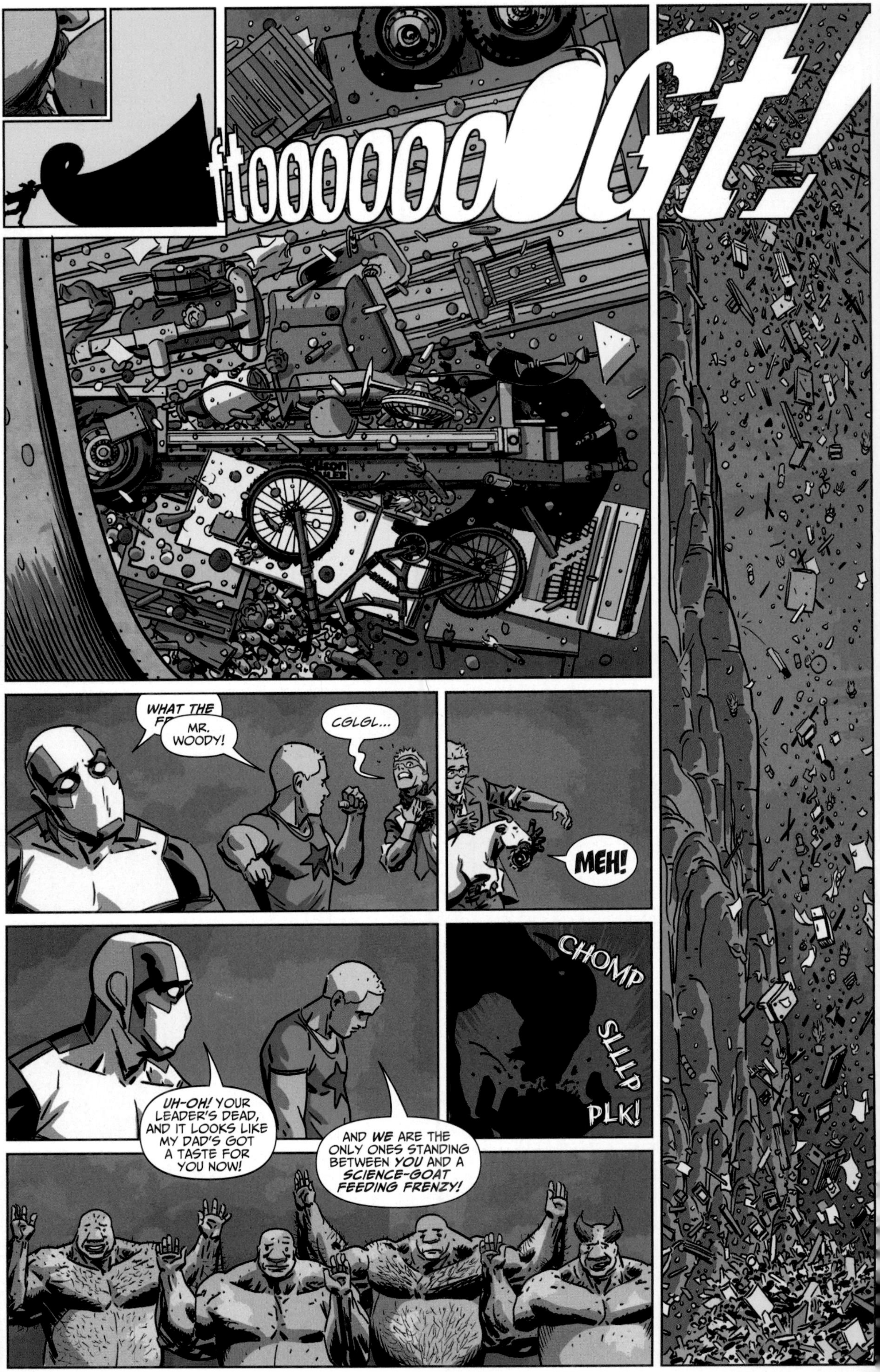
ftooooooOGT!
WHAT THE F—
MR. WOODY!
CGLGL...
MEH!
CHOMP
SLLLP
PLK!
UH-OH! YOUR LEADER'S DEAD, AND IT LOOKS LIKE MY DAD'S GOT A TASTE FOR YOU NOW!
AND WE ARE THE ONLY ONES STANDING BETWEEN YOU AND A SCIENCE-GOAT FEEDING FRENZY!

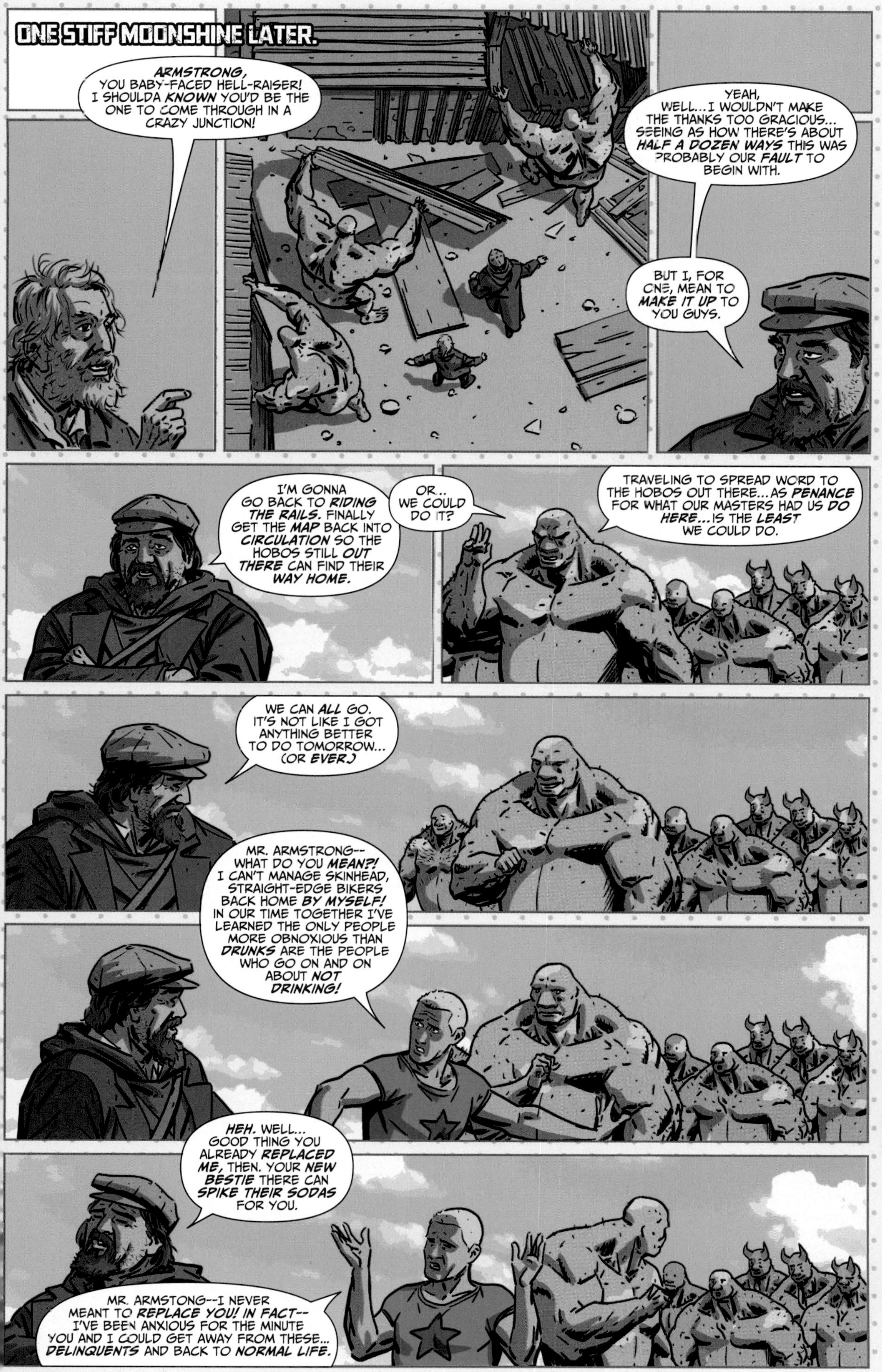
ONE STIFF MOONSHINE LATER.
ARMSTRONG, YOU BABY-FACED HELL-RAISER! I SHOULDA KNOWN YOU'D BE THE ONE TO COME THROUGH IN A CRAZY JUNCTION!
YEAH, WELL... I WOULDN'T MAKE THE THANKS TOO GRACIOUS... SEEING AS HOW THERE'S ABOUT HALF A DOZEN WAYS THIS WAS PROBABLY OUR FAULT TO BEGIN WITH.
BUT I, FOR ONE, MEAN TO MAKE IT UP TO YOU GUYS.
I'M GONNA GO BACK TO RIDING THE RAILS. FINALLY GET THE MAP BACK INTO CIRCULATION SO THE HOBOS STILL OUT THERE CAN FIND THEIR WAY HOME.
OR... WE COULD DO IT?
TRAVELING TO SPREAD WORD TO THE HOBOS OUT THERE... AS PENANCE FOR WHAT OUR MASTERS HAD US DO HERE... IS THE LEAST WE COULD DO.
WE CAN ALL GO. IT'S NOT LIKE I GOT ANYTHING BETTER TO DO TOMORROW... (OR EVER.)
MR. ARMSTRONG-- WHAT DO YOU MEAN?! I CAN'T MANAGE SKINHEAD, STRAIGHT-EDGE BIKERS BACK HOME BY MYSELF! IN OUR TIME TOGETHER I'VE LEARNED THE ONLY PEOPLE MORE OBNOXIOUS THAN DRUNKS ARE THE PEOPLE WHO GO ON AND ON ABOUT NOT DRINKING!
HEH. WELL... GOOD THING YOU ALREADY REPLACED ME, THEN. YOUR NEW BESTIE THERE CAN SPIKE THEIR SODAS FOR YOU.
MR. ARMSTONG--I NEVER MEANT TO REPLACE YOU! IN FACT-- I'VE BEEN ANXIOUS FOR THE MINUTE YOU AND I COULD GET AWAY FROM THESE... DELINQUENTS AND BACK TO NORMAL LIFE.

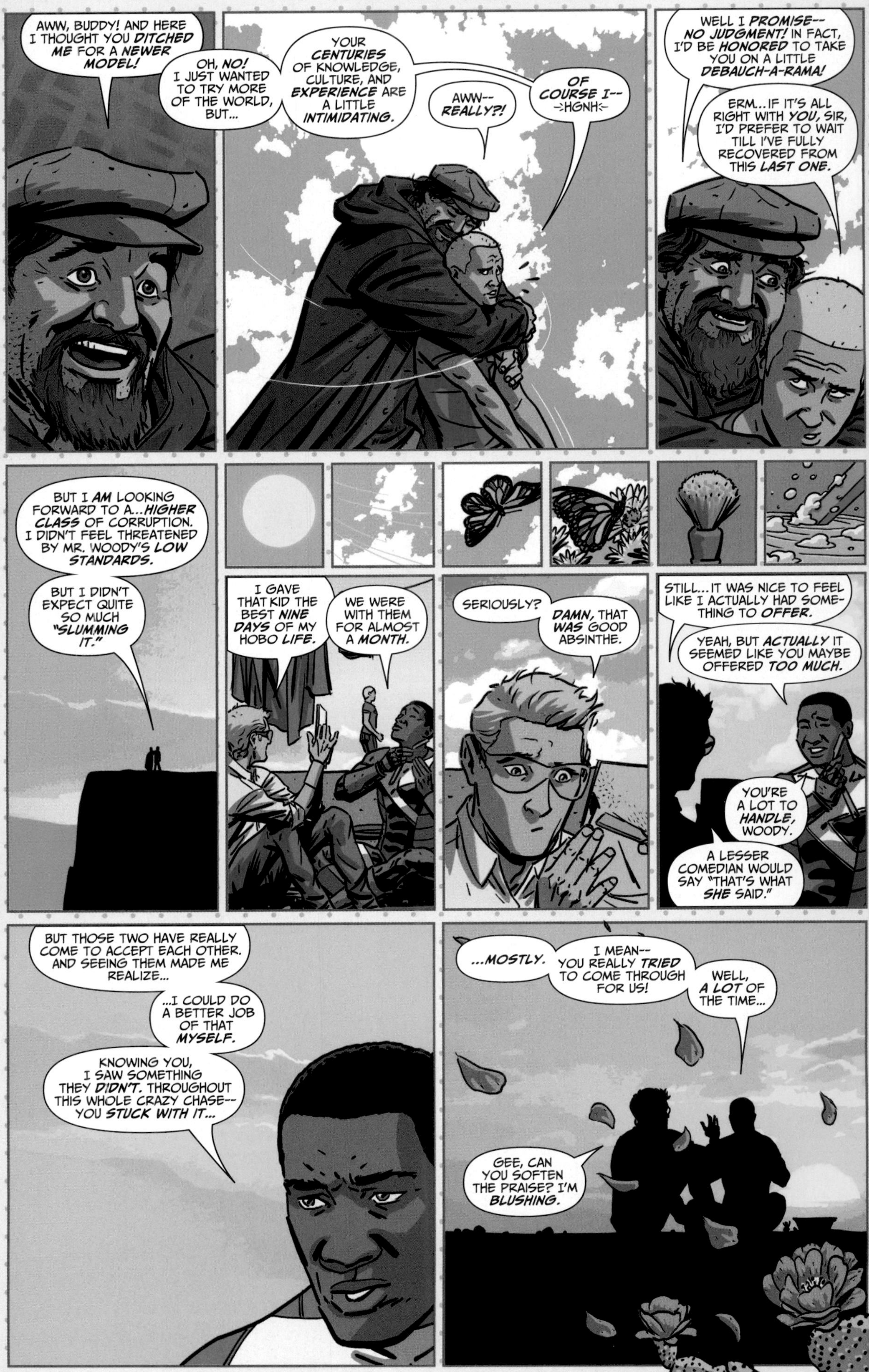
AWW, BUDDY! AND HERE I THOUGHT YOU DITCHED ME FOR A NEWER MODEL!
OH, NO! I JUST WANTED TO TRY MORE OF THE WORLD, BUT...
YOUR CENTURIES OF KNOWLEDGE, CULTURE, AND EXPERIENCE ARE A LITTLE INTIMIDATING.
AWW-- REALLY?!
OF COURSE I-- HGNH
WELL I PROMISE-- NO JUDGMENT! IN FACT, I'D BE HONORED TO TAKE YOU ON A LITTLE DEBAUCH-A-RAMA!
ERM...IF IT'S ALL RIGHT WITH YOU, SIR, I'D PREFER TO WAIT TILL I'VE FULLY RECOVERED FROM THIS LAST ONE.
BUT I AM LOOKING FORWARD TO A...HIGHER CLASS OF CORRUPTION. I DIDN'T FEEL THREATENED BY MR. WOODY'S LOW STANDARDS.
BUT I DIDN'T EXPECT QUITE SO MUCH "SLUMMING IT."
I GAVE THAT KID THE BEST NINE DAYS OF MY HOBO LIFE.
WE WERE WITH THEM FOR ALMOST A MONTH.
SERIOUSLY?
DAMN, THAT WAS GOOD ABSINTHE.
STILL...IT WAS NICE TO FEEL LIKE I ACTUALLY HAD SOMETHING TO OFFER.
YEAH, BUT ACTUALLY IT SEEMED LIKE YOU MAYBE OFFERED TOO MUCH.
YOU'RE A LOT TO HANDLE, WOODY.
A LESSER COMEDIAN WOULD SAY "THAT'S WHAT SHE SAID."
BUT THOSE TWO HAVE REALLY COME TO ACCEPT EACH OTHER. AND SEEING THEM MADE ME REALIZE...
...I COULD DO A BETTER JOB OF THAT MYSELF.
KNOWING YOU, I SAW SOMETHING THEY DIDN'T. THROUGHOUT THIS WHOLE CRAZY CHASE-- YOU STUCK WITH IT...
...MOSTLY.
I MEAN-- YOU REALLY TRIED TO COME THROUGH FOR US!
WELL, A LOT OF THE TIME...
GEE, CAN YOU SOFTEN THE PRAISE? I'M BLUSHING.

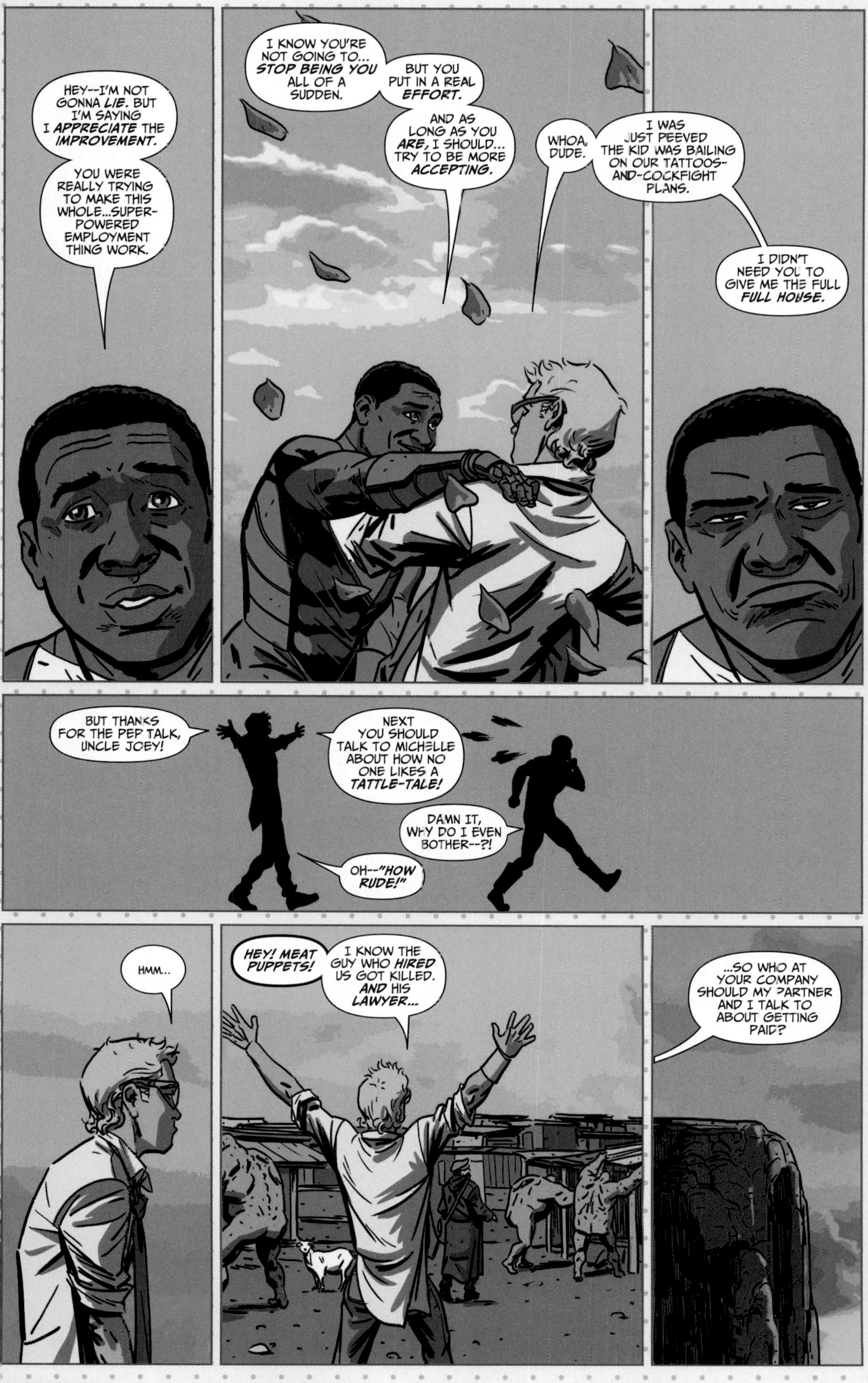
HEY--I'M NOT GONNA *LIE.* BUT I'M SAYING I *APPRECIATE* THE *IMPROVEMENT.*
YOU WERE REALLY TRYING TO MAKE THIS WHOLE...SUPER-POWERED EMPLOYMENT THING WORK.
I KNOW YOU'RE NOT GOING TO... *STOP BEING YOU* ALL OF A SUDDEN.
BUT YOU PUT IN A REAL *EFFORT.*
AND AS LONG AS YOU *ARE,* I SHOULD... TRY TO BE MORE *ACCEPTING.*
WHOA, DUDE.
I WAS JUST PEEVED THE KID WAS BAILING ON OUR TATTOOS-AND-COCKFIGHT PLANS.
I DIDN'T NEED YOU TO GIVE ME THE FULL *FULL HOUSE.*
BUT THANKS FOR THE PEP TALK, UNCLE JOEY!
NEXT YOU SHOULD TALK TO MICHELLE ABOUT HOW NO ONE LIKES A *TATTLE-TALE!*
DAMN IT, WHY DO I EVEN BOTHER--?!
OH--*"HOW RUDE!"*
HMM...
HEY! MEAT PUPPETS!
I KNOW THE GUY WHO *HIRED* US GOT KILLED. *AND HIS LAWYER...*
...SO WHO AT YOUR COMPANY SHOULD MY PARTNER AND I TALK TO ABOUT GETTING PAID?

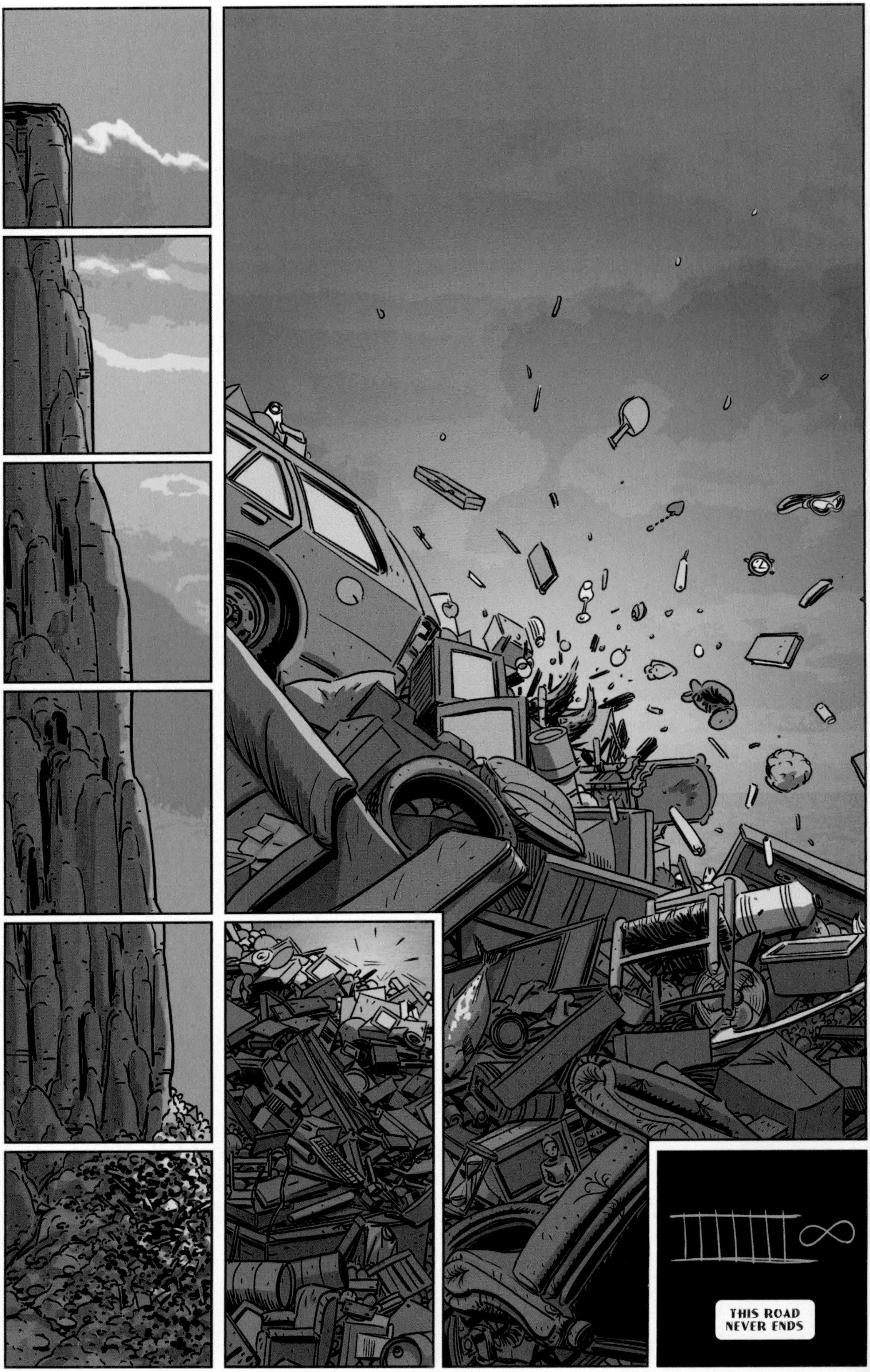
THIS ROAD
NEVER ENDS

the DELINQUENTS

the BOARD GAME!

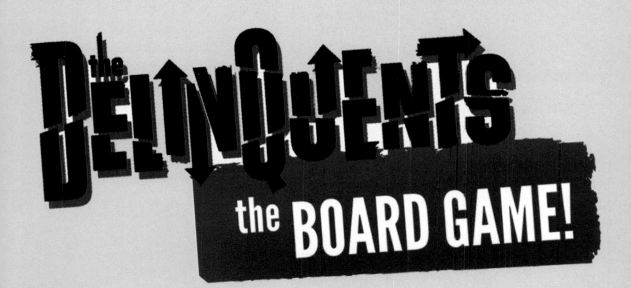

ARCHER

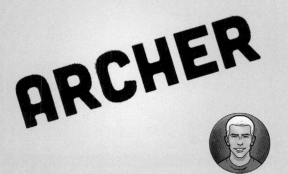

ARCHER

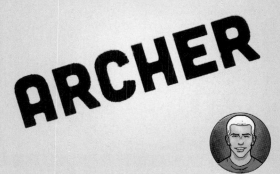

ARCHER

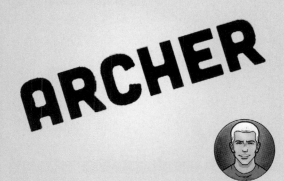

ARCHER

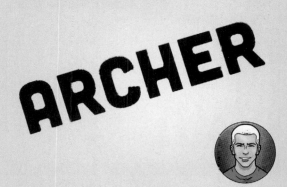

ARCHER

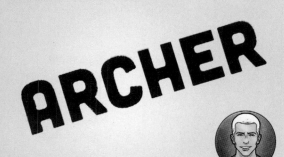

ARCHER

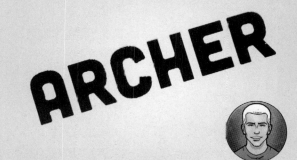

THE DELINQUENTS the BOARD GAME!

OFFICIAL GAME RULES:

1. DELINQUENTS THE BOARD GAME is played with two dice. Choose a player to go first, then rotate turns clockwise around your party.
2. Each player rolls both dice ONCE per turn unless specified by a draw card or player power.
3. Move forward the number of spaces designated by your dice roll. First person to land on or past the finish line wins.
4. When landing on a state with a requested action, perform said action(s) before the next player can roll!
5. If a player lands in jail, they are to remain there until they roll a seven. This can take multiple turns.

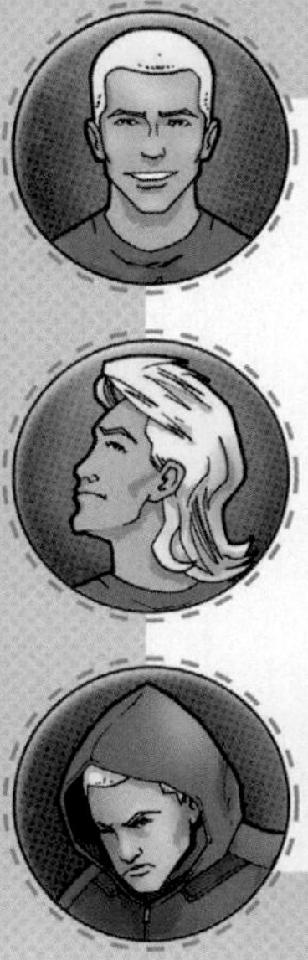

ARCHER

BIO: Raised by a fundamentalist religious cult, Obadiah Archer had only one purpose in life...
kill Armstrong Anni-Padda!
After breaking free from his Sect, Archer partnered with Armstrong and used his vast abilities to combat evil around the world!

PLAYER POWER!

RELIGIOUS ROLLER: If both of your dice are the same number, you've been saved! Move ten spaces ahead of your roll!

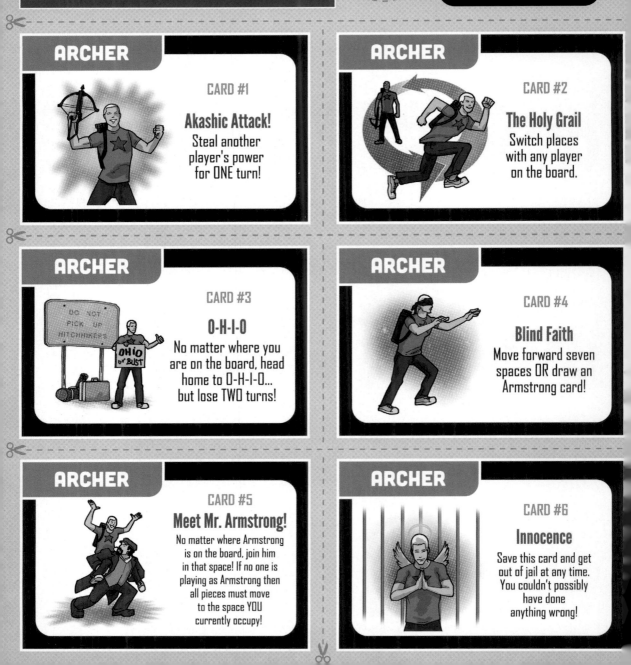

ARCHER

CARD #1

Akashic Attack!

Steal another player's power for ONE turn!

ARCHER

CARD #2

The Holy Grail

Switch places with any player on the board.

ARCHER

DO NOT PICK UP HITCHHIKERS
OHIO or BUST

CARD #3

O-H-I-O

No matter where you are on the board, head home to O-H-I-O... but lose TWO turns!

ARCHER

CARD #4

Blind Faith

Move forward seven spaces OR draw an Armstrong card!

ARCHER

CARD #5

Meet Mr. Armstrong!

No matter where Armstrong is on the board, join him in that space! If no one is playing as Armstrong then all pieces must move to the space YOU currently occupy!

ARCHER

CARD #6

Innocence

Save this card and get out of jail at any time. You couldn't possibly have done anything wrong!

the DELINQUENTS
the BOARD GAME!

WOODY

WOODY

WOODY

WOODY

WOODY

WOODY

The DELINQUENTS the BOARD GAME!

OFFICIAL GAME RULES:

1. DELINQUENTS THE BOARD GAME is played with two dice. Choose a player to go first, then rotate turns clockwise around your party.
2. Each player rolls both dice ONCE per turn unless specified by a draw card or player power.
3. Move forward the number of spaces designated by your dice roll. First person to land on or past the finish line wins.
4. When landing on a state with a requested action, perform said action before the next player can roll! Only one state action per turn!
5. If a player lands in jail, they are to remain there until they roll a seven. This can take multiple turns.

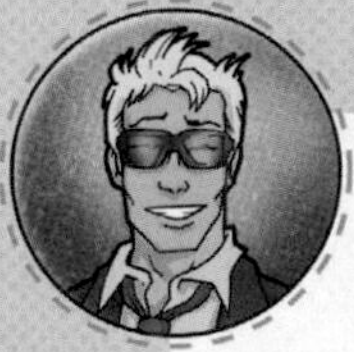

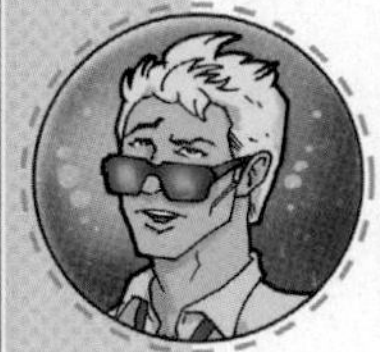

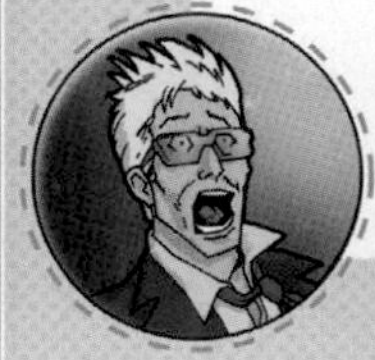

WOODY

BIO: A life-long con man looking for a fresh start, Woody Henderson was investigating his father's murder when he and his adopted brother, Eric, accidentally got their powers. The brothers were bound by experimental energy wristbands, which must be KLANG-ed together every 24 hours or the brothers will disperse into atoms!

PLAYER POWER!

CON ARTIST:
If Woody lands exactly five spaces behind any player, he gets to switch places with them!

WOODY

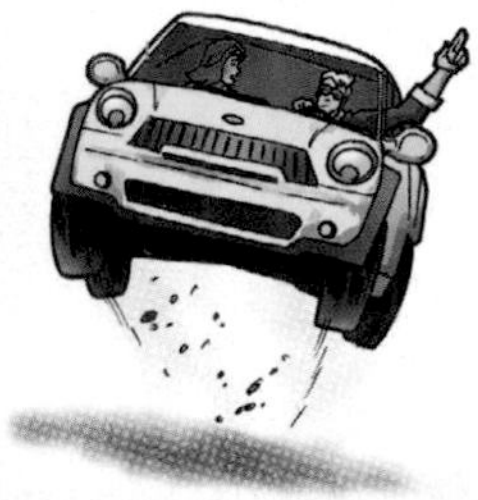

CARD #1

Come On and Take a Free Ride!

Hitch a ride! Move forward four spaces.

WOODY

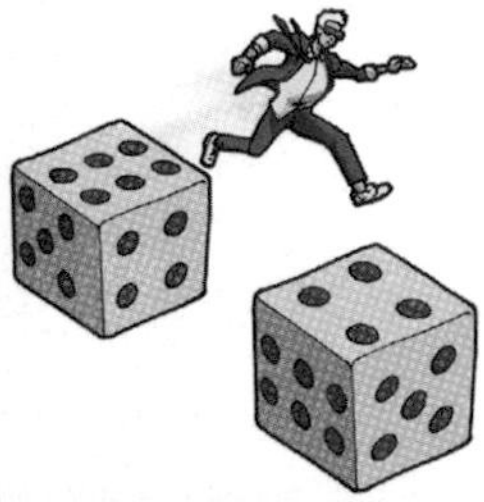

CARD #2

Dicey Proposition

Roll again!

WOODY

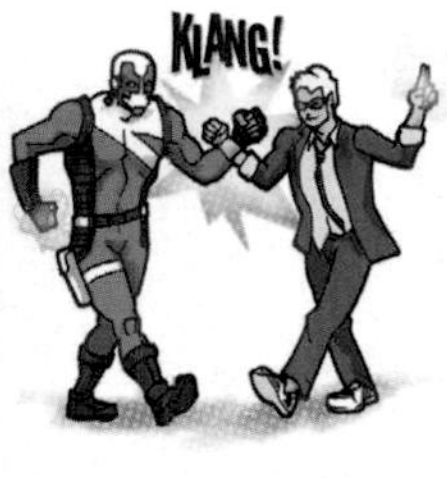
KLANG!

CARD #3

KLANG!

If Quantum is on the board, move him backward or forward to Woody's position.

WOODY

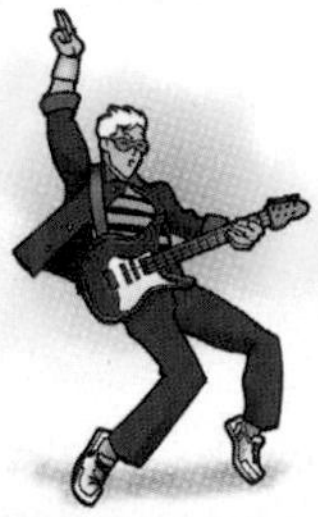

CARD #4

Jailhouse Rock

The food is great in the slammer, but hold this card to get out of jail immediately!

WOODY

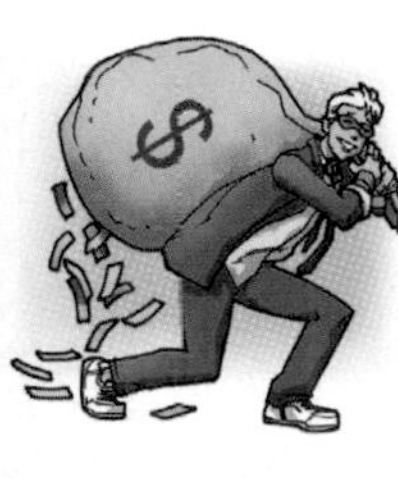

CARD #5

Heroes For Cash

Save the day and move everyone else forward five spaces! As payment, roll twice in a row on your next turn!

WOODY

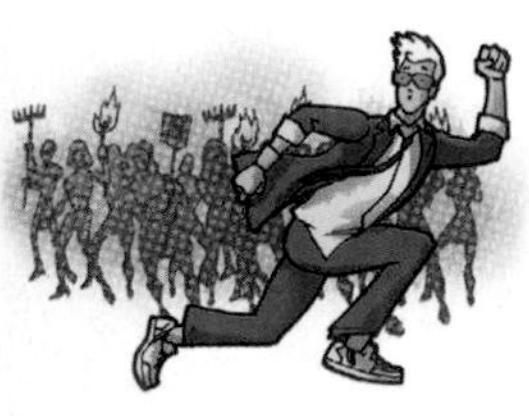

CARD #6

On The Run!

Dash ahead four spaces! Move all other players back four spaces!

the DELINQUENTS

the BOARD GAME!

ARMSTRONG

ARMSTRONG

ARMSTRONG

ARMSTRONG

ARMSTRONG

ARMSTRONG

THE DELINQUENTS: the BOARD GAME!

ARMSTRONG

BIO: An immortal with a penchant for drinking (heavily), Armstrong has lived many lives during his millennia on Earth. Now, Armstrong reunites with his conspiracy-busting best buddy Obadiah Archer (and some guys named Quantum and Woody) to search for the lost treasure of the Hobo King!

PLAYER POWER!

IMMORTAL ROLLER:
Anytime you roll a seven, you get an EXTRA turn! Complete your turn and roll again!

OFFICIAL GAME RULES:

1. DELINQUENTS THE BOARD GAME is played with two dice. Choose a player to go first, then rotate turns clockwise around your party.

2. Each player rolls both dice ONCE per turn unless specified by a draw card or player power.

3. Move forward the number of spaces designated by your dice roll. First person to land on or past the finish line wins.

4. When landing on a state with a requested action, perform said action before the next player can roll! Only one state action per turn!

5. If a player lands in jail, they are to remain there until they roll a seven. This can take multiple turns.

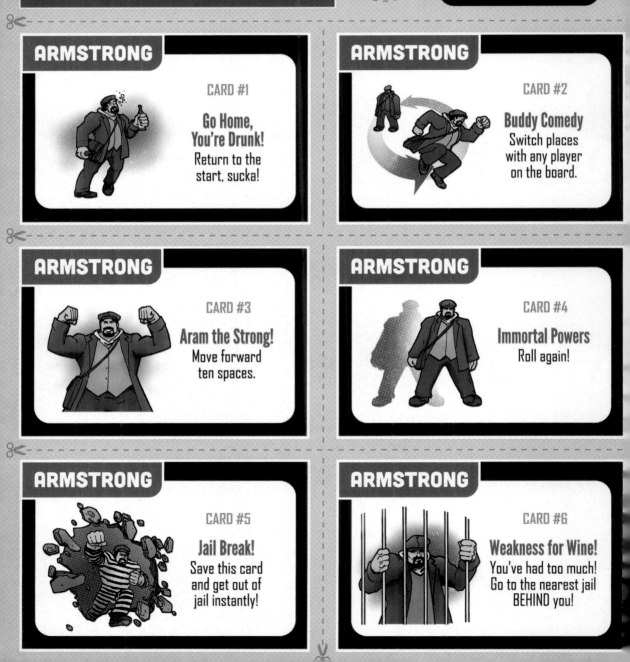

ARMSTRONG

CARD #1

Go Home, You're Drunk!
Return to the start, sucka!

ARMSTRONG

CARD #2

Buddy Comedy
Switch places with any player on the board.

ARMSTRONG

CARD #3

Aram the Strong!
Move forward ten spaces.

ARMSTRONG

CARD #4

Immortal Powers
Roll again!

ARMSTRONG

CARD #5

Jail Break!
Save this card and get out of jail instantly!

ARMSTRONG

CARD #6

Weakness for Wine!
You've had too much! Go to the nearest jail BEHIND you!

the DELINQUENTS
the BOARD GAME!

QUANTUM

QUANTUM

QUANTUM

QUANTUM

QUANTUM

QUANTUM

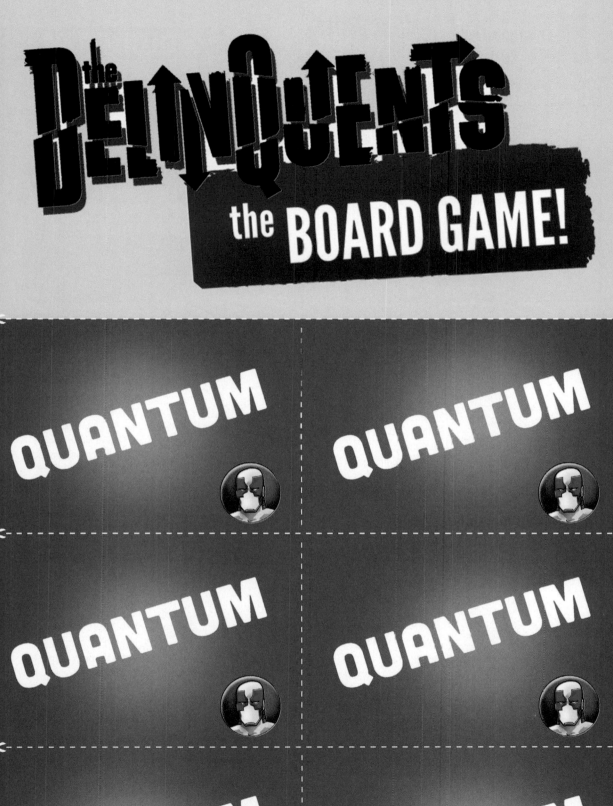

the DELINQUENTS the BOARD GAME!

OFFICIAL GAME RULES:

1) DELINQUENTS THE BOARD GAME is played with two dice. Choose a player to go first, then rotate turns clockwise around your party.
2) Each player rolls both dice ONCE per turn unless specified by a draw card or player power.
3) Move forward the number of spaces designated by your dice roll. First person to land on or past the finish line wins.
4) When landing on a state with a requested action, perform said action before the next player can roll! Only one state action per turn!
5) If a player lands in jail, they are to remain there until they roll a seven. This can take multiple turns.

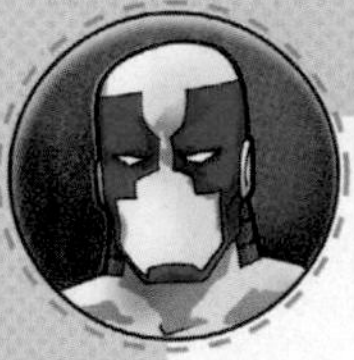
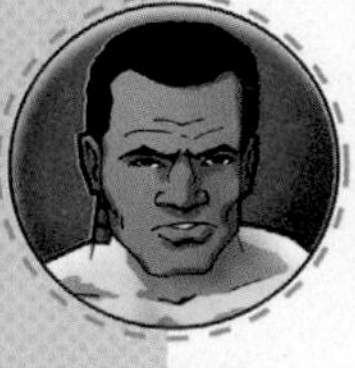
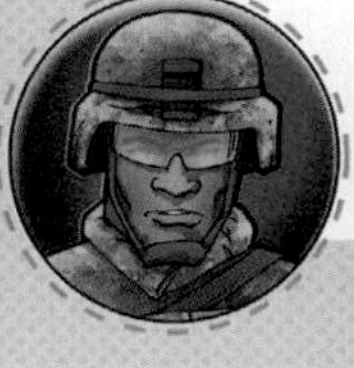

QUANTUM

BIO: A former soldier of the United States Army, Eric Henderson now works as a "Hero For Cash" alongside his adopted brother Woody. Each brother has a powerful control band that gives them incredible powers, but must be KLANG-ed together every 24 hours or the brothers will disintegrate into energy.

PLAYER POWER!

LEADER OF THE PACK:
Quantum cannot be placed in jail, provided he is in the lead!

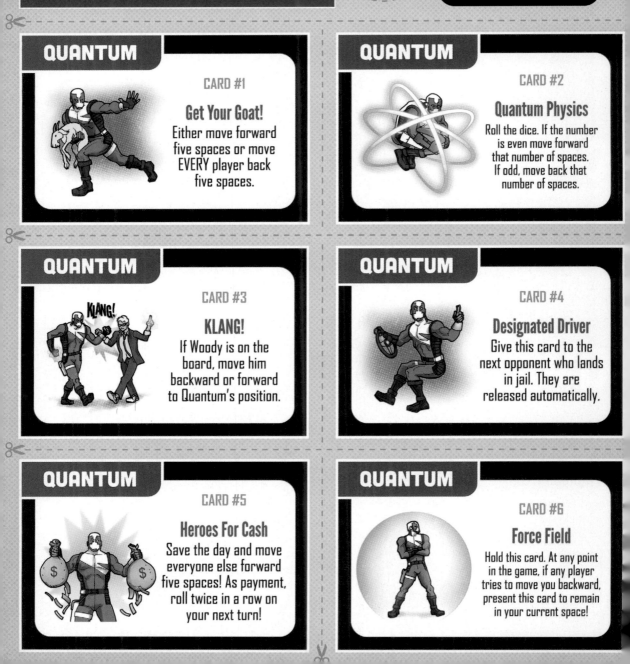

QUANTUM

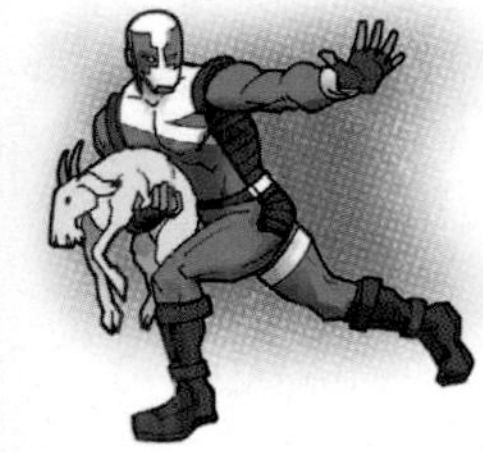

CARD #1

Get Your Goat!
Either move forward five spaces or move EVERY player back five spaces.

QUANTUM

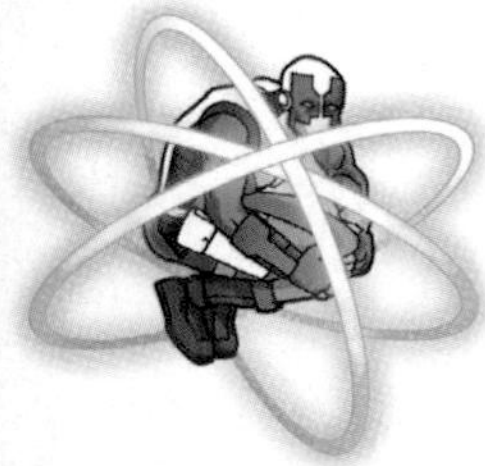

CARD #2

Quantum Physics
Roll the dice. If the number is even move forward that number of spaces. If odd, move back that number of spaces.

QUANTUM

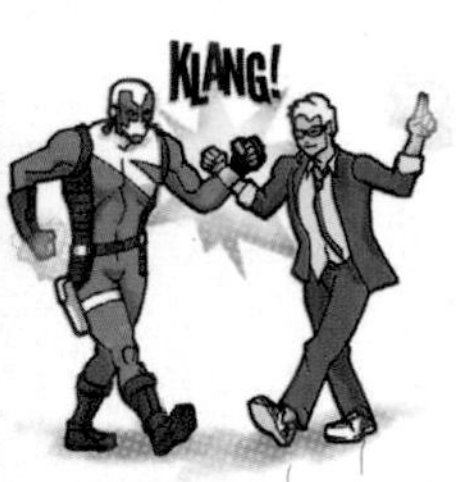
KLANG!

CARD #3

KLANG!
If Woody is on the board, move him backward or forward to Quantum's position.

QUANTUM

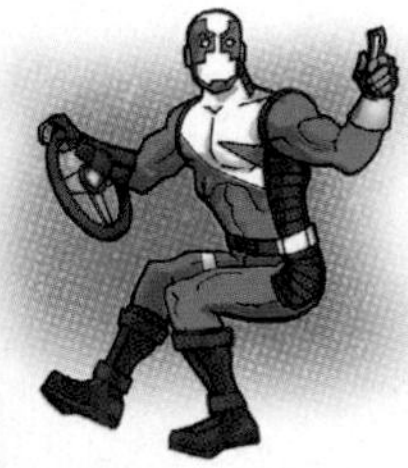

CARD #4

Designated Driver
Give this card to the next opponent who lands in jail. They are released automatically.

QUANTUM

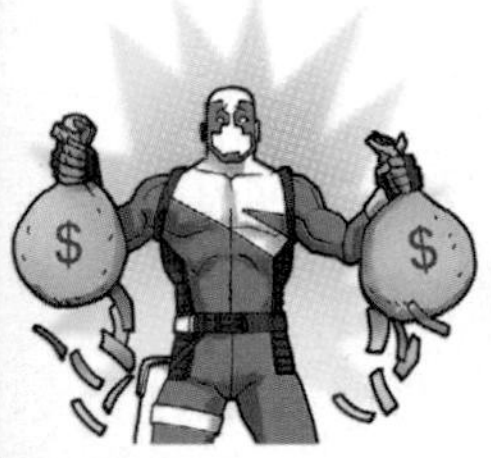
$
$

CARD #5

Heroes For Cash
Save the day and move everyone else forward five spaces! As payment, roll twice in a row on your next turn!

QUANTUM

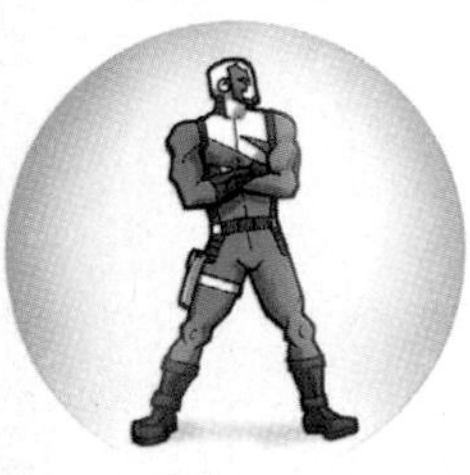

CARD #6

Force Field
Hold this card. At any point in the game, if any player tries to move you backward, present this card to remain in your current space!

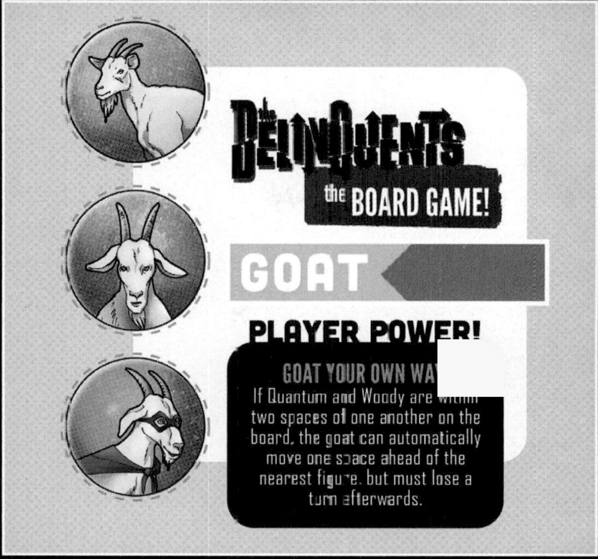
The DELINQUENTS
the BOARD GAME!
GOAT
PLAYER POWER!
GOAT YOUR OWN WA
If Quantum and Woody are within two spaces of one another on the board, the goat can automatically move one space ahead of the nearest figure, but must lose a turn afterwards.

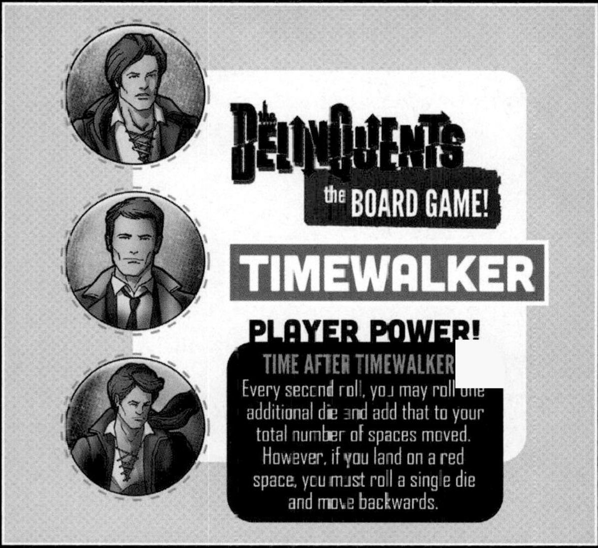
The DELINQUENTS
the BOARD GAME!
TIMEWALKER
PLAYER POWER!
TIME AFTER TIMEWALKER
Every second roll, you may roll one additional die and add that to your total number of spaces moved. However, if you land on a red space, you must roll a single die and move backwards.

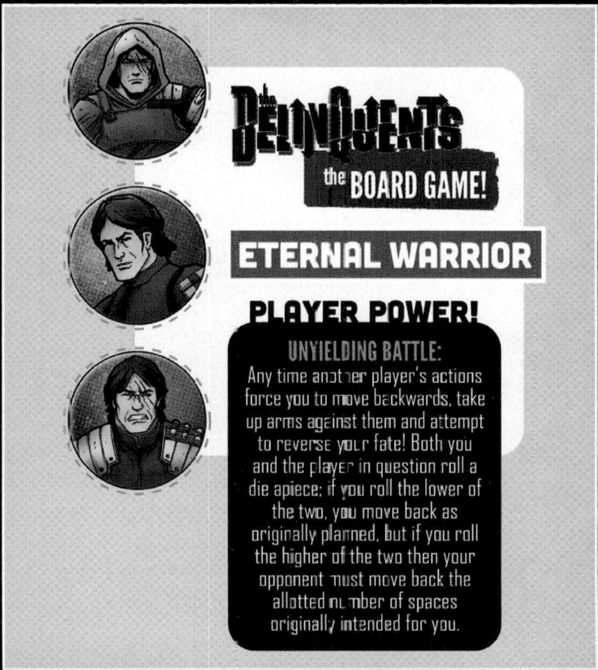
The DELINQUENTS
the BOARD GAME!
ETERNAL WARRIOR
PLAYER POWER!
UNYIELDING BATTLE:
Any time another player's actions force you to move backwards, take up arms against them and attempt to reverse your fate! Both you and the player in question roll a die apiece; if you roll the lower of the two, you move back as originally planned, but if you roll the higher of the two then your opponent must move back the allotted number of spaces originally intended for you.

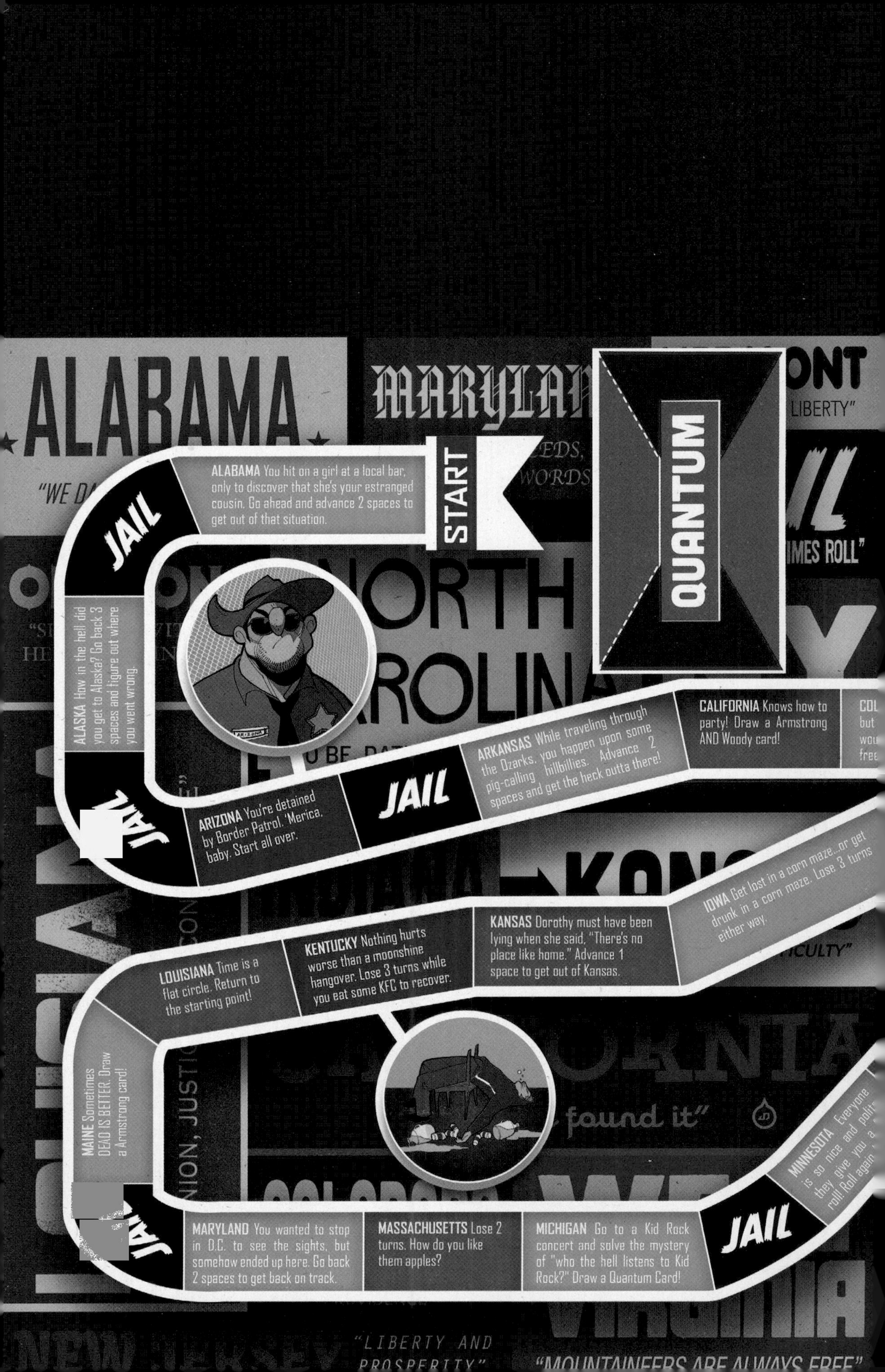START
QUANTUM
ALABAMA You hit on a girl at a local bar, only to discover that she's your estranged cousin. Go ahead and advance 2 spaces to get out of that situation.
JAIL
ALASKA How in the hell did you get to Alaska? Go back 3 spaces and figure out where you went wrong.
JAIL
ARIZONA You're detained by Border Patrol. 'Merica, baby. Start all over.
JAIL
ARKANSAS While traveling through the Ozarks, you happen upon some pig-calling hillbillies. Advance 2 spaces and get the heck outta there!
CALIFORNIA Knows how to party! Draw a Armstrong AND Woody card!
IOWA Get lost in a corn maze...or get drunk in a corn maze. Lose 3 turns either way.
KANSAS Dorothy must have been lying when she said, "There's no place like home." Advance 1 space to get out of Kansas.
KENTUCKY Nothing hurts worse than a moonshine hangover. Lose 3 turns while you eat some KFC to recover.
LOUISIANA Time is a flat circle. Return to the starting point!
MAINE Sometimes DEAD IS BETTER. Draw a Armstrong card!
JAIL
MARYLAND You wanted to stop in D.C. to see the sights, but somehow ended up here. Go back 2 spaces to get back on track.
MASSACHUSETTS Lose 2 turns. How do you like them apples?
MICHIGAN Go to a Kid Rock concert and solve the mystery of "who the hell listens to Kid Rock?" Draw a Quantum Card!
JAIL
MINNESOTA Everyone is so nice and polite they give you a roll! Roll again
ALABAMA
"WE DA
MARYLAN
LIBERTY"
"LIBERTY AND PROSPERITY"
"MOUNTAINEERS ARE ALWAYS FREE"
NORTH CAROLINA
found it"

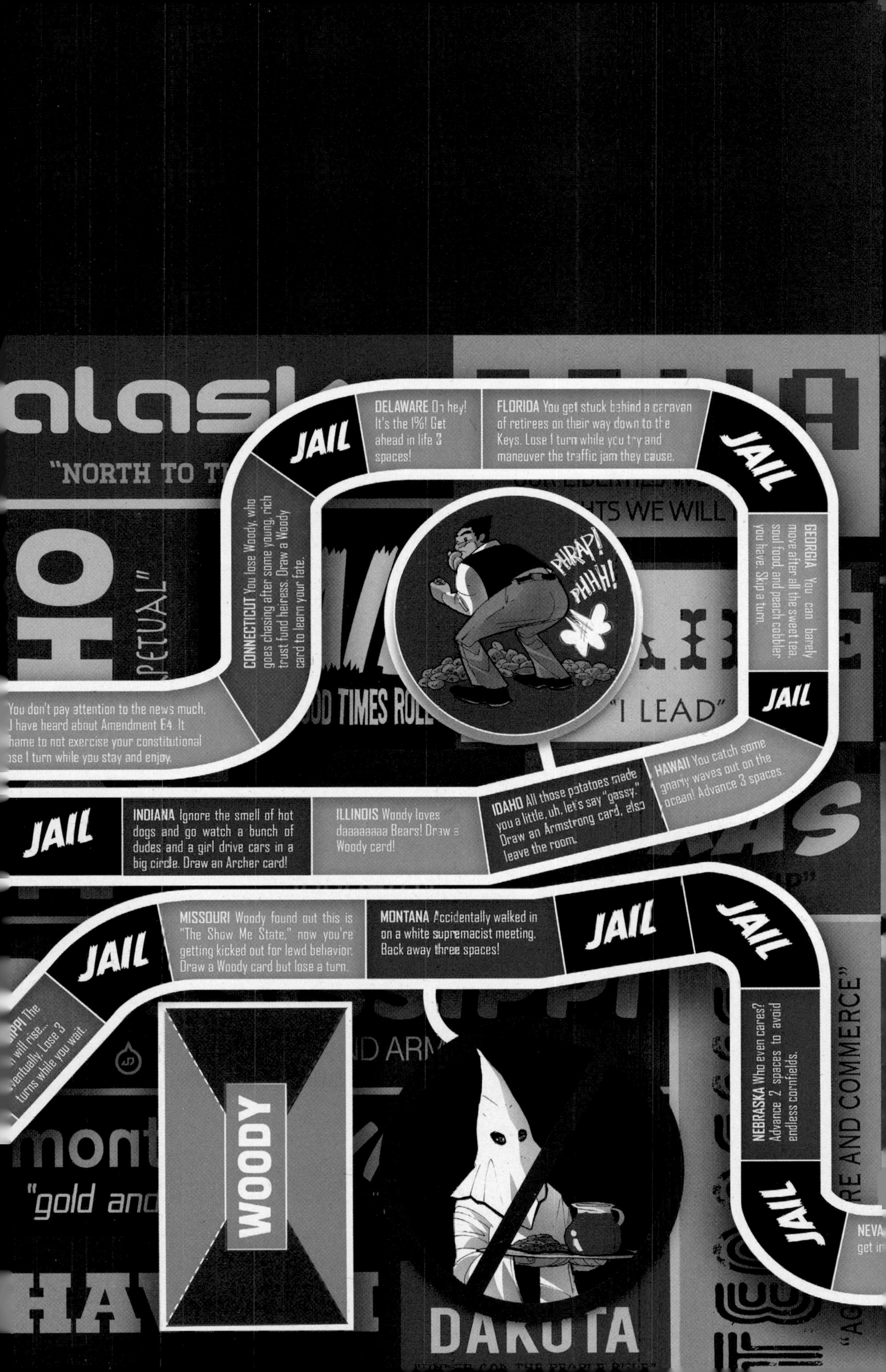

DELAWARE Oh hey! It's the 1%! Get ahead in life 3 spaces!
FLORIDA You get stuck behind a caravan of retirees on their way down to the Keys. Lose 1 turn while you try and maneuver the traffic jam they cause.
JAIL
JAIL
CONNECTICUT You lose Woody, who goes chasing after some young, rich trust fund heiress. Draw a Woody card to learn your fate.
GEORGIA You can barely move after all the sweet tea, soul food, and peach cobbler you have. Skip a turn.
PHRAP! PHHH!
JAIL
You don't pay attention to the news much, I have heard about Amendment E4. It hame to not exercise your constitutional ose 1 turn while you stay and enjoy.
HAWAII You catch some gnarly waves out on the ocean! Advance 3 spaces.
IDAHO All those potatoes made you a little, uh, let's say "gassy." Draw an Armstrong card, also leave the room.
JAIL
INDIANA Ignore the smell of hot dogs and go watch a bunch of dudes and a girl drive cars in a big circle. Draw an Archer card!
ILLINOIS Woody loves daaaaaaaa Bears! Draw a Woody card!
JAIL
MISSOURI Woody found out this is "The Show Me State," now you're getting kicked out for lewd behavior. Draw a Woody card but lose a turn.
MONTANA Accidentally walked in on a white supremacist meeting. Back away three spaces!
JAIL
JAIL
IPPI The will rise... ventually. Lose 3 turns while you wait.
NEBRASKA Who even cares? Advance 2 spaces to avoid endless cornfields.
WOODY
JAIL
NEVA get ir
alask
"NORTH TO TH
HO
PETUAL"
HTS WE WILL
OOD TIMES ROLL
"I LEAD"
ND ARM
mont
"gold and
HAW
DAKOTA
RE AND COMMERCE"
"AG

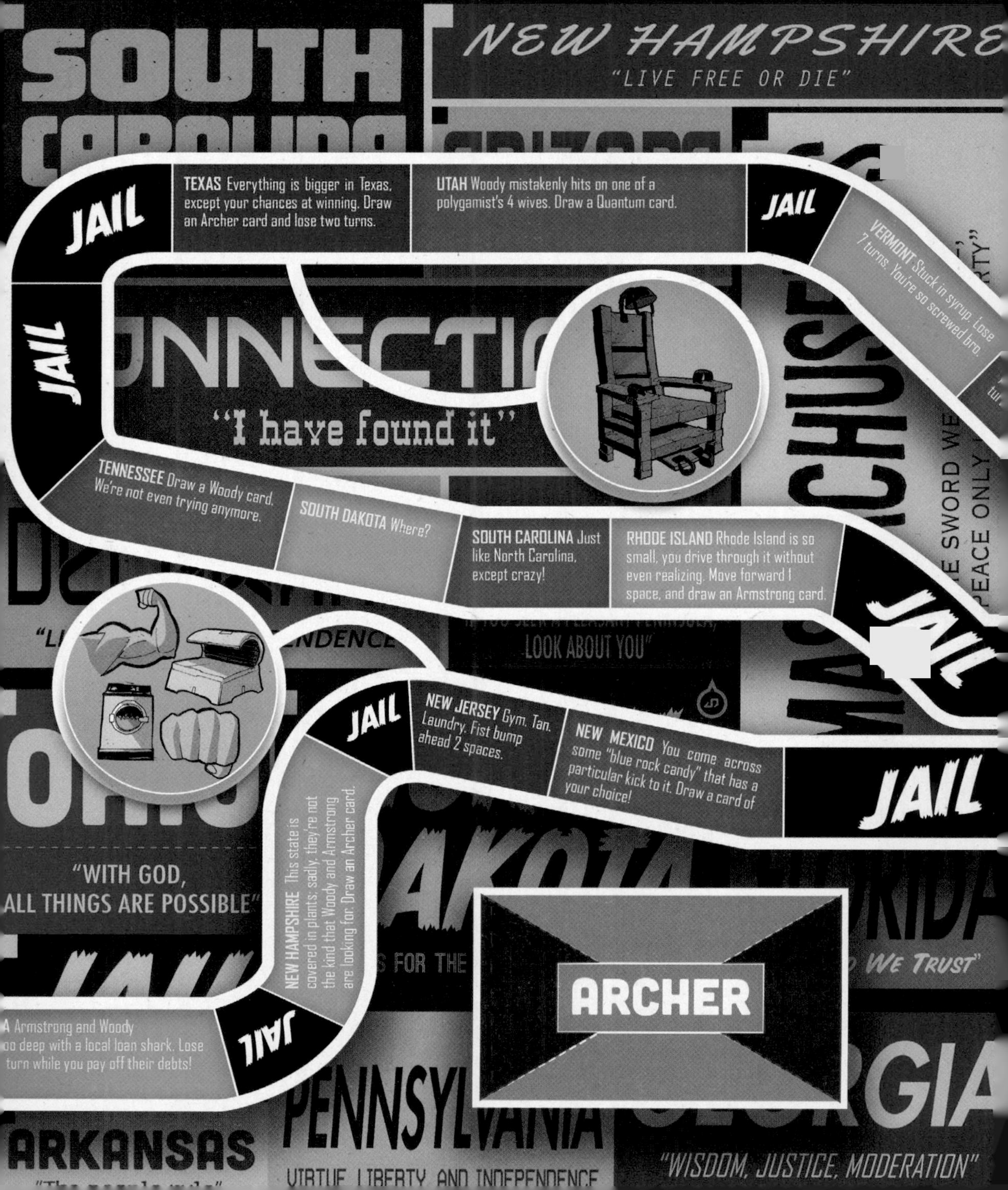

SOUTH
NEW HAMPSHIRE
"LIVE FREE OR DIE"
JAIL
TEXAS Everything is bigger in Texas, except your chances at winning. Draw an Archer card and lose two turns.
UTAH Woody mistakenly hits on one of a polygamist's 4 wives. Draw a Quantum card.
JAIL
VERMONT Stuck in syrup. Lose 7 turns. You're so screwed bro.
JAIL
"I have found it"
TENNESSEE Draw a Woody card. We're not even trying anymore.
SOUTH DAKOTA Where?
SOUTH CAROLINA Just like North Carolina, except crazy!
RHODE ISLAND Rhode Island is so small, you drive through it without even realizing. Move forward 1 space, and draw an Armstrong card.
JAIL
LOOK ABOUT YOU"
JAIL
NEW JERSEY Gym. Tan. Laundry. Fist bump ahead 2 spaces.
NEW MEXICO You come across some "blue rock candy" that has a particular kick to it. Draw a card of your choice!
JAIL
"WITH GOD, ALL THINGS ARE POSSIBLE"
NEW HAMPSHIRE This state is covered in plants; sadly, they're not the kind that Woody and Armstrong are looking for. Draw an Archer card.
ARCHER
Armstrong and Woody go deep with a local loan shark. Lose turn while you pay off their debts!
JAIL
PENNSYLVANIA
VIRTUE, LIBERTY, AND INDEPENDENCE
ARKANSAS
"WISDOM, JUSTICE, MODERATION"

ARMSTRONG

FINISH

WYOMING The goat uses her laser vision to enhance the eruptive powers of Old Faithful. Advance to finish as you ride the eruption.

AS IT GOES

R COUNTRY BATTLE

WISCONSIN Armstrong makes a comment about how the Packers suck. Go back 2 spaces to avoid an attack from angry Cheese Heads. Draw a Woody card.

...VA You joined a fraternity. Now get hazed for 3 ...you can escape!

JAIL

WASHINGTON You take up the local trend of wearing socks with sandals, which helps you blend in, but destroys your self-respect and slows you down. Go back 1 space.

WEST VIRGINIA Hillbillies vs. rednecks. Who you got? Draw an Armstrong card.

JAIL

JAIL

PENNSYLVANIA So much for the "City of Brotherly Love." Eric and Woody get arrested after Woody accidently "KLANGs" the Liberty Bell. Lose a turn while you get those bros out of the dangerous Philly jail.

OREGON You are attacked by a pack of fixie-riding hipsters.

OKLAHOMA OⅢⅢ00000000...ok, screw it. Just lose a turn.

NEW YORK Be sure to visit Valiant HQ! Actually don't, that's crazy. Draw a Woody card.

JAIL

**ATIONAL UNION"

OHIO Now that LeBron is back there, draw an Archer card!

"LET THE WELFARE ... OPL...
BE THE SUPR...

JAIL

NORTH CAROLINA The goat gets carried away and eats an entire tobacco field. Draw a Quantum card to learn your fate.

NORTH DAKOTA You come across some dude putting another guy into a wood-chipper. Don't even wanna know what that's about. Let's draw an Armstrong card.

"EQUALITY BEFORE THE LAW"

GALLERY

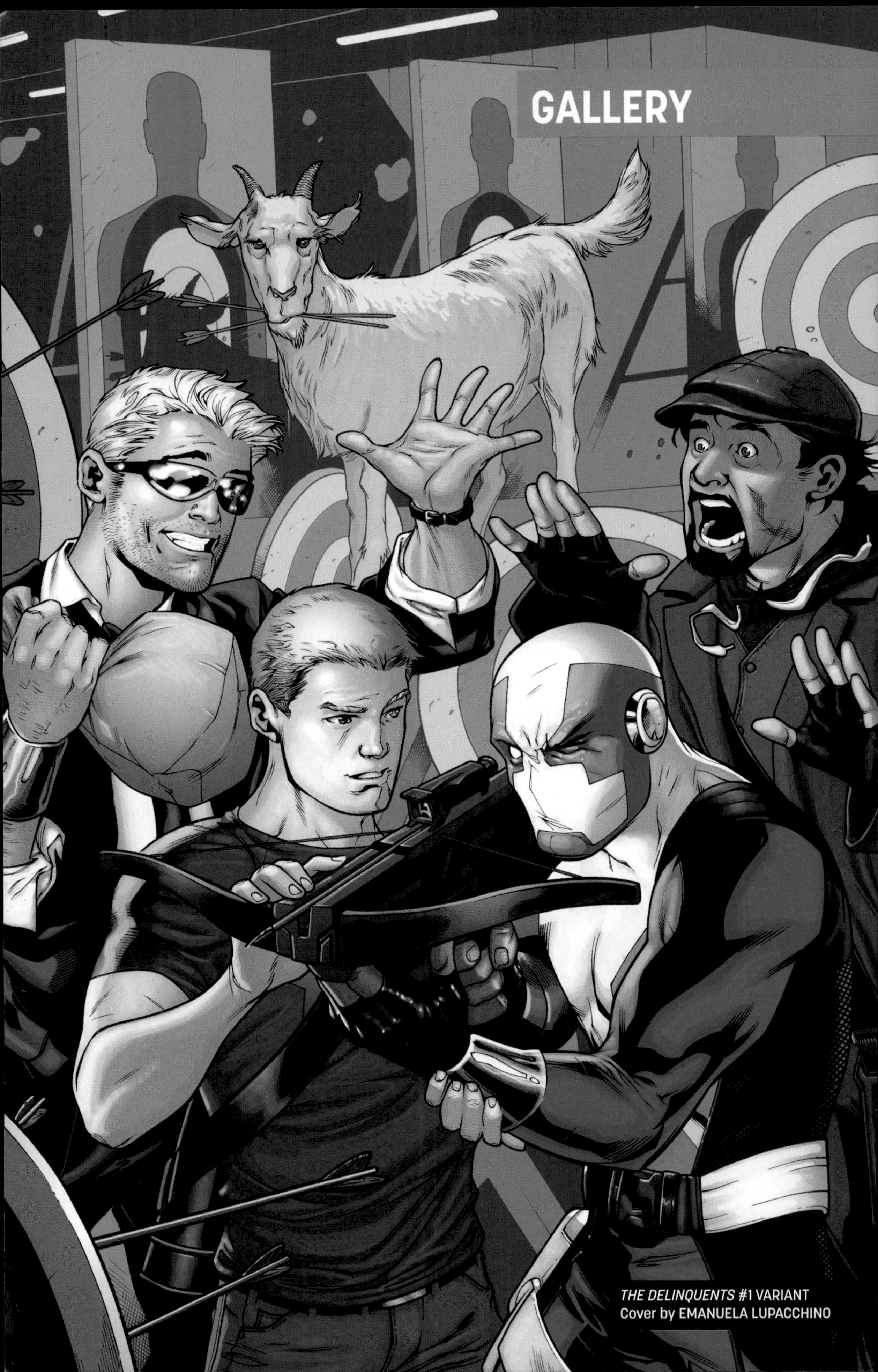

THE DELINQUENTS #1 VARIANT
Cover by EMANUELA LUPACCHINO

THE DELINQUENTS #2 VARIANT
Cover by SHAWN CRYSTAL

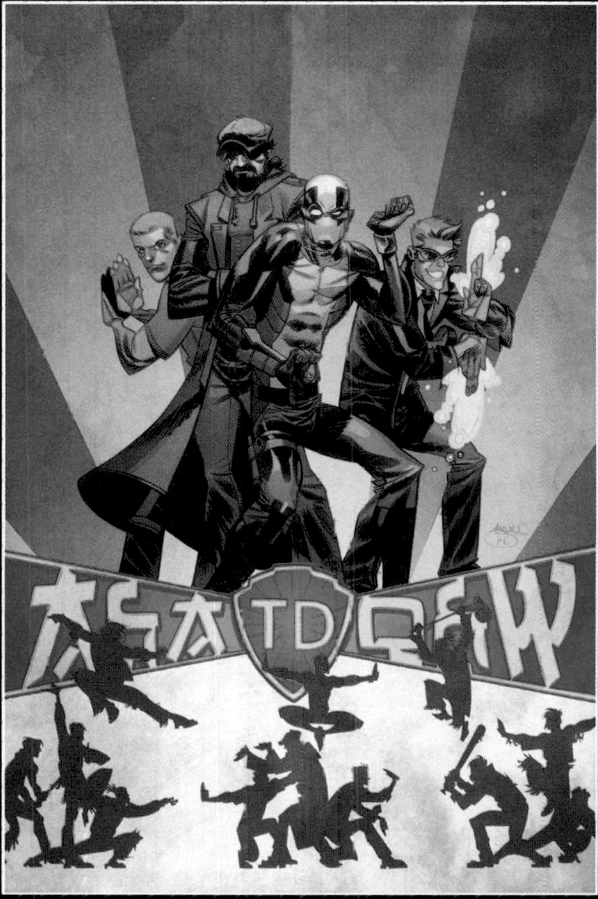
TD

THE DELINQUENTS #3 VARIANT
Cover by KHARI EVANS

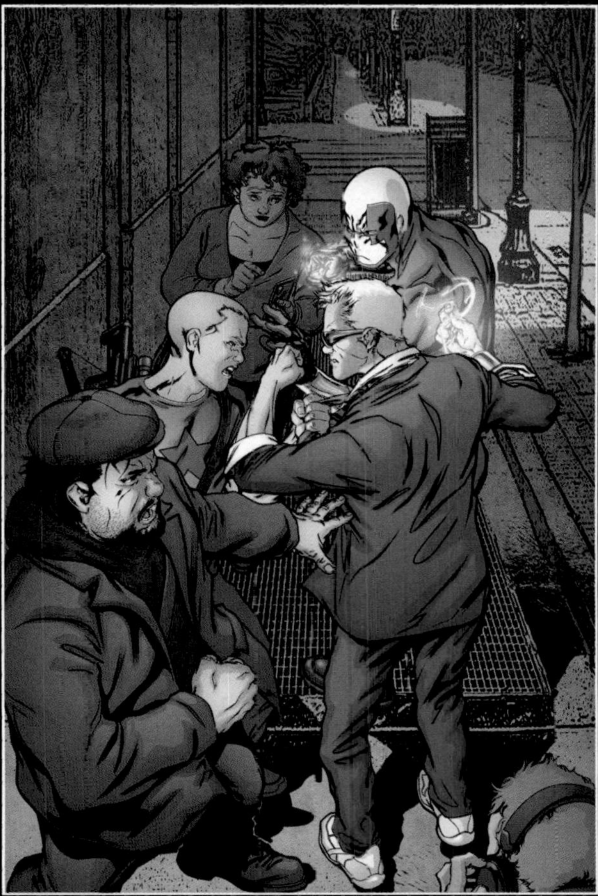

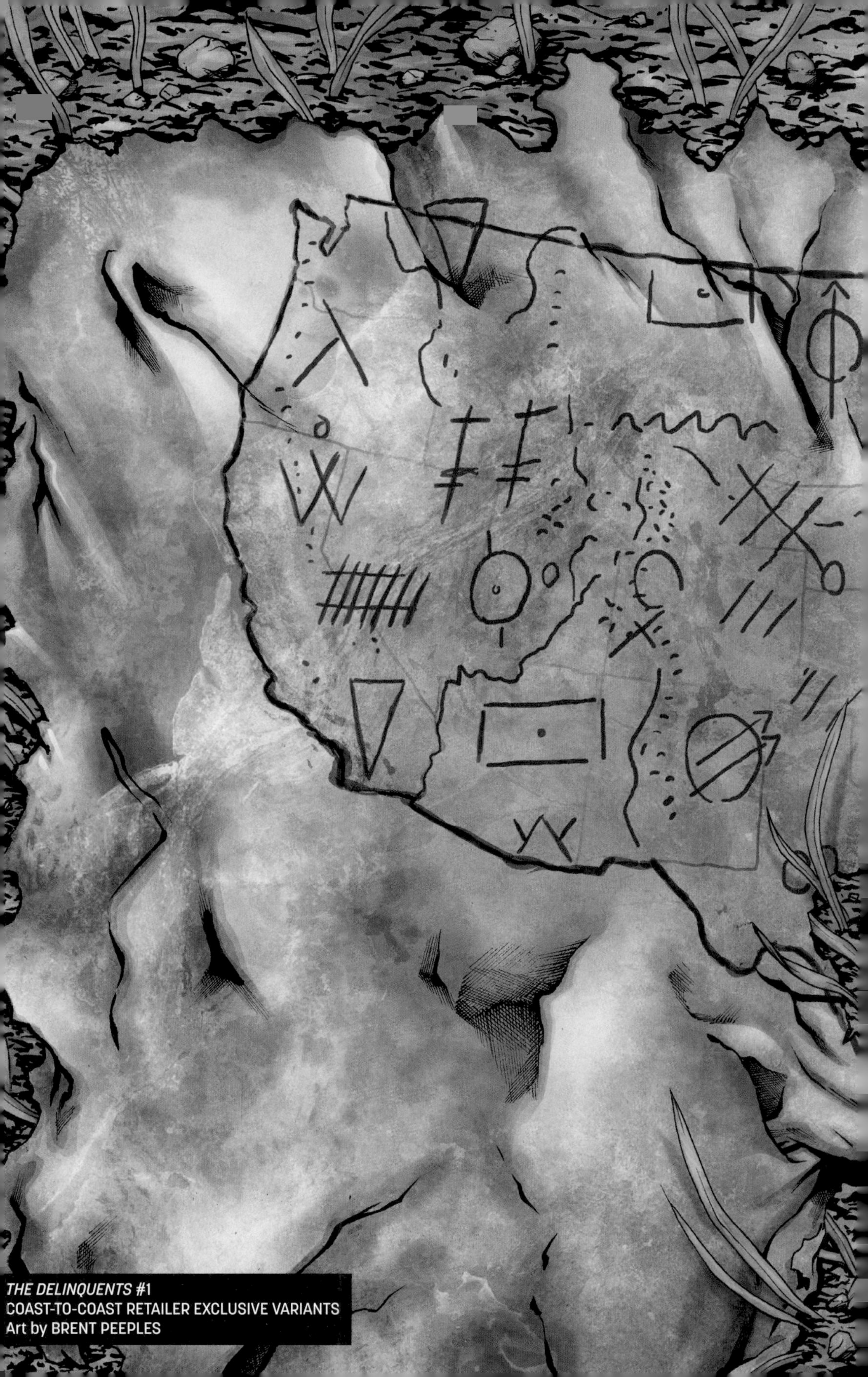

THE DELINQUENTS #1
COAST-TO-COAST RETAILER EXCLUSIVE VARIANTS
Art by BRENT PEEPLES

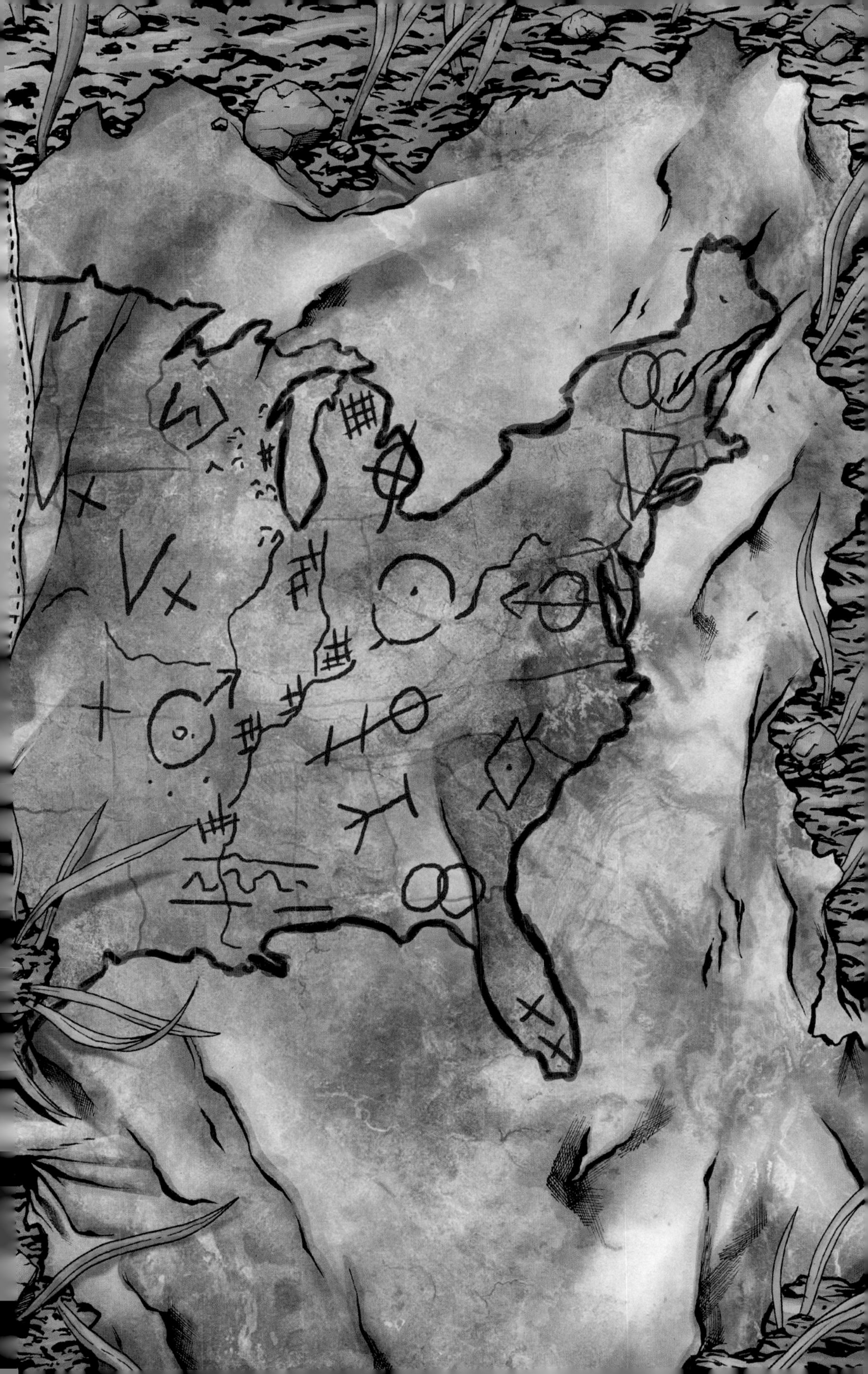

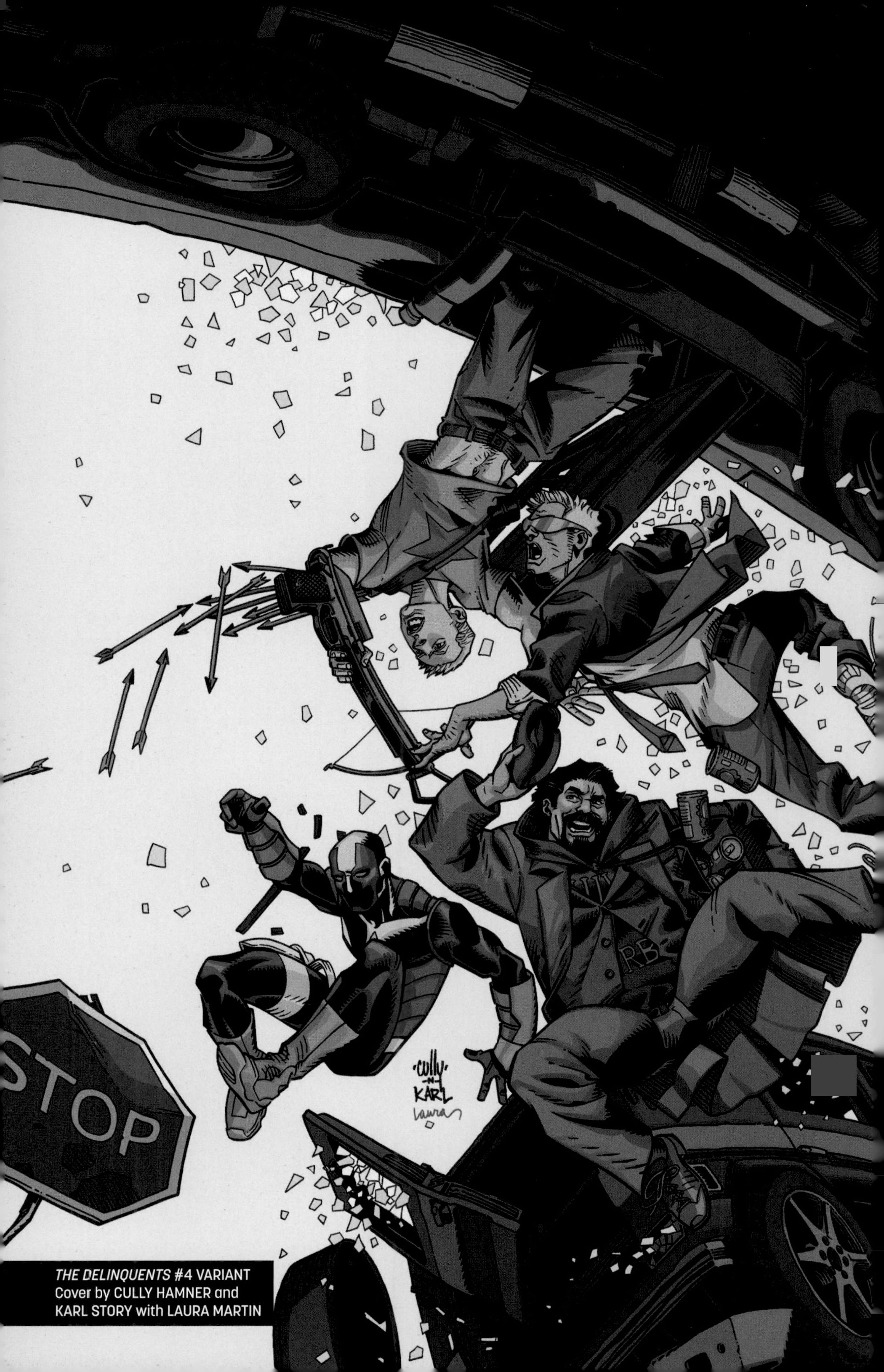
STOP
CULLY -N- KARL
Laura

THE DELINQUENTS #4 VARIANT
Cover by CULLY HAMNER and
KARL STORY with LAURA MARTIN

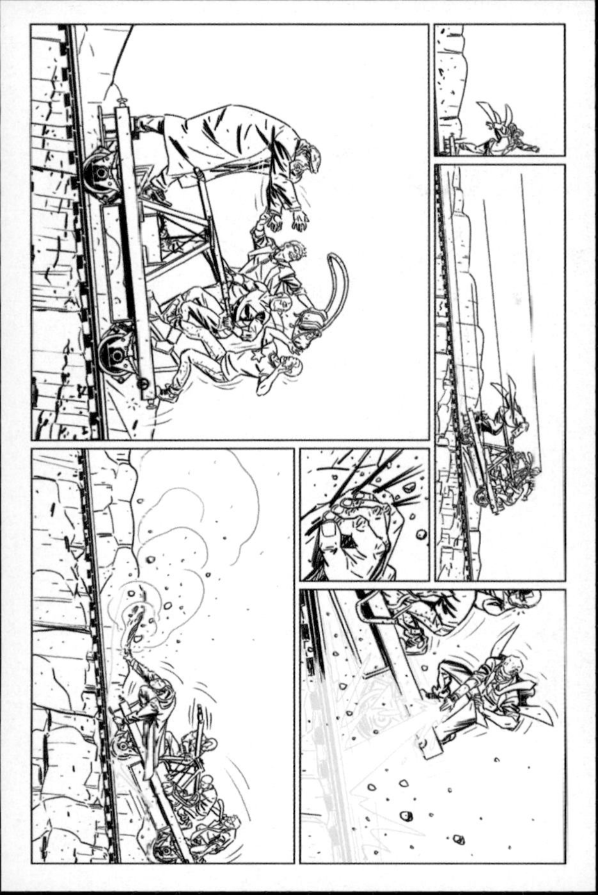

THE DELINQUENTS #4, p.5
Art by KANO

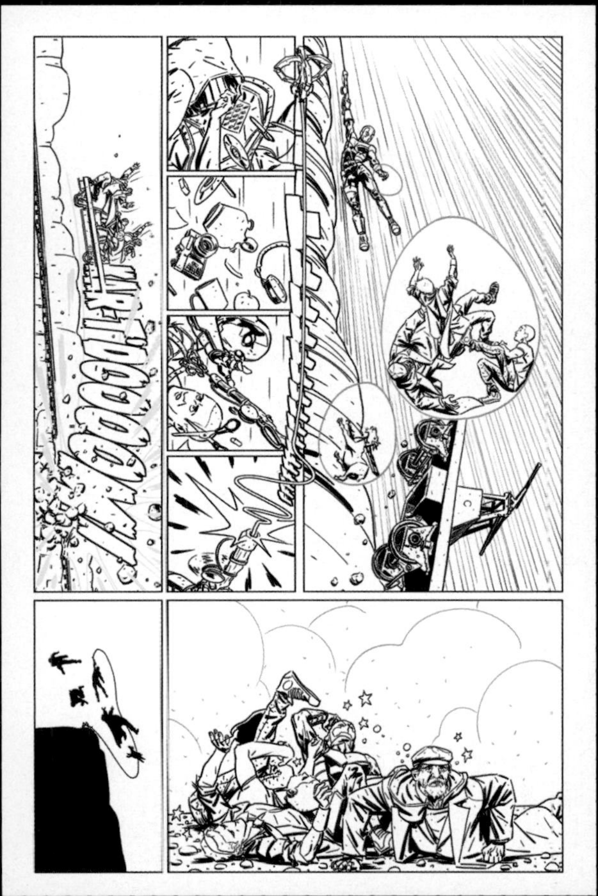

THE DELINQUENTS #4, p.6
Art by KANO

THE DELINQUENTS #4, p.7
Art by KANO

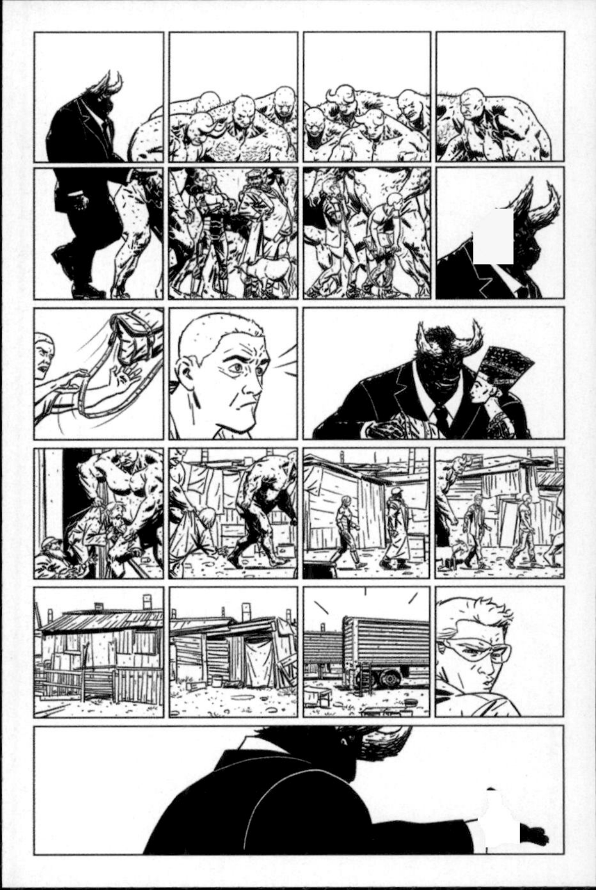

THE DELINQUENTS #4, p.8
Art by KANO

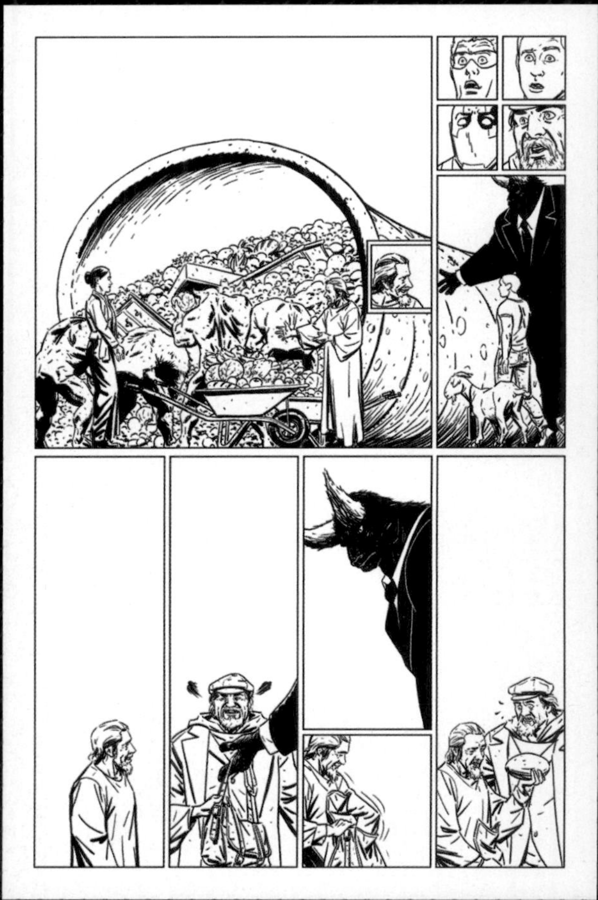

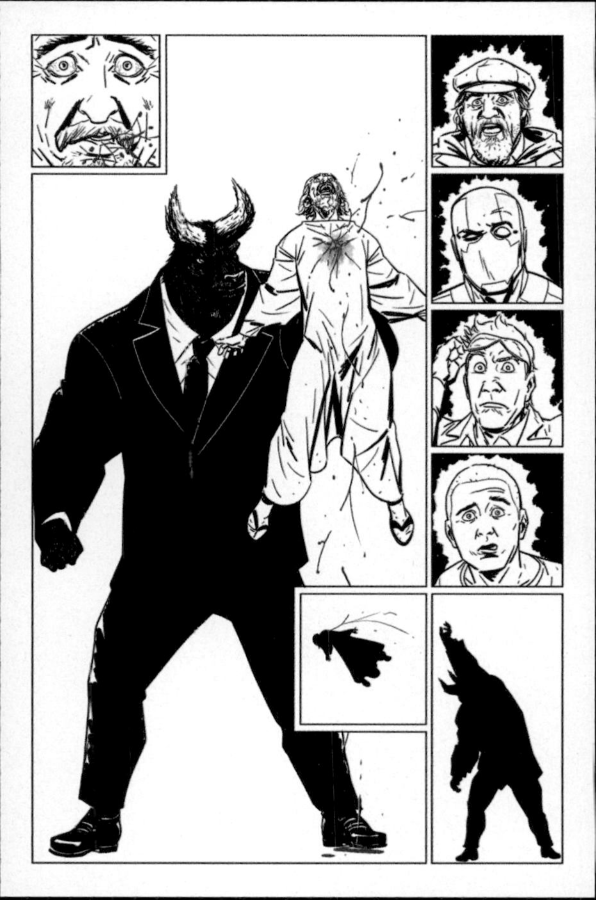

THE DELINQUENTS #4,
Art by KANO

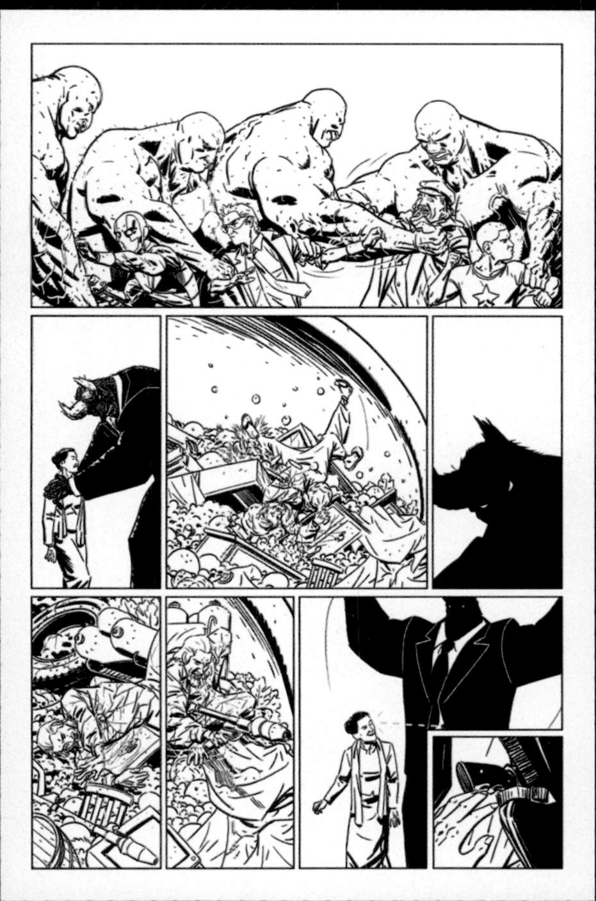

THE DELINQUENTS #4,
Art by KANO

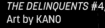

VALIANT® DELUXE HARDCOVERS

ROBERT VENDITTI | CARY NORD | LEE GARBETT
TREVOR HAIRSINE | STEFANO GAUDIANO | MOOSE BAUMANN
VALIANT
X-O MANOWAR
DELUXE EDITION 1

X-O MANOWAR DELUXE EDITION BOOK 1

Writer: Robert Venditti | Artists: Cary Nord, Lee Garbett, and Trevor Hairsine
ISBN: 9781939346100 | Diamond Code: AUG131497 | Price: $39.99 |
Format: Oversized HC

Aric of Dacia, a fifth-century Visigoth armed with the universe's most powerful weapon, is all that stands between the Earth and all-out annihilation at the hands of the alien race that abducted him from his own time. Stranded in the modern day, X-O Manowar's battle against the Vine will take him into the shadows with the lethal operative known as Ninjak–and launch a quest for vengeance that will bring an alien empire to its knees. The Vine destroyed Aric's world. Now he will give them war.

Collecting X-O MANOWAR #1-14 and more than 20 pages of bonus materials!

JOSHUA DYSART | KHARI EVANS | TREVOR HAIRSINE
MICO SUAYAN | IAN HANNIN
VALIANT
HARBINGER
DELUXE EDITION 1

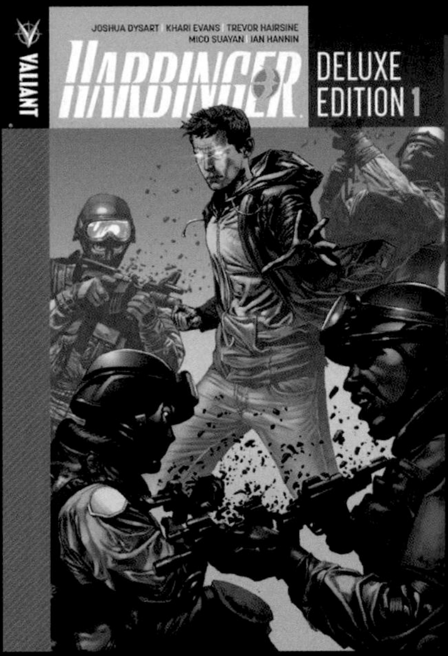

HARBINGER DELUXE EDITION BOOK 1

Writer: Joshua Dysart | Artists: Khari Evans, Trevor Hairsine, Barry Kitson, and Lee Garbett
ISBN: 9781939346131 | Diamond Code: SEP131373 | Price: $39.99 | Format: Oversized HC

Outside the law. Inside your head. You've never met a team of super-powered teenagers quite like the Renegades. Skipping across the country in a desperate attempt to stay one step ahead of the authorities, psionically powered teenager Peter Stanchek only has one option left–run. But he won't have to go it alone. As the shadowy corporation known as the Harbinger Foundation draws close on all sides, Peter will have to find and recruit other unique individuals like himself...other troubled, immensely powerful youths with abilities beyond their control. Their mission? Bring the fight back to the Harbinger Foundation's founder Toyo Harada–and dismantle his global empire brick by brick...

Collecting HARBINGER #0-14 and more than 20 pages of bonus materials!

DUANE SWIERCZYNSKI | MANUEL GARCIA
BARRY KITSON | ARTURO LOZZI | STEFANO GAUDIANO
VALIANT
BLOODSHOT
DELUXE EDITION 1

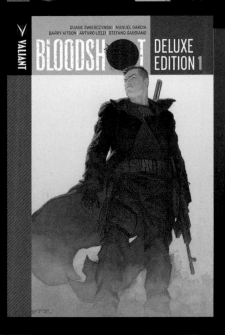

BLOODSHOT DELUXE EDITION BOOK 1

Writer: Duane Swierczynski | Artists: Manuel García, Barry Kitson, Matthew Clark, and Arturo Lozzi
ISBN: 9781939346216 | Diamond Code: JAN141376 | Price: $39.99 | Format: Oversized HC

You have no name, just a project designation. They call you Bloodshot, but the voices inside your head call you "daddy, "sir," "commander," "comrade"–whatever it takes to motivate you to get the job done. But after so many missions and so many lives, you're finally ready to confront your handlers at Project Rising Spirit and find out who you really are. You'd better move quickly, though, because your former masters don't like it when a billion-dollar weapons project goes rogue. And wherever you go, all hell is sure to follow...

Collecting BLOODSHOT #1-13 and more than 20 pages of bonus materials!

VALIANT® DELUXE HARDCOVERS

VALIANT
FRED VAN LENTE | CLAYTON HENRY
EMANUELA LUPACCHINO | PERE PÉREZ
ARCHER & ARMSTRONG
DELUXE EDITION 1

ARCHER & ARMSTRONG DELUXE EDITION BOOK 1

Writer: Fred Van Lente | Artists: Clayton Henry, Emanuela Lupacchino, Pere Pérez, and Álvaro Martínez

ISBN: 9781939346223 | Diamond Code: FEB141484 | Price: $39.99 | Format: Oversized HC

Join one of the most acclaimed adventures in comics as naive teenage assassin Obadiah Archer and the fun-loving, hard-drinking immortal called Armstrong unite to stop a plot ten thousand years in the making! From the lost temples of ancient Sumeria to modern-day Wall Street, Area 51, and beyond, Valiant's conspiracy-smashing adventurers are going on a globe-trotting quest to bring down the unholy coalition of cultists known as the Sect–and stop each of history's most notorious conspiracies from remaking the world in their own insane image.

Collecting ARCHER & ARMSTRONG #0-13 and more than 20 pages of bonus materials!

VALIANT
HARBINGER WARS
DELUXE EDITION 1

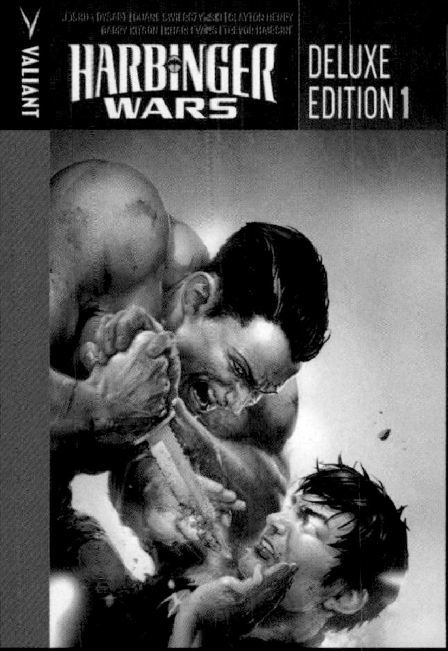

HARBINGER WARS DELUXE EDITION

Writer: Joshua Dysart & Duane Swierczynski | Artists: Clayton Henry, Pere Pérez, Barry Kitson, Khari Evans, Trevor Hairsine, Mico Suayan, and Clayton Crain

ISBN: 9781939346322 | Diamond Code: MAR141422 | **Price: $39.99 | Format: Oversized HC**

Re-presenting Valiant's best-selling crossover event in complete chronological order!

When an untrained and undisciplined team of super-powered test subjects escapes from Project Rising Spirit and onto the Vegas Strip, Bloodshot and the Harbinger Renegades will find themselves locked in battle against a deadly succession of opponents–and each other. As the combined forces of the H.A.R.D. Corps, Bloodshot, and omega-level telekinetic Toyo Harada all descend on Las Vegas to vie for control of Rising Spirit's deadliest assets, the world is about to discover the shocking price of an all-out superhuman conflict...and no one will escape unscathed. Who will survive the Harbinger Wars?

Collecting HARBINGER WARS #1-4, HARBINGER #11-14, BLOODSHOT #10-13, material from the HARBINGER WARS SKETCHBOOK, and more than 20 pages of bonus materials!

VALIANT
JUSTIN JORDAN | PATRICK ZIRCHER
NEIL EDWARDS | LEE GARBETT
SHADOWMAN
DELUXE EDITION 1

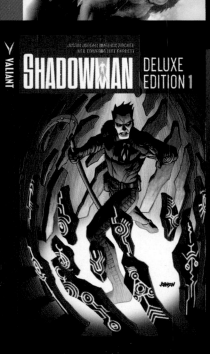

SHADOWMAN DELUXE EDITION BOOK 1

Writers: Justin Jordan and Patrick Zircher | Artists: Patrick Zircher, Neil Edwards, Lee Garbett, Diego Bernard, Roberto de la Torre, Mico Suayan, and Lewis LaRosa

ISBN: 9781939346438 | Price: $39.99 | Format: Oversized HC | COMING SOON

There are a million dreams in the Big Easy. But now its worst nightmare is about to come true. As the forces of darkness prepare to claim New Orleans as their own, Jack Boniface must accept the legacy he was born to uphold. As Shadowman, Jack is about to become the only thing that stands between his city and an army of unspeakable monstrosities from beyond the night. But what is the true cost of the Shadowman's otherworldly power? And can Jack master his new abilities before Master Darque brings down the wall between reality and the otherwordly dimension known only as the Deadside?

Collecting SHADOWMAN #0-10 and more than 20 pages of bonus materials!

VALIANT®

TRADE PAPERBACKS

VALIANT
TO KILL A KING
UNITY

UNITY VOL. 1: TO KILL A KING
ISBN: 9781939346261 | Diamond Code: JAN141356 | Price: $14.99 | Format: TP

UNITY VOL. 2: TRAPPED BY WEBNET
ISBN: 97819393463461 | Diamond Code: MAY141658 | Price: $14.99 | Format: TP

VALIANT
BY THE SWORD
X-O MANOWAR

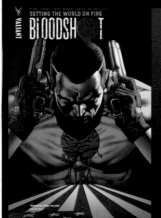

X-O MANOWAR VOL. 1: BY THE SWORD
ISBN: 9780979640995 | Diamond Code: OCT121241 | Price: $9.99 | Format: TP

X-O MANOWAR VOL. 2: ENTER NINJAK
ISBN: 9780979640940 | Diamond Code: JAN131306 | Price: $14.99 | Format: TP

X-O MANOWAR VOL. 3: PLANET DEATH
ISBN: 9781939346087 | Diamond Code: JUN131325 | Price: $14.99 | Format: TP

X-O MANOWAR VOL. 4: HOMECOMING
ISBN: 9781939346179 | Diamond Code: OCT131347 | Price: $14.99 | Format: TP

X-O MANOWAR VOL. 5: AT WAR WITH UNITY
ISBN: 9781939346247 | Diamond Code: FEB141472 | Price: $14.99 | Format: TP

X-O MANOWAR VOL. 6: prelude to armor hunters
ISBN: 9781939346407 | Diamond Code: JUN141513 | Price: $14.99 | Format: TP

VALIANT
SETTING THE WORLD ON FIRE
BLOODSHOT

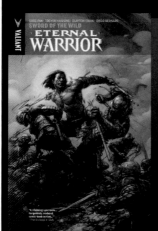

BLOODSHOT VOL. 1: SETTING THE WORLD ON FIRE
ISBN: 9780979640964 | Diamond Code: DEC121274 | Price: $9.99 | Format: TP

BLOODSHOT VOL. 2: THE RISE AND THE FALL
ISBN: 9781939346032| Diamond Code: APR131280 | Price: $14.99 | Format: TP

BLOODSHOT VOL. 3: HARBINGER WARS
ISBN: 9781939346124 | Diamond Code: AUG131494 | Price: $14.99 | Format: TP

BLOODSHOT VOL. 4: H.A.R.D. CORPS
ISBN: 9781939346193 | Diamond Code: NOV131275 | Price: $14.99 | Format: TP

BLOODSHOT VOL. 5: GET SOME!
ISBN: 9781939346315 | Diamond Code: JUN141514 | Price: $14.99 | Format: TP

VALIANT
SWORD OF THE WILD
ETERNAL WARRIOR

ETERNAL WARRIOR VOL. 1: SWORD OF THE WILD
ISBN: 9781939346209 | Diamond Code: NOV131271 | Price: $9.99 | Format: TP

ETERNAL WARRIOR VOL. 2: ETERNAL EMPEROR
ISBN: 9781939346292 | Diamond Code: APR141439 | Price: $14.99 | Format: TP

VALIANT® TRADE PAPERBACKS

VALIANT
OMEGA RISING
HARBINGER

HARBINGER VOL. 1: OMEGA RISING
ISBN: 9780979640957 | Diamond Code: NOV121345 | Price: $9.99 | Format: TP

HARBINGER VOL. 2: RENEGADES
ISBN: 9781939346025 | Diamond Code: MAR131332 | Price: $14.99 | Format: TP

HARBINGER WARS (MINI-SERIES)
ISBN: 9781939346094 | Diamond Code: JUL131325 | Price: $14.99 | Format: TP

HARBINGER VOL. 3: HARBINGER WARS
ISBN: 9781939346117 | Diamond Code: JUL131326 | Price: $14.99 | Format: TP

HARBINGER VOL. 4: PERFECT DAY
ISBN: 9781939346155 | Diamond Code: DEC131331 | Price: $14.99 | Format: TP

HARBINGER VOL. 5: DEATH OF A RENEGADE
ISBN: 9781939346339 | Diamond Code: JUL141498 | Price:$19.99 | Format: TP

HARBINGER VOL. 6: OMEGAS
ISBN: 9781939346384 | Diamond Code: NOV141706 | Price: $14.99 | Format: TP

VALIANT
THE MICHELANGELO CODE
ARCHER & ARMSTRONG

ARCHER & ARMSTRONG VOL. 1: THE MICHELANGELO CODE
ISBN: 9780979640988 | Diamond Code: JAN131309 | Price: $14.99 | Format: TP

ARCHER & ARMSTRONG VOL. 2: WRATH OF THE ETERNAL WARRIOR
ISBN: 9781939346049 | Diamond Code: MAY131314 | Price: $14.99 | Format: TP

ARCHER & ARMSTRONG VOL. 3: FAR FARAWAY
ISBN: 9781939346148 | Diamond Code: OCT131350 | Price: $14.99 | Format: TP

ARCHER & ARMSTRONG VOL. 4: SECT CIVIL WAR
ISBN: 9781939346254 | Diamond Code: DEC131317 | Price: $14.99 | Format: TP

ARCHER & ARMSTRONG VOL. 5: MISSION: IMPROBABLE
ISBN: 9781939346353 | Diamond Code: APR141438 | Price: $14.99 | Format: TP

VALIANT
BIRTH RITES
SHADOWMAN

SHADOWMAN VOL. 1: BIRTH RITES
ISBN: 9781939346001 | Diamond Code: FEB131168 | Price: $9.99 | Format: TP

SHADOWMAN VOL. 2: DARQUE RECKONING
ISBN: 9781939346056 | Diamond Code: AUG131482 | Price: $14.99 | Format: TP

SHADOWMAN VOL. 3: DEADSIDE BLUES
ISBN: 9781939346162 | Diamond Code: NOV131282 | Price: $14.99 | Format: TP

SHADOWMAN VOL. 4: FEAR, BLOOD, AND SHADOWS
ISBN: 9781939346278 | Diamond Code: MAR141410 | Price: $14.99 | Format: TP

SHADOWMAN VOL. 5: end times
ISBN: 9781939346377 | Diamond Code: JUN141515 | Price: $14.99 | Format: TP

VALIANT
THE WORLD'S WORST SUPERHERO TEAM
QUANTUM AND WOODY!
KLANG.

QUANTUM AND WOODY VOL. 1: THE WORLD'S WORST SUPERHERO TEAM
ISBN: 9781939346186 | Diamond Code: SEP131374 | Price: $9.99 | Format: TP

QUANTUM AND WOODY VOL. 2: IN SECURITY
ISBN: 9781939346230 | Diamond Code: JAN141365 | Price: $14.99 | Format: TP

VALIANT®

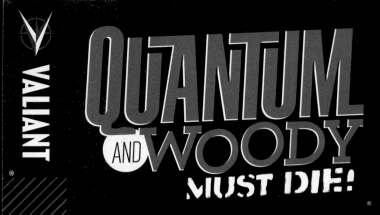

QUANTUM AND WOODY MUST DIE!®

MULTIPLE HARVEY AWARD NOMINEE JAMES ASMUS (QUANTUM AND WOODY, THE DELINQUENTS) AND EISNER AWARD-WINNING ARTIST STEVE LIEBER (*The Superior Foes of Spider-Man*) ARE HERE TO BRING THE MOST TALKED-ABOUT, MOST AWARD-NOT-WINNING-EST HEROES IN COMICS TO A WHOLE NEW HIGH! UNFORTUNATELY, THERE ARE A BUNCH OF PEOPLE THAT WOULD LIKE TO KILL THEM UP THERE.

They came. They saw. They pissed off a whole lotta folks. And now a team of mystery vigilantes has singled out the world's worst superhero team for complete and utter destruction. Their first target: their minds! But who are these all-new enemies? Are Quantum and Woody hitting it off with a sexy duo of cat burglars? And, dear god, what have they done to the goat? Is this the real life? Is this just fantasy? *Sex Criminals* isn't the only comic that can quote Queen, comics fans - here come Quantum and Woody! (Or so they think! [Trippy, right?!])

Collecting QUANTUM AND WOODY MUST DIE! #1-4 along with VALIANT-SIZED QUANTUM AND WOODY #1, start reading here as the writer James Asmus and artist Steve Lieber bring the most talked-about duo of semi-professional heroes in comics to a whole new high!

JAMES ASMUS | STEVE LIEBER | DAVE McCAIG
VALIANT
QUANTUM AND WOODY
MUST DIE!

TRADE PAPERBACK
ISBN: 978-1-939346-62-9